Baskets from Nature's Bounty

ELIZABETH JENSEN

INTERWEAVE PRESS

Quote on page 109:
Wildwood Flower by A.P. Carter
© 1935 by Peer International Corporation
Copyright renewed. International copyright secured.
All rights reserved. Used by permission.

All baskets made by the author, except page 124 and Chapter 10.

Editor: Rick Mastelli
Designer: Deborah Fillion
Author's technical drawings rendered by Steve Buchanan
Botanical drawings: Rob Proctor
Photography, except where noted: © Image & Word
Black-and-white photos of author's baskets, and
photos on pages 143-145, 148, 157, 190-193: © Sheila Silvernail
Copy editor: Betsy Strauch
Production: Image & Word

Interweave Press
201 East Fourth Street
Loveland, CO 80537
(303) 669-7672

Library of Congress Catalog Number 91-30752
ISBN 0-934026-69-6
First printing: 9:91OB12500
Printed in the United States of America

Library of Congress Cataloging-in-Publication Data

Jensen, Elizabeth J., 1933-
      Baskets from nature's bounty / Elizabeth Jensen.
         p.   cm.
      Includes bibliographical references and index.
      ISBN 0-934026-69-6 : $24.95
      1. Basket making. 2. Plants, Useful. 3. Fiber plants.
   I. Title.
   TT879.B3J462   1991   91-30752
   746.41'2—dc20   CIP

FOR MY MOTHER AND TO THE MEMORY
OF MY FATHER, BOTH OF WHOM TAUGHT ME
TO LOVE AND RESPECT WORK *FATTO A MANO*,
MADE BY HAND.

I AM DEEPLY GRATEFUL to my mentors, students, and fellow basketmakers for inspiration and a healthy spirit of competition.

I also wish to thank the many basketmakers who submitted photos for the gallery. Their patience and understanding are appreciated.

For special interest shown from the very beginning and continued encouragement and support, I wish to thank Shereen LaPlantz.

The following people generously supplied needed information on plants: Misti Washington, Betz Salmont, Vivian Aron, Myrna Brunson, Rita Buchanan, and Jim Roix.

I am thankful to Rob Proctor whose exquisite botanical drawings add a note of elegance to the chapter on plants; and to Steve Buchanan whose talented pen gave to my technical drawings an additional and appealing dimension.

Rita Buchanan was kind enough to verify and amend the section on plant dyes. Her expertise is very much appreciated.

Sheila Silvernail, who took the black-and-white photos of my baskets, merits praise. Her work, patience, and companionship were deeply appreciated. I'm grateful also to Rick Mastelli and Deborah Fillion of Image & Word for the rich and well-planned color photos that appear throughout the book.

I am indebted to Interweave's publisher, Linda Ligon. Her kindness and consideration throughout all the phases of manuscript preparation gave me a deep feeling of security and confidence that will ever be remembered.

I commend and thank Betsy Strauch for her diligence in meticulously copyediting the manuscript, especially the Harvest Calendar.

It was a pleasure to work directly with Rick Mastelli, my editor, from whom I learned so much and who corrected in a kind and gentle way.

I am grateful to Deborah Fillion, book designer, for the thrill and privilege of observing the pages blossom under her capable hands.

The staff at the New York Botanical Garden, Brookfield Craft Center, and the American Indian Archeological Institute helped to propel me on my way. Barrie Kavasch encouraged and advised me in many areas. Thank you.

Also thanks to family and friends for just being there and for listening—Margaret, Rusty, Mary, Pidg, Jan, and especially Joe.

Above all, I thank the Lord for the joy of seeing this book come to fruition.

Contents

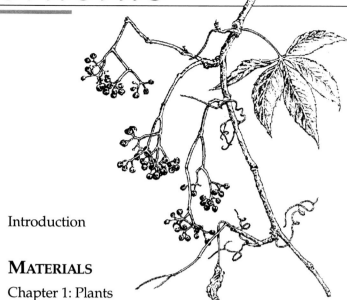

Introduction

And God said, Behold, I have given you every herb-bearing seed, which is upon the face of all the earth, and every tree, in which is the fruit of a tree yielding seed.

—GENESIS 1:29

*D*esign, color, form, and structure can be learned from observing the works of creation. Many animals have been endowed with built-in baskets. The pouches of the kangaroo, koala, and opossum serve as cradles for their young. The camel's hump is a storage tank for reserves of fat, and chipmunks have loose cheek skin that forms pouches for carrying nuts. The honeybee has pollen-carrying baskets on its hind legs, as well as a special stomach for transporting nectar to the hive.

Other creatures, not provided with built-ins, make their baskets. The spider weaves her web basket to snare prey. Larvae spin and fashion cocoons to protect themselves during the pupal state. Birds, those master basketmakers, build nests in which to rear their young, and some fish construct bubble nests to conceal their eggs.

Even the properties of the materials we use can inform our work. Vines wrap around trees, posts, and themselves to create strong, functional structures. Natural fibers, from cotton to wood, grow into materials that are valued for their softness, stiffness, flexibility or strength. Even after the plants have discarded them, needles and leaves can mat into sumptuous surfaces.

Many of our lessons come from the past. People in every early civilization needed to carry home nuts, berries, herbs, and meat from their foraging and hunting expeditions. Expediently, nature has provided each habitable region in the world with plants that can be woven into baskets to fill that need.

Archeological studies indicate that basketmaking is the oldest craft. The methods used for making baskets in our earliest cultures are still used today. Despite centuries of civilization, invention and progress, a basket still cannot be made by machine. Modern technology has, of course, produced metal and plastic items that have replaced many containers and utensils originally made of basketry. How many of us, when using a metal sifter or carrying water in a glass jug or zinc canteen, are conscious that these activities were once performed with a handmade basket?

Today, our society encourages us to purchase everything—from homes, food, and apparel to the most trivial items our hearts may desire. How foreign is the thought that any commodity cannot be had for a price. Most of the time we even fail to wonder where an item came from, what it was made of, or what went into preparing it for the consumer. When we need or want something, we simply buy it.

Baskets have served so many needs that the list seems endless, from gathering, storing, drying, cooking, and serving to furniture, clothing, vehicles, musical instruments, and even boats. The list of plants used for making baskets is similarly extensive. Indeed, basket styles and types have been determined largely by the plants available to make them. Size, of course, is a matter of the function the basket has been made to serve. There are baskets small enough to fit through a lady's finger ring and large enough in which to put the lady!

For most of us, the need for baskets in which to carry home food from the woods no longer exists. But baskets admirably continue to serve us in many ways. As well as being useful, they can satisfy our desire to own or create a work of art or history—or to keep a tradition alive.

When you make your first basket from natural material, no matter how crudely woven, you'll find it will have a warmth and charm not found in baskets made from store-bought or commercially prepared materials. I believe those souls, brave or fortunate enough to return to living off the land enjoy a security and composure that our modern society doesn't share. Weaving baskets from nature's bounty is one small way that we can capture that wonderful feeling of getting back to the earth. Harvesting the plants we use is, to me, one of the most enjoyable phases of the art of basketmaking. It can consume many hours, composing much of the feeling that goes into making a basket. Each step puts us more in tune with our ancestors, who had neither shops nor supply houses but lived in harmony with the earth and her stores.

My intent in writing this book is to share with you a common love for the hills, swamps, woodlands, roadsides, and gardens around us reflected in beautiful and useful baskets woven from nature's bounty.

How this book is organized

This book begins with the bounties of nature—the plants around us. In Chapter 1 you'll find a concise list of well-known plants found in many areas of the country. This list (on page 4) is grouped by materials, and should give you ideas for substitutions within the groups. Use what is available to you. Only a few of them can keep you occupied for years. And experiment. That's half the fun of basketmaking.

In the rest of the chapter I offer my own experiences regarding the materials I am most familiar with. Those common to the Northeast necessarily weight the list. A few others are included that I have received from basketmakers and friends. Trading materials is an extra pleasure, making possible experimentation with a wider selection of plants.

The section on materials concludes with an extensive Harvest Calendar, in which more than 200 plants are listed alphabetically by common name, followed by the scientific name, the part of the plant and the technique that have been successfully used, notes and comments, and the range and habitat of the plant. A list cross-referencing the Latin names begins on page 184.

The second section of the book describes the techniques of basketmaking, categorized by type of basket. It will enable you to start from the simplest forms and proceed to your own personal variations and combinations. Directions for project baskets, illustrating various techniques in the category and highlighting the use of particular materials, are given toward the end of each chapter.

At the end of the chapters on wickerwork, splintwork, and twining, you will find summary charts—a recap of some basic weaves with possible patterns using color. Most of these weaves are fully described in the text. The charts are designed to give you easy access to stroke and color "formulas" for arriving at pattern variations.

In the final chapter is pictured the work of basketmakers across the country, both traditional and contemporary. This inspiring exhibit depicts many of the techniques in this book using materials from nature's bounty.

The book concludes with several appendices, including an annotated tool kit (page 190) and a glossary (page 188) which defines the terms as I've used them in this book. The words for basket types, weaves, and parts often differ from one geographical area or culture to another. While this may be fascinating, it can also be confusing. It is doubtful whether a universal glossary can ever be created or accepted. I suggest that before you begin to work on techniques you study this section and keep a bookmark there.

—Elizabeth Jensen
Bridgewater, Connecticut
September 1991

Materials

*N*ature's storehouses are vast. With over
300,000 plants recorded and described
according to the system set up by Linnaeus
in the 1700s, it would be difficult, indeed,
to find an area in the world that did not
yield some plant suitable for basketmaking.
In our wanderings through field and fen,
there seems always to be more plants to try.

Basketry materials can be gathered at
practically any time of the year. I collected
my first vines while on skis in the middle of
January. In many instances we need look no
farther than our own backyards.

Chapter 1

Yellow iris (*Iris pseudacorus*).

Plants

A winding wall of mossy stone,
Frost-flung and broken, lines
A lonesome acre thinly grown
With grass and wandering vines.

Without the wall a birch-tree shows
Its drooped and tasselled head;
Within, a stag-horned sumach grows,
Fern leafed, with spikes of red.

—JOHN GREENLEAF WHITTIER

Virginia creeper.

Many types of round material, such as vines and twigs, and soft material, such as cattail, iris, and daylily leaves, are quite easy to locate, harvest, and prepare. These are described first in this chapter, along with materials that can be taken from trees without cutting them down. Pine needles, leaf stems, pods, withes, and even roots are included here. The latter part of this chapter deals with material that can be harvested from trees only by felling them, such as splints and some barks.

Listing plants by the type of material they yield is intended to help the beginner on his or her first gathering expedition. The list on page 4 is by no means exhaustive, but I have had experience with many of the species and plant materials there. More information can be found in the Harvest Calendar that begins on page 31.

Before you go out gathering, make certain you are familiar with the protected plants in your state and always practice good conservation methods when harvesting any type of natural material. Gather only if there is an abundance of material, and always leave some for next year's growth.

It's a good idea to keep records. Information on a label tied to a sample of each type of plant may have the following: name of plant, part of plant, place and date of harvest, preparation, and remarks. A sample label might look like the one at right.

Now let's go out and gather some material. Take your pruning shears, knife, and string, and let's see what we can find.

VINES

This group includes many obvious choices for basketmakers; vines are perfect in their length and pliability. In many cases, very little work is required to begin weaving with them immediately after gathering. If storing, simply remove the leaves and use a length of cord or heavy yarn to tie them into coils 8 to 10 inches in diameter so that they will fit in a pot for soaking later on. As with many basket materials, drying first and resoaking before using helps to minimize shrinkage in the finished basket. Vines lend themselves well to wickerwork techniques whether used stripped or unstripped. Stripping the bark is easiest when the vines are green.

Weeping Willow
Roots
Calter Valley,
  bottom of hill
  near bridge
Harvested: 5/1/91
Boiled for 4 hours

COMMON BASKET PLANTS

VINES AND RUNNERS
Akebia
Bittersweet
Clematis
Coralberry
Grape
Honeysuckle
Ivy
Kudzu
Morning Glory
Raspberry, Blackberry, etc.
Strawberry
Vinca
Virginia Creeper
Wisteria

WOODY SHOOTS
Apple (and other fruit)
Ash
Black Walnut
Dogwood
Elm
Hazelnut
Maple
Mulberry
Paper Mulberry
Redbud
Red Osier Dogwood
Sassafras
Sumac
Sycamore
Willow

LEAVES
Bamboo
Bear Grass
Cattail
Crocosmia
Daffodil
Daylily
Dracaena
Flax
Iris
Palm
Pampas Grass
Pandanus
Phragmites
Sedge
Sweet Flag
Sweet Grass
Yucca

GRASS OR GRASSLIKE
Bulrush
Oats
Redtop
Rice
Ricegrass
Rush
Rye
Sedge
Sweet Grass
Sweet Vernal Grass
Timothy
Wheat

STALKS AND STEMS
Bamboo
Cane
Cattail
Corn
Giant Chain Fern
Goldenrod
Maidenhair Fern
Palm
Phragmites
Tule

FIBERS FROM LEAVES, STEMS, OR BARK
Agave
Basswood Bark
Dogbane (Hemp)
Flax
Milkweed
Mother-in-Law's Tongue
Nettle
Spanish Moss
Yucca

MISCELLANEOUS
Black Walnut leaf stems
Catalpa pods
Corn husks
Date Palm seed heads
Eucalyptus pods
Martynia pods
Phragmites pods
Pine needles
Seaweed

ROOTS
Balm of Gilead
Bittersweet
Balsam Poplar
Black Birch
Brake Fern
Bulrush
California Nutmeg
Cedar
Douglas Fir
Hemlock
Pine
Red Alder
Redwood
Sassafras
Sedge
Spruce
Sumac
Willow
Yucca

BARK
Basswood
Bitternut Hickory
Bittersweet
Black Walnut
Cedar
Cherry
Elm
Hemlock
Maple
Mulberry
White Birch
White Pine
Willow
Wisteria
Yew

SPLINTS
Ash
Elm
Hickory
Maple
Oak

Akebia *(Akebia quinata)*

The generic name for this semievergreen vine was Latinized from the Japanese name for the plant; the species name, *quinata*, refers to its five leaflets. If you have access to a stand of akebia, you are lucky indeed. The vine is strong, pliable, and attractive, and it can be used stripped or unstripped. Though it takes some work to remove the bark, the fine, white, supple material that results is well worth the effort. The wrapped border pictured on page 67 attests to the wonderful pliability of the stripped vines.

Akebia can and usually does take over an area, completely covering other shrubs and trees. My neighbor has been trying to eradicate it from her property for years. Fortunately for me, she has not succeeded and allows me to come and harvest all I want.

Choose vines that are on the ground away from other shrubs or fences. These runners are looking for a support to climb on. In their search for the fastest route to a fence or pole, they will be growing long and straight and, for the most part, free of leaves. Strip any leaves that do occur by running your hand down the vine. A few nodes may mark where the vine is trying to establish roots; however, in the spring, before new growth has started, these nodes are nearly absent. This is the best time to gather the vine, although I have gathered it in midsummer and midwinter as well.

Akebia vines running along the ground can reach lengths of 35 to 40 feet. Coil each vine separately and tie the coils into bundles for easy carrying. I attach a hook made from a metal coat hanger to my jeans belt and hang the coils on the hook. This frees both hands for clipping and coiling.

Akebia *(Akebia quinata)*.

If you wish to strip off the bark, boil the coils for six hours, then rub them with a plastic mesh pot scrubber. Boiling will also kill any insect eggs and may strengthen the fibers. Coil the vines again to dry and store. Akebia can be stored for months or even years until you're ready to use it. Soak the coiled vines in warm water for at least an hour, or until they are pliable enough to work with. Akebia may also be worked green, but in drying it will shrink in diameter and cause the weave to loosen up a bit.

Honeysuckle *(Lonicera japonica)*

This aggressive vine has been common in basketmaking for a long time. Where winters are warm, this plant is an evergreen. It forms dense tangles, climbing over underbrush and fences or sprawling over the ground. The fragrant white or yellowish flowers bloom from April to July.

Gather and prepare as for akebia. Honeysuckle is best used stripped, because the bark is shreddy and may peel off just from handling. But don't let this stop you from trying it unstripped. Some people like "hairy" baskets. If you do want to peel it, boiling for three or four hours will enable you to slip the bark off the hollow vines quite easily.

Bittersweet
(Celastrus scandens).

Bittersweet *(Celastrus scandens)*

This is a strong, aggressive vine—woodier or more fibrous than honeysuckle or akebia but not as slippery when stripped. Asian Bittersweet *(C. orbiculatus)* is similar, but with nearly circular leaves.

Look for orange "clouds" on the branches of naked trees in an autumn or winter woodland. These are tangled clusters of bittersweet fruits, beautiful orange-red berries that provide food for songbirds, grouse, pheasant, and bobwhite. Learn to recognize the vine in other seasons by memorizing the shape of the leaf and where it grows, as it may be gathered anytime. When gathering, wear gloves because the small buds, set nearly at right angles to the stem, are sharp. The vines may be used stripped or unstripped. Use the bark for wrapping, as for rims. To strip, insert a knife into the end and peel back. This must be done when the vine is still green. Bittersweet is protected in some areas—make sure you gather only where it's growing in abundance and there are no restrictions.

Wisteria *(Wisteria* spp.)

"One man's poison is another man's bread." A friend wanted to eradicate a wisteria vine that had completely taken over a large maple tree as well as a long, sloping bank alongside her lawn. The beautiful, long clusters of fragrant purple blossoms created a fantastic canopy on the branches of the maple and all surrounding shrubs, many of which were dead or dying. I gathered all the wisteria I could, from ⅛-inch-thick stems to vines ¾ inch in diameter.

This vine is supple yet marvelously strong. Climbing up trees, posts, or itself, it forms tight coils, but along banks or the ground, it will grow straight for 20 to 30 feet. It can be used stripped or unstripped. Bark can be used for wrapping.

Blackberries, Raspberries, Dewberries (*Rubus* spp.); Roses (*Rosa* spp.)

Berry vines (also known as brambles) vary in strength and length. Some raspberry canes can grow as long as 12 feet. In some areas, people have traditionally used these canes for the stitching material in coiled rye baskets. I have not been so successful with the canes in my area. I have, however, found great delight in making tiny wicker-work baskets of wild strawberry vines growing at the edge of my driveway. These can be 4 feet long and remain a pinkish red.

Most berry and rose vines have thorns. Remove these by drawing the vine from tip to base through your closed hand protected by a heavy glove or by drawing the vine through a notch cut in a tree stump.

Grape *(Vitis* spp.)

Grapevines can be gathered anytime. They are ideal for large, strong baskets. The vines are easily split, and the half-round sections can be used for rims and especially for hoops and frames in rib baskets. Keep the vines soaked while working.

I have seen huge rib baskets made completely of grapevines. They were rather rustic, because the vine is so coarse, but they were unquestionably strong. If you remove the shreddy bark, grape does look somewhat more refined. You can use the bark itself for cores in coiling and for small areas of dark color in wickerwork and splintwork.

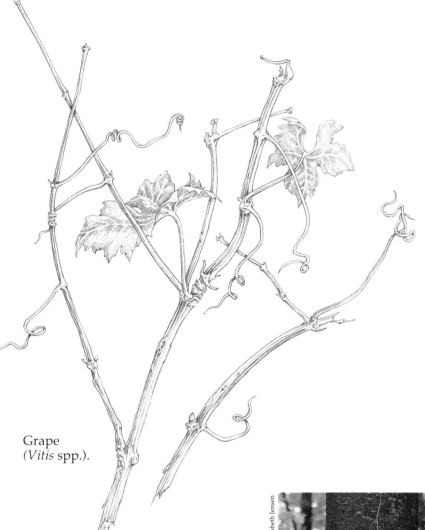

Grape
(*Vitis* spp.).

Virginia Creeper (*Parthenocissus quinquefolia*)

This plant has five pointed and toothed leaves arranged like spokes of a wheel. You will recognize it in the fall, a beautiful scarlet vine climbing high up into trees and around telephone poles and fence posts. Small blue berries appearing in August are sought by birds, mice, and chipmunks. The nodes and bumps give this plant an interesting texture when woven. It can be used freshly gathered or stored.

Virginia creeper
(*Parthenocissus quinquefolia*).

Basket willow
(*Salix purpurea*).

WOODY SHOOTS

Almost any tender shoot from a hardwood tree, as well as those from many shrubs, can be used to weave baskets. Rods, as basketmakers usually refer to them, can be gathered from apple, pear, and other fruit trees, maple, sassafras, flowering dogwood, paper mulberry, elm, and hazelnut, to name a few.

Stumps from felled trees will often sprout straight new shoots or suckers. Roadsides, fence rows, and railroad tracks are good places to look for sprouting stumps—any area that is cut back often, encouraging new growth. The same stump may yield shoots year after year.

I collect suckers and shoots 1 to 2 feet long from most plants; rods from shrubs such as willow and red osier dogwood can be 3 or 4 feet long, sometimes longer. The diameter may range from ⅛ inch to ¼ inch. Tie them into bundles 3 or 4 inches around and store them tip end down to keep individual shoots from slipping out, or bunch them in paper bags, butt end down. Woody shoots are generally used in wickerwork or for ribs.

Willow (*Salix* spp.)

There are many species of willow, also known as sallow, in this country. A few even occur as creeping shrubs. It would be worthwhile to experiment with any wild willows that grow in your area. Some basketmakers prefer wild willows to cultivated species.

Although willow for basketry is not cultivated in this country to the extent it once was, some basketmakers today do maintain willow beds on a smaller scale. Species worth cultivating include *S. purpurea, S. viminalis, S. nigra,* and *S. triandra*. Not all species need rich, damp soil. Some make attractive and useful hedges; pruned every year, these can produce a good supply of rods for basketmaking.

Some basketmakers who cultivate willow and pollard it (cutting back new growth to the trunk) prefer spring harvesting. Others prefer fall after the leaves have dropped. Spring harvesting produces *white* willow, as the material peels easily and then can be dried in the sun. *Brown* willow is willow dried with the bark left on. *Buff* willows are brown willows that have been boiled and peeled. Boiling with the bark, which contains tannic acid, produces the buff color. Willow rods can be split into flat elements called skeins. These are often combined with rods in traditional willow baskets.'

The bark of many willow shrubs and trees can be used for splintwork, plaiting, and cordage. (The same willow shoot can yield both bark and peeled rod.) The diagonal plaited basket described on page 98 is made of willow bark.

To strip off the bark, split the base with your fingernail or a knife so that the rod is divided into thirds. Hold all three sections of bark at once and peel them back to the tip end. If you pull all sections at the same time, you will have greater success getting wider, longer pieces.

Weeping willow (*S. babylonica*) wands or rods can often be gathered without harm to the tree by pruning a few from this tree and a few from that. In the spring, weeping willows often drop slender wands; you can quickly and easily gather large numbers from the ground while walking through a willow grove. Coil and secure bundles and immerse in water as soon as possible if using them immediately—or coil them and let dry before storing. Soak before using.

The sallow knows
the basket maker's thumb.
–RALPH WALDO EMERSON

Flowering Dogwood *(Cornus florida)*

Flowering dogwood is beautiful in so many ways. In spring, its familiar white blooms (actually bracts) grace our woods and yards. In fall, the leaves turn wine red, and the fruits ripen scarlet, providing food for wildlife. In winter, the tree is easily recognized by its lovely, irregular crown and numerous flower buds. The alligator-hide pattern of the reddish brown bark identifies the tree any time of the year. The genus name stems from the Latin word *cornu,* "horn," referring to the hardness of the wood. The species name means "flowering." The common name is believed to have come from "dagger-wood" (or "dag-wood") because its hard wood was used to make daggers, skewers, and other implements.

Straight young shoots growing up from stumps or out of the lower trunk can be used as for other wicker material. They are typically deep wine in color and 18 to 24 inches long. I store them loosely in brown paper bags, butt end down, to keep the tips from being bent or damaged. Dried shoots can also be tied into bundles. Soak before using, as with other rods.

Most dogwood cut for commercial purposes is made into spindles and bobbins for weaving. Needles carved of the hard, close-grained wood are a great help in coiling and for wrapping rims. The sapwood will be easily recognized by its beautiful pink color; dogwood tools are a pleasure to use and own. Directions for making needles are given in Tools, page 192.

Red Osier Dogwood *(Cornus stolonifera)*

The red stems of the red osier dogwood brighten up the winter landscape. The shrub prefers wet areas, and grows to 10 feet tall. You can encourage straight growth by selective pruning. Gather rods in the spring before the leaf buds open, and you'll find them wonderfully pliable. The red bark can be peeled and used for other techniques, leaving the osiers white underneath, or you can use them unstripped. Prepare and use as basket willow. A similar species, silky dogwood *(C. amomum),* can be used the same way.

Red osier dogwood *(Cornus stolonifera).*

Elizabeth Jensen

LEAVES

I like this group. Generally thought of as softer and kinder to hands and wrists than woody splints or rods, leaves nevertheless range from very soft or delicate to tough and sturdy. A subtle variety of color can be found in the leaves of different plants: the pale tan of daylily and daffodil, the gray-green of cattail, the russet and tan of iris, and the brown or greenish brown of yucca. Color can be affected by time of harvest and method of storage and preparation. (Generally speaking, the later you harvest, the browner will be the color; the darker the storage area, the more of the original color will remain.) Leaves lend themselves to twining, coiling, braiding, stitching, and plaiting.

Siberian iris
(Iris sibirica).

Iris or Flag *(Iris* **spp., but especially** *I. sibirica)*

If you are going to cultivate iris for weaving, try *I. sibirica.* I have found this species to be superior to others I have worked with. Iris leaves should be gathered in the fall. At this time they are as strong as they will ever get, since their growth is now complete. After frost has hit them, they will turn beautiful shades of tan and rust. If gathered before the first frost and dried and stored in a dark place, much of the green color may be kept. Cut the leaves off as low as possible, but leave the roots in the ground for next year's growth. Spread the leaves on a rack or screen to dry. Tie into bundles for storage. To use, soak in warm water and wrap in towels to mellow; or just wrap in wet towels and leave overnight.

Daffodil *(Narcissus* **spp.)**

Try any of the hundreds of cultivated varieties of narcissus, daffodil, and jonquil. Gather when you clean your narcissus beds, and use and prepare as for iris. The daffodils I tried seemed to hold more water than iris. Remove as much water as possible by wrapping in towels after soaking; otherwise, as the leaves dry, the weave of your basket will loosen.

Daylily *(Hemerocallis fulva)*

Harvest, prepare, and use as for iris leaves. They may dry a little lighter in color than most iris, with which they can be used.

Wet, marshy areas are a good source of cattail leaves and stalks.

Cattail *(Typha latifolia)*

Harvest the leaves when the seed heads or "cattails" are brown. With a knife, cut off a few inches above the root. Separate the leaves and wash off the jellylike substance at the base; otherwise, it will harden and be difficult to remove later. Cut off any parts that are ant-riddled. Now spread out the washed and trimmed leaves, turning frequently to promote drying and prevent mildew. Tie in bundles and store upright. When ready to weave, soak in warm water. Drain and mellow under wet towels for a few hours. The center pith of the leaf will hold water like a blotter or sponge. Squeeze out the excess moisture by running the length of the leaves between your closed fingers. I know of a weaver who puts his cattail through a hand-operated clothes wringer. Very often, I do not soak mine, but simply wrap them in wet, hot towels for a few hours. Experience will tell you just how wet the towels should be to prevent over-wetting and the need for squeezing. If excess water is not removed, the weave will open up considerably as the material dries. Cattail can be used for twining, coiling, and plaiting. You can slit it easily by running your fingernail along its length. The narrow pieces can be braided.

Cattail
(Typha latifolia).

GRASS OR GRASSLIKE MATERIALS

Grasses are found in almost every habitat of the world. They all need drying or curing and are useful for coiling, braiding, stitching, plaiting, and fine twining.

Sweet Grass (*Hierochloe odorata*); Sweet Vernal Grass (*Anthoxanthum odoratum*)

Various species of sweet-smelling grasses are used for twining and coiling, and with splintwork. Dry these long-bladed grasses slowly in the shade to hold their color. They are sometimes bunched and braided for storage. To use, soak in warm water for 10 to 15 minutes and wrap in towels. Some of these grow along the shore, and some grow in meadows. You can use these one strand at a time or braid them into one long continuous strand.

Sedge (*Carex* spp.).

The New England and Great Lakes Indian tribes are noted for their beautiful baskets of black ash splint and sweet grass. Farther south, descendants of slaves brought from Africa to work the rice plantations in South Carolina weave their Gullah or Low Country baskets of sweet grass and palmetto strips.

Sedge (*Carex* spp.)

There are hundreds of species of sedge throughout the United States. Found in wetlands, they form elevated tussocks which may in time provide a base for shrubs and trees. If rubbed one way, the undersides of leaves of some species will grip and cut your skin. Sedge grows on my property in a low, saucer-shaped depression that was once (and occasionally still is) a pond. The long, thin, grasslike leaves, triangular in cross section, are quite strong. Cut them above the roots, spread to dry, tie in bundles at the base, and hang, tip end down, to store. Soak in warm water to use.

Sedge is marvelous for braiding into one continuous strand, and it can also be used for twining and coiling. Western Indians split sedge roots for coiled baskets.

Rye (*Secale cereale*) and Other Grains

Gather these when ripe or when you see farmers making hay. Harvest time varies, depending on the variety, intended use, and locality. Weavers on Attu, the westernmost of the Aleutian Islands, harvested wild rye in November if they wanted the grass to be white. If they wanted it yellow, they would harvest in July. They would hang it to dry in the shade for a few weeks, then bring it indoors to finish the curing. No sun would be allowed to shine on it throughout the curing, which took a month or more. Other weavers elsewhere have complete success with sun-drying methods. Turn them occasionally until dry, and tie for storage.

STALKS

The words stalk and stem are often used interchangeably. I tend to think of stalks as more rigid than stems. Stalks lend themselves to splintwork and plaiting—techniques that utilize their rigidity. They can also be simply lashed together to form mats. Common stalks include corn, bamboo, phragmites, and cattail.

River Cane (*Arundinaria gigantea* spp. *tecta*)

This stalk, which thrives in our Southern states, takes dye well. It can be found in many colorful baskets, both contemporary and historical. The split outer portion of the stem was used shiny side out by the Choctaws, Chickasaws, Cherokees, Seminoles, and Chitimacha tribes.

Bamboo (*Bambusa* spp.)

Many of us associate bamboo with tropical climes. However, the panda of Tibet thrives on bamboo shoots, so we should not be surprised to see it growing in our northern states. I recently gathered sheaths (the husky outer covering shed from the stalk) from a wonderful stand of bamboo growing in western Connecticut. Master Gardener Miles Aborn grows the bamboo for fishing rods and fences around his vegetable gardens. I soaked the already dry 8-inch-long sheaths and split them into strands, out of which I produced some very strong cordage. I look forward to working with the stalks themselves when the patch needs thinning.

Bamboo (*Bambusa tuldoides*).

Yucca (*Yucca* spp.).

FIBERS FROM PLANT PARTS

Fibers from many plants are used in the manufacture of threads, cords, and ropes, from large hawsers on ships, rope bridges, and cowboy lassos to the very finest of linen. Agave, sisal, hemp, jute, maguey, abaca, flax, sansevieria, and other plants have fibers that can be separated from the rest of the plant. Methods for separating include pounding, soaking, retting (or rotting), chewing, pulling, combing, or a combination of these. The basketmaker will find thread and cordage made from these fibers to be useful for stitching, coiling, twining, lashing, knotting, and handlemaking.

Cordage is made from at least two strands of material, each one twisted separately in one direction, then twisted together (or *plied*) in the opposite direction. Between the palms or on the thigh, both movements can be done almost simultaneously. Knot the ends together and place the strands in your left palm or on your thigh. The knot should be on the left and the other ends separated. With your right palm, roll the strands away from you and as the twist in the individual strands travels back toward the knot, the strands will start to ply the opposite way in-

to one thick strand. Keep the two strands separated until they have enough twist in them before allowing them to ply together.

It is not necessary to isolate the fibers of some plants. Cordage can also be made from plant parts, either whole or split, as with grasses, leaves, husks, and inner barks. Instead of rolling these, you can twist the individual strands with one hand, while holding the strands together in your other hand. Give each strand a few twists *away* from you. As you alternate from one strand to the other, give them a half-twist together *toward* you. You'll be surprised at how quickly you'll have a plied cord.

Mother-in-Law's Tongue or Snake Plant (*Sansevieria trifasciata*)

In northern states, Mother-in-law's tongue is a common potted plant, but it has become naturalized in the South. When I began to work leaves I had cut months before, I was amazed at how much water they retained. They had turned a translucent cream color. When I began lightly striking them with a rawhide mallet, water splashed out. Soon, the pulp broke away, exposing fine, pure-white fibers (see photo, below left).

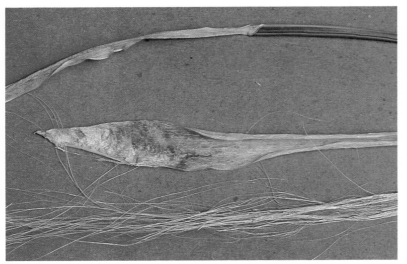

Pounding the leaves of Mother-in-law's tongue (Sansevieria trifasciata) *removes the pulp, exposing and separating long, strong fibers, ideal for cordage. From top to bottom: a whole leaf, a partially worked leaf, and the separated exposed fibers.*

Examples of cordage made from whole plant parts. From left to right: yucca, ti, cattail, iris, corn husk (natural and dyed with black walnut hulls), and cedar inner bark.

Yucca (*Yucca* spp.)

Several species of yucca are used in basket-making. In my yard I have two plants of *Yucca filamentosa*. The name *filamentosa* signals the fibrous nature of the plant; just looking at it, the fibers seem to jump right out at you.

Yucca was traditionally used by Hopi Indians and other pueblo tribes in the making of shallow bowls, sifters, and mats. Tribes from California and North Carolina used yucca for basketmaking, also. The leaf was usually split into fine strands and plaited. The roots of some species, red in color, were split and used in the weaving of figures and other decorations. The leaves of other species were gathered while young and still pale so that they would accept dye well. Still others were used for stitching material and cordage because of the strength of their fibers.

I made my yucca cordage by soaking the entire dried leaves, then lightly pounding to soften. I split them by running a needle down through the length of each and twisted the resulting strips into cord.

MISCELLANEOUS PLANT PARTS

Various parts of diverse plants have found their way into basketry. It may seem strange to employ generally short, stiff plant parts like husks, pods, or seed heads for basketry, but some very interesting—sometimes amazing—things have been done with them. Usually they're worked in as accents or decoration, but whole baskets can be made from some in this group.

Catalpa (*Catalpa bignonioides* and *C. speciosa*)

The catalpa is also called cigar tree, and the pods are called Indian cigars. The large, heart-shaped leaves and showy white flower clusters identify this tree. In the northern United States, it may reach a height of 50 feet. The fruit—pods, which may be as long as 24 inches—turn brown in fall and remain on the tree into early winter. They can be gathered from the ground during winter, after they drop off. They usually split open at this time, releasing the beans inside. If they haven't split, the beans can be removed when the pods are soaked before using. Soak for an hour or more. Pods can be used whole or split. After soaking, cut down the length of the pod with scissors. You can use wide pieces for plaiting or coarse splintwork. Very fine lengths can be grouped and used as a core in coiling (see the photo on page 132).

Corn Husks

Collect the husks whenever you have corn on the cob for dinner. Separate and dry, turning frequently. The dried husks dye well. I store my corn husks loosely in paper bags, boxes, or baskets. To use, I soak and split them. Corn husks are strong and durable. They can be plaited into long strips and stitched together as in coiled baskets or braided rugs and mats, or used for handles and surface decoration. The Nez Perce Indians made beautiful twined bags of corn husks and hemp, sometimes decorated with embroidery in wool.

Catalpa seedpod
(*Catalpa* spp.).

Maidenhair fern (*Adiantum pedatum*), shown dried, below.

Maidenhair Fern (*Adiantum pedatum*)

West Coast Indians used the split stems of this fern in twined baskets. Because the stems break so easily, I would suggest that only experienced basketmakers use this plant. It does not grow in abundance in my area so I am jealously guarding a few stems gathered from our woods every fall before the ferns are killed by frost. I now have a small bundle of beautiful mahogany-colored strands waiting to be woven into a special basket, perhaps as overlay. I simply gathered the fronds and let them dry indoors. When they are perfectly dry, I will carefully rub off the leaflets. They should be soaked for one hour before using.

Giant Chain Fern (*Woodwardia spinulosa*)

This is another fern used by western Indians. It is found in moist shade, as the maidenhair is. Gather in the fall or winter. The inside of the stalk is the part used. To get to it, pound with a rock on the flatter side of the stem. Then twist to separate the outer sections, which you discard. What's left is the inner, light green material. Dry this and tie it into bundles for storage. Soak for fifteen minutes in hot water before using.

I was able to get some flat, light green stringy strands from a species of *Woodwardia* growing in my woods using this method. They dried to a lovely, soft, creamy yellow.

Sensitive Fern (*Onoclea sensibilis*)

The common sensitive fern is readily recognized in autumn when the leaves have died back and the stems supporting the dark brown, fertile spikes are left standing tall. Pull the stem straight up so that it doesn't bend. These can be used in wickerwork with the spore cases left attached to make a distinguishing contrast on a light-colored basket. It's a good idea to spray the spore sacks with fixative or hair spray to prevent the minute spores from dropping.

Pine Needles (also called Pine Straw) (*Pinus* spp.)

The longleaf pine (*P. palustris*), also called southern pine or Georgia pine, and the slash pine (*P. elliottii*) have long been used as core material in coiled baskets. Other pines may yield suitable needles also, but the two mentioned have the longest, as long as 12 to 18 inches.

In late spring or summer, branches can be gathered and dried in the sun before the needles are removed, or needles can be gathered after they have fallen to the ground in the fall. Try to gather those that have not lain on the ground for long, as they tend to become brittle. They should be washed in a weak solution of detergent and rinsed well. Let them dry in the shade to keep them green—or in the sun to turn them brown. Tie them into bundles to keep the needles straight. Cut off the stem ends and wrap in damp towels when ready to use. Take care not to leave them wrapped for more than several hours, as they will mildew. You can also put them in a plastic bag with a small amount of water until pliable enough to use.

Sycamore Leaf Stems (*Platanus occidentalis*)

This large lowland tree is recognized by its patchy brown bark and white inner bark that stands out in a green landscape. It is often found along riverbanks. The small fruits, sometimes called buttonballs, are 1 to 1½ inches in diameter and hang on slender stems. (As I look with my binoculars now—late May—I can see the small balls or buttons formed by the female flower which appear when the leaves unfold in early May.)

In the fall, when the leaves drop, I gather them and cut away the leaf from the leaf stalk or petiole. The wide hollow stalk end (where the leaf base covers the bud) makes a good decorative element. Simply spread the stems to dry and store in a basket. Soak for at least one hour before using.

Black Walnut Leaf Stems (*Juglans nigra*)

I owe much to my niece, Shelly, who really discovered black walnut leaf stems for me. I had been teaching basketmaking to a small group of young children, including Shelly and her older sister, Elizabeth, ages five and seven at the time. A short time later, Shelly found some black walnut leaf stems in her yard. She gathered a bundle and proclaimed to her mother that she would give them to Auntie for basketmaking because they were so "bendable." I have been using them ever since.

My favorite month is October. This is the time to gather black walnut leaf stems. They fall to the ground here in New England from the middle to the end of the month and the beginning of November, or about the same time the nuts fall. (Gather some nuts while you are about it—to use for dyeing, page 159.) Most of the leaflets will already have fallen off the stems. Remove the few remaining leaflets and spread the stems to dry. Tie in neat bundles to store. To use, soak for two hours in warm to hot water. The leaf stems are quite wide at the butt end; this makes them ideal for ornamentation or added textural interest. Some may be as long as 24 inches and can be used for spokes or weavers.

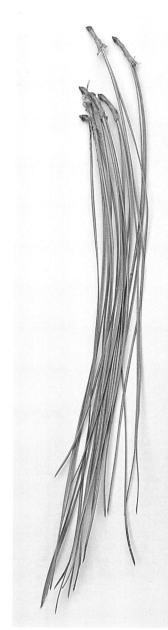

Pine needles
(*Pinus palustris*).

Black walnut leaf stems
(*Juglans nigra*).

ROOTS

Roots afford a variety of textures and colors to the basketmaker. They're interesting not only for the many ways they can be used (from stitching and lacing to ribs, rims, and even whole baskets) but for how they are harvested and prepared. They tend to be less readily available than other plant parts, so when a tree is uprooted or when a ditch is being dug, take advantage and gather roots. On the other hand, roots from some trees, conifers in particular, can be gathered without apparent harm to the tree. Most roots run close to the surface, and digging a 6-inch layer of soil may net you a few usable roots. Most are strong and pliable and can be split. Pine, redwood, spruce, hemlock, willow, and alder, as well as western species of yucca are a few whose roots have been used.

Brake fern or bracken
(Pteridium aquilinum).

Brake Fern or Bracken (*Pteridium aquilinum*)

Bracken is found nearly all the world over. Look in woods and fields for a large, coarse fern with a three-parted triangular blade. Carefully follow a root down until you reach the horizontal rootstock. This may be as long as 15 feet and very deep in the ground, thus making it impervious to ice and cold. Because of this, the brake fern is one of the most prolific and widespread of all the ferns.

Lay the washed rootstock on a flat board and strike with a rawhide or wood mallet. This will crush the pulp and outer skin and enable you to break it away. Try to keep the long, flat root from twisting as you pound it. A light pounding is all that's necessary. In the center you will find two dark brown flat, leathery, and somewhat soapy, flexible strands which are the parts to use. Discard the white strings, outer skin, and crushed pulp. Scrape the dark flat strands clean with your fingernail or a sharp knife. These will be a rather uniform $1/16$ to $1/8$ inch wide and very strong. Dry to store. Soak before using. They can be used for ornamental work in coiled and twined baskets or as weaving strands. Shorter pieces can be removed from the individual roots growing up from the rootstock.

Flat Material

It is the poet who makes the truest use of the pine, who does not fondle it with an axe, or tickle it with a saw, or stroke it with a plane. It is the poet who loves it as his own shadow in the air, and lets it stand.

—HENRY DAVID THOREAU

THE POET DOES WELL TO let the tree stand, but there are times when a tree must come down, or comes down accidentally. Flat material, whether bark or splint, is more difficult to come by than round material. After all, it takes a good many years to grow a tree.

Watch for housing developments going up in your area, or excavations of any kind. Many trees are cut down to clear land and may be free for the asking. Check with tree removal experts if you are looking for a specific tree. They often must remove a tree from someone's yard, and a phone call may procure it for you. Electrical storms can result in fallen trees. Call the owner or your power company to see if any may be available. Trees or products from trees can also be obtained from fence and firewood suppliers, foresters, and sawmills.

The easiest material to work with comes from straight, clear stock, although plenty of good splints or bark can be had from the better sections of trees that are old, crooked, or twisted. Straight, smooth bark is usually a good indicator that the material underneath is the same. Often a newly down or dying tree will yield useful bark or splint.

BARK

When gathering bark, try to select a young tree in a wooded area that needs thinning. Removing the bark from around a tree (girdling it) will kill it. Look for trees that have just been cut down. Cedar bark can often be collected from fence posts. Pieces of the outer bark of white birch can almost always be found lying on the ground near the tree. It may still be useful long after the tree has fallen. Carefully gather up the pieces and store where they will not be crushed.

The inner bark from most evergreens can be used, as well as that of some hardwoods. Many traditional baskets are distinguished for the colors and patterns of such inner bark: black from the black walnut, brown from cherry, and yellow from hickory.

Take bark in the spring, when new growth makes the bark easy to separate. With a drawknife, remove the rough outer bark, leaving the surface beneath smooth and even. The bark from some trees, such as basswood and slippery elm, can be removed and used with the outer bark left on. But for most trees, you have to get past the hard, crusty outer surface to the still-green layers beneath. This inner bark can then be scored down to the wood and peeled by inserting and "walking" the knife under the cut strip. Keep runout to a minimum by pulling slowly in line with the strip, rather then bending it up. Widths of 1 to 2 inches are generally convenient to gather and store. Later you can cut them into narrower strips, if necessary. I have gathered hemlock and spruce bark up to 6 inches wide.

Eastern red cedar
(*Juniperus virginiana*).

Eastern Red Cedar (*Juniperus virginiana*)

Though not a true cedar (*Cedrus* spp.), this is the tree that is used for cedar chests, cabinets, panels, and fence posts. The outer bark provides excellent tinder. The small dark blue berries, covered with a whitish bloom, are eaten by opossums and birds.

A few years ago I was given three large trash bags full of bark taken from fence posts. I was delighted with the thoughtful gift, but certainly had my work cut out for me. I set a few planks across sawhorses and worked under the shade of a nearby tree so the sun wouldn't dry out the bark. For the next few days, I worked on the strips. I kept them on the wet grass, covered with the trash bags and scrap pieces of bark to keep them damp and pliable. Some of the strips were as wide as 4 or 5 inches. I laid each strip on the plank work table and scraped the outer, shreddy bark off with a knife. Some of the strips had to be cut into narrower, workable widths. Next, I split each strip as follows (see photos of a similar process for hemlock bark on page 23): First cut the end off square and insert the knife into the end exactly in the middle. Lever the knife back and forth to separate the halves. Take the knife out and put both thumbs into the split, holding the strip below the split with the fingertips of both hands exerting equal pressure as you continue to pull the strip apart. If the split begins to run to one side, pull down more on the thick side until the sides are equal again. You will be able to split some pieces almost paper thin. Leave other pieces thicker, so that you will have a variety from which to choose. Drape them in half over a clothesline to dry somewhat so that they don't mildew. Select pieces of equal length, width, and thickness and tie them loosely into neat bundles for storage.

Red Maple (*Acer rubrum*)

In autumn, the brilliance of the red maple, also called swamp or scarlet maple, adds greatly to the beauty of our eastern forests. The fall foliage is one of many reasons for its Latin name. The leaf stems may be tinged with red also, as is the inner bark. On a young tree, the outer bark is gray and smooth. The inner bark is one of the loveliest (and best behaved) that I have worked with. Score down to the wood. Remove in 1-inch strips and store as for other barks. The bark of young trees is thin enough for very fine or small baskets.

Red maple *(Acer rubrum).*

Basswood or American Linden (*Tilia americana*)

This is a compact, symmetrical tree, 70 to 90 feet high, that is native to the eastern half of our country as far south as Florida and Texas. It has perfect, five-petaled, fragrant white or cream-colored flowers that appear in June or July after the leaves are fully developed. The flowers, which secrete nectar in great abundance and are therefore alluring to bees, play an important role in the honey industry. (Another name for this tree is the bee-tree.) The broad, heart-shaped, fine-toothed leaves are 5 to 10 inches long and taper rapidly to a point, sometimes from uneven bases. The light-colored wood is prized for woodenware and is also used for boxes, veneer, excelsior, and paper pulp.

The strength of the fibrous inner bark of this tree makes it extremely desirable for weaving as well as for cordage and ropemaking. It can be split very thin. Score the bark (no need to drawknife off the outer bark) for the length of the log and remove as previously described.

Soaking basswood bark for two to four weeks will cause much of the soft tissue to rot or fall away, leaving the somewhat slippery fibrous material, ideal for cordage and plaiting. The process can be hastened by pounding or simmering in water and wood ashes.

The linden in the fervors of July Hums with a louder concert.

—WILLIAM CULLEN BRYANT

American linden *(Tilia americana).*

HARVESTING HEMLOCK BARK

The inner bark of hemlock, as that of hickory, red maple and others, is best taken in the spring, when the sap begins to flow and the bark easily separates from the wood. The first step is to remove the crusty outer bark. A drawknife permits fine, level slices to be made without cutting into the soft, fibrous layer beneath. Some of the scaly, red outer bark may remain without compromising the quality of the material. Note the two stumps cut with V notches to make a handy workbench.

Use a knife to score a couple of lines, about ¼ inch deep, delineating the width of the strip you want to take. Begin fairly narrow, say, 1 inch. Then use the knife to begin prying the strip up. If the bark is coming easily, you can cut wider strips, up to one-third the circumference of the log, peeling with no runout at all.

Eastern hemlock *(Tsuga canadensis)*.

Eastern Hemlock *(Tsuga canadensis)*

Of necessity, several hemlocks had to be cut down on my property. I love hemlock trees and enjoy their beauty as well as their usefulness in supplying us with bark and roots for basketmaking. This tall, lovely evergreen tree of eastern forests has delicate foliage and perfectly formed, tiny brown cones. The thick, beautiful, cinnamon-red inner bark is very easily taken in spring and summer. Remove the scaly, rough outer bark with a drawknife or large straight knife. With a pointed knife, cut a straight line the length of the log through the inner bark. Cut another line a few inches away from the first. Insert the knife and slide and walk it under the strip as you peel it back. If there are no branches, you can remove the entire bark in a few wide sections. When wet, this lovely inner bark looks and feels like leather.

Hemlock roots can be stripped and split. Dry to store, soak before using.

SPLITTING HEMLOCK BARK

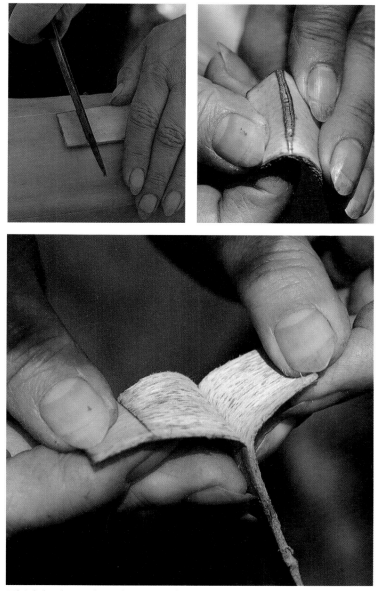

Thick bark can be split. Near the end of the strip, score halfway through the thickness, bend away from the knife cut, and peel the two halves apart. Separate slowly, controlling the direction of the split with tension to keep the halves even. The split will run toward the half you bend more.

Paper Birch *(Betula papyrifera)*

Also called white birch, canoe birch, and silver birch. Birch-bark containers have long been made by Native Americans. Many of these baskets were not actually woven, but made of wide sections of bark laced at the corners. Some were beautifully decorated with dyed porcupine quills. Others were scratched or etched on the surface, revealing a contrasting color beneath. The pieces of bark that are found on the ground in our woodlands usually consist only of the outer layer. These thin pieces can be used where strength is not a concern; however, the Indian birch-bark baskets and canoes were made with the entire thickness of bark, resulting in a very strong container.

Generally, the orange inner bark was used on the outside, and the white outer bark was on the inside.

I once had the pleasure of gathering birch bark with Jim Roix, who has worked with white birch bark for a number of years, making containers as well as baskets woven of narrow strips of bark. Jim claims he has gathered birch bark every month of the year, but March and early April are best. (It was right after Christmas when we gathered ours.) Jim had access to a lovely stand of white birch and said debarking will not kill the tree if you carefully remove only the outer layer. When he selected a tree, he made a vertical cut anywhere from 1 to 2 feet long and then two cuts around the tree at the top and bottom of this first cut. He then beveled the edge of one side of the vertical cut with a sharp curved knife. This enabled him to insert a wide putty knife into the cut and work the edge loose. When he had worked the bark back far enough to get a good grip on it, he'd pull straight out from the trunk all the way around the tree. Jim says he never fights with a tree. If he perceives that it is refusing to give up its bark, he just goes to another tree. Look for a tree with lenticels (dark spots) far apart; such trees will yield the largest, smoothest pieces. Some of the bark will split and the thinner layers can be used, but a solid piece of non-splitting bark makes the best containers.

Birch bark is best used fresh, when it is most flexible, although it can be stored for months. Soaking it may make it delaminate or become brittle. Heating it may help to make it more pliable, but use caution, as it is extremely flammable.

Paper birch
(Betula papyrifera).

Red Mulberry *(Morus rubra)*

The wood of the mulberry is very hard and durable and is used for fence posts and in shipbuilding. The Choctaw Indians of Mississippi and Louisiana made coarse cloth from the inner bark after macerating it in hot water and ashes. The fibrous inner bark, especially that of the roots, can be twisted into cordage (see page 14).

Black Willow *(Salix nigra)*

Returning to our campground at a music festival one summer, I noticed someone had left great slabs of muddy bark on my car. It appeared to be black willow, at least there were some growing nearby along the river. I took the whole mess home, dried it, and stored it in my shed. A few years later I pulled it out and discovered how beautiful it is. I scraped off the outer bark with a knife and the soft dark inner bark was a joy to work with. I still don't know who to thank for it!

SPLINTS

I do not recommend cutting down a tree for splints unless you have help to work it immediately, as most trees will give up their splints only when green. This is a good group project. Start early in the morning when you are fresh and can work all day at it. Besides those listed here, other trees that yield splints include hickory, cottonwood, sassafras, and northern white cedar.

White oak
(Quercus alba).

White Oak *(Quercus alba)*

Making splints from white oak is no easy task and requires many hours of labor to split out the workable section of the tree. With some help from a friend, I was able to get some fairly good splints from a white oak found in my woods. The tree was about 5 inches in diameter. I looked for one with a straight trunk that was relatively free of branches. We cut it into 8-foot lengths, then split the larger pieces in half using wedges and a maul (both made from a piece of dogwood, though iron wedges will do).

Splitting the smaller sections is best done with a froe: Place the butt end of the log (or log section) against the base of a stump and rest the other end on a piece of firewood or such. Place the froe in the center of the end and strike it with the maul until it is buried

HARVESTING WHITE OAK SPLINTS

Preparing oak splints can be arduous work, and it helps to have the right tools. Begin with a pair of wedges and a maul, and split the log in half, then in quarters, leap-frogging the wedges down the length of the log, above. Place a froe on the end of the blank and tap it in with a maul, top right. Then alternately pry the split open and slide the froe deeper into the split, right.

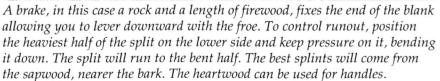

A brake, in this case a rock and a length of firewood, fixes the end of the blank allowing you to lever downward with the froe. To control runout, position the heaviest half of the split on the lower side and keep pressure on it, bending it down. The split will run to the bent half. The best splints will come from the sapwood, nearer the bark. The heartwood can be used for handles.

Remove the bark, by peeling or with a drawknife, and continue splitting the blanks with a froe until your splints are less than ½ inch thick.

Now use a knife to start thinner splints (top), prying and pulling the wood apart (middle). When you get material too thin to split further (about ¼ inch), use a drawknife and shaving horse (bottom) to even the thickness.

in the log. Now put down the maul and try levering the log apart. The smaller the section, the more likely this will work. If it doesn't, continue striking the froe where it protrudes from each side of the log, but alternate this maul work with attempts at levering. You can apply more force to the handle if you steady the far end of the blade with your opposite hand, or place your foot at the point where the handle is attached. It also helps if the other end of the log is fixed, say, wedged under a heavy rock or log— something you can lever against. The difficulty is in keeping the split in the center. When the split runs off center, exert pressure (pulling or pushing) on the thicker section of wood. If you're striking the froe, sometimes tilting it toward the thicker side helps to straighten the split. Split the log into quarters or eighths, depending on its size. When you have pieces no more than a few inches thick, still using the froe and maul, separate the heartwood (darker in color) from the sapwood. The heartwood can be used for handles, rims, and hoops. Next, remove the bark by splitting or drawknifing it off. The sections that remain will be halved again and again. Keep some ¼ inch thick for rims and handles, and split others down to ¹⁄₁₆ inch; thin these further by scraping with a knife.

When the sections are too thin to accept the froe, tap a knife down onto the end, just deep enough to make room for your fingers, at which point you will actually be ripping or *riving* the wood with your hands. If the split runs off center, pull down more on the thicker side and it should straighten.

Now you can use a drawknife and shaving horse to make the splints smooth. You can also smooth splints by holding them on your thigh (protected by a piece of heavy leather) and scraping with a sharp knife. Then trim them to width with shears, looped and tie into bundles for storage. You may have to soak them for hours to make them pliable enough for weaving.

White ash *(Fraxinus americana),* top, and black ash *(F. nigra),* bottom.

Red Maple (*Acer rubrum*)

While having some of my land cleared, I had a red maple cut down. Before I could stop the sawyer, he had cut the log into 4-foot lengths. I usually prefer longer pieces, but these worked out fine. I was able to stand the sections on end, straight up, and strike the froe with the maul from above. This seemed to work better for me. I did, however, remove the bark before I split the log out. I was anxious to save as much of the beautiful inner bark as I could, as splitting would cause a lot of waste.

White Ash (*Fraxinus americana*) and Black Ash (*F. nigra*)

Black ash, also called basket ash, is found in wet areas. Since most of my property is sloping and well drained, I have no black ash, but I do have white ash. Both are good for splints and can be worked the same way.

I once watched a demonstration of black ash splintmaking by an Indian couple from upstate New York. The woman was weaving, and the man was explaining how the splints were made. Someone in the audience asked how he could tell the difference between white ash and black ash. The Indian looked at him with a direct, hard gaze, hesitated—and then answered calmly but firmly, "An Indian can tell." No one dared ask him any further questions. The drawing at left shows that the white ash has long leaflet stems; black ash leaflets have no stems.

Ash trees will release their splints only after long and vigorous pounding that crushes the relatively large cells of the early-growth wood, allowing the annular layers to separate. A heavy maul is used for this, one made from a section of very hard wood about 4 to 5 inches in diameter and 12 to 18 inches long. Mine is made from dogwood; hickory is good, too. Carve away one end of it until it is comfortable in your hand.

Spring is the best time for making ash splints. Select a straight tree free of lower branches, from 3 to 12 inches in diameter. Cut the tree into pieces 4 to 8 feet long. Try to split the tree the same day it is cut; otherwise it will have to be kept from drying out. Storing it in a pond is traditional; complete submersion has the advantage of inhibiting mold growth. To remove the bark, a drawknife works best. Work carefully so as not to cut into the sapwood. When all of the bark has been removed, move the log to a firm, level piece of ground on which to do the pounding. Protect the log from dirt by laying strips of soft bark or hay under it. Grass may stain. An old rug works great. Now commence to pound the whole length of the log along 2 inches of the circumference at a time. Pound and then pound some more. Then have your partner do the same thing. Look at the end of the log and you will eventually see the outer layers begin to separate. Insert a knife into the separation and work it along the log to remove it. If it sticks in any one area, pound some more. Turn the log and repeat all around. Continue layer by layer, down to the darker heartwood, which can also be split out and used for handles and rims.

If the layers you remove are thicker than you want them, they can be split again by inserting a knife into the end and pulling apart by bending the halves down. Keep your thumbs in the split, and hold the splint just below the split, applying pressure with the fingers of both hands as you separate the halves. If the split begins to run off center, bend the thicker side more and the split will run toward that side.

Scissors work well to cut splint into desired widths. Sort your splints by thickness and widths; loop and tie them into neat bundles for storage. Soak splints well before using.

HARVESTING ASH SPLINTS

Ash requires persistent pounding (top) before it will yield its splint. Eventually, the growth rings will separate, and you can lift the splint with a knife (middle). You can thin the splint further by splitting it in half (bottom). If the split begins to run off center, bend the thicker side more.

Chapter 2

Harvest Calendar

Along the river's summer walk,
The withered tufts of asters nod;
and trembles on its arid stalk
The hoar plume of the golden-rod.

And on a ground of sombre fir,
The azure-studded juniper,
The silver birch its buds of purple shows
And scarlet berries tell where bloomed the sweet wild rose.
—JOHN GREENLEAF WHITTIER

Harvesting materials is one of my favorite parts of basketmaking. This Harvest Calendar is compiled from my field notes, my collection and curing records, workshops, discussions with other basketmakers, and the sources listed in the back of this book. There are necessarily gaps in this chart, particularly in plants not found in the Northeast. In some cases I have not named a particular species because various species in the same genus (iris or grape, for instance) may be used and prepared similarly. In other cases it may be difficult to distinguish species, as in the blackberries and raspberries. You may be more familiar with the characteristics of some of the species that grow in your area. Feel free to add information and to fill in the gaps. Plants used for dyeing can be found in the chart beginning on page 161.

Some entries come from historic texts and modern field guides that offer spotty information about how certain plants have been used, only that they played a part in a culture's basketmaking activities. I've included these, leaving the unknowns blank, because we should be encouraged to experiment and rediscover what were common understandings among early makers.

The scientific classification of plants is in continual flux. It is not uncommon for a plant to carry more than one name, having been discovered simultaneously by different botanists in separate areas. The prolific variety of common names also works at odds with the scientific mission to eliminate confusion. (If you know a plant by its Latin name, you can find its common name in the alphabetized list beginning on page 184.) Many older texts, still useful, carry outdated nomenclature. I have tried to strike a balance between the old and the new, the common and the scientific. But you should amend things as you see fit.

For most plants, the range/habitat column lists the place of origin as well as where the plant grows now. A few of the plants grow in tropical climates, but are available from greenhouses and conservatories. Often you can pick up discarded fronds or leaves. Be certain to find out whether they have been sprayed with insecticide before using them as food containers.

Note that a material harvested in the spring may yield entirely different results in texture, color, and strength than the same material harvested in summer, fall, or winter. Again, I say—experiment! And record your findings.

PLANT	PART	TECHNIQUE	SEASON	PREPARATION AND NOTES	RANGE, HABITAT
Agave American Aloe, Century Plant, Maguey, Sisal *Agave americana,* *A. cantala, A. deserti,* *A. lecheguilla, A. parryi,* *A. shawii, A. sisalana,* *Manfreda virginica*	Fibers in leaves	Coiling: stitching Twining Cordage Tying	Anytime	Set leaf over log. Pound with stick until pulp falls away. Or soak dried leaf, then remove fibers. Wear gloves to protect hands.	Gardens, hillsides, roadsides of sw. U.S. *M. virginica:* Se. U.S. n. to Ohio.
Ailanthus Tree-of-Heaven *Ailanthus altissima*	Leaf stems Bark	Wickerwork Splintwork Plaiting Lacework	Fall	Gather leaf stems when they drop in the fall. Allow to dry for storage. Soak only enough to become pliable. Fast growing. Male blossoms have foul odor.	China. Widely nat. across temperate N. Amer.
Akebia, Five-Leaf *Akebia quinata*	Vines	Wickerwork Twining Rib baskets: weavers	Anytime	Strip leaves, coil; dry to store or work green. Boil to remove bark. Similar to honeysuckle when stripped, but akebia is stronger. A marvelous material.	Japan, China, Korea. Introd. in zones 4 to 8.
Alder, Red *Alnus oregona*	Roots	Coiling: stitching	Early spring Fall	Gather near river bank, where long, flexible roots are exposed.	Se. Alaska s. to cen. Calif.; local in n. Id.
Allspice Strawberry Shrub, Sweet Shrub *Calycanthus floridus,* *C. occidentalis*	Shoots Bark Splints	Wickerwork	Spring Summer	Used by Indians of Mendocino Co., Calif. Crushed flowers smell like strawberries.	*C. floridus:* Rich woods, Fla. to Va. Hardy farther north. *C. occidentalis:* Calif.

Apple
Malus spp.
	Shoots
	Suckers
	Branches
		Wickerwork
		Rib baskets:
		  hoops
		  ribs
			Spring
			Summer
				Use thin, straight, flexible shoots green. Tie heavier branches to desired shape when green and let season for handles and ribs.	Eurasia. Nat. and cult. from Ga. and N. Mex. to s. Canada.

Aralia, Japanese *Fatsia japonica*	Leaf stems	Wickerwork Coiling: core	Anytime	Dry until just pliable.	Japan. Cult. as foliage plant outdoors in warm regions, indoors elsewhere.
Aristea *Aristea* spp.	Leaves	Plaiting Twining	Fall Winter	Leaves dry almost black.	S. Afr. Greenhouses. gardens in warm climates.
Artichoke *Cynara scolymus*	Leaves	Plaiting Twining		Use whole or stripped.	Eur. Cult. as vegetable.

Ash, Black
Fraxinus nigra
	Trunk	Splintwork
		Plaiting
		Coiling:
		  stitching
		Rib baskets:
		  hoops
		  ribs
		  weavers
			Spring
			Summer
				See pages 28 to 29.	Swamps and streambanks of ne. N. Amer.

PLANT	PART	TECHNIQUE	SEASON	PREPARATION AND NOTES	RANGE, HABITAT

Ash, White
Fraxinus americana
	Trunk	Splintwork
		Plaiting
		Coiling:
		  stitching
		Rib baskets:
		  hoops
		  ribs
		  weavers
			Spring
			Summer
				See pages 28 to 29.	Deep, rich soils of
					se. Canada, e. U.S.
					to Fla. and Tex.

	Leaf stems	Wickerwork	Fall	Gather leaf stems in the fall when they drop.	
Aspen: *See* Cottonwood					

Bamboo
Bambusa spp.
	Stems
	  whole
	  or split
	Leaves
		Splintwork
		Plaiting
				Cut at base.	Chiefly Asia. Cult.
					as ornamentals,
					timber. Sprouts
					in warm climates.

Banana *Musa* x *paradisiaca*	Stems	Coiling: stitching Plaiting Twining			Cult. in tropics for edible fruit; as ornamental in greenhouses.

Basswood
American Linden
Tilia americana
	Inner bark	Splintwork
		Plaiting
		Coiling
		  stitching
		Twining
		Rib baskets
		  weavers
		Cordage
				Soak log for 1 or 2 weeks.
				Score length of log with
				knife. Lift strip by
				peeling back, inserting
				and walking knife
				when necessary.
				(*See also* pages 22
				to 23.)
					Moist woods of cen.
					and e. N. Amer.

Beachgrass *Ammophila arenaria,* *A. breviligulata*	Stems	Coiling: core Twining		Split white stems.	*A. arenaria:* Eur. Nat. from Wash. to Calif. *A. breviligulata:* Ne. N. Amer.
Birch, Black Sweet birch *Betula lenta*	Roots Root bark	Wickerwork Coiling: stitching Twining	Anytime	Gather the roots whenever a tree must be cut down. Strip and split or use whole.	S. Me., sw. through Appalachians to n. Ala.

PLANT	PART	TECHNIQUE	SEASON	PREPARATION AND NOTES	RANGE, HABITAT

Birch, White
    Paper Birch, Canoe Birch
    Betula papyrifera
	Bark	Wickerwork
		Plaiting
		Lacework
			Spring
			Summer
				Small pieces of outer bark may be found lying on ground in woods anytime. Full-thickness bark must come from living tree. *See* page 24.	Alaska e. to Labr., s. into n. U.S.; local in mountains of N.C.

Bird-of-Paradise
    Strelitzia reginae
	Split leaf
	stems
		Twining
		Plaiting
		Coiling:
		    core
		    stitching
				Cut at base after flowering or when thinning. Dry. Soak to use.	S. Afr. Gardens in warm climate; greenhouses.

Bittersweet, American
    Celastrus scandens
Bittersweet, Oriental
    C. orbiculatus
	Vines
	Vine bark
	Roots
	Root bark
		Wickerwork
		Coiling:
		    core
		    stitching
		Twining
			Spring
			Summer
			Fall
				Use green or coil to dry and store. Soak to use. Strip when green if desired. Root may be stripped and split.	*C. scandens:* Que. s. to N.C. and N. Mex. *C. orbiculatus:* Japan, China. Escaped from cult. N.Y. s.

Blackberry
    Rubus spp.
	Vines
	Shoots
		Wickerwork
		Coiling:
		    core
		    stitching
			Anytime
			Spring
			    is best
				Use heavy gloves.	Widespread in N. Amer.

Blue-Joint
    Reed Bentgrass
    Calamagrostis canadensis,
    C. c. var. *scabra*
	Stems	Ornament		Used as overlay on spruce root for white pattern by Tlingit of Alaska. (O.T. Mason)	N. and cen. N. Amer.

Bluestem: *See* Grass, Broom Beard					
Bracken: *See* Fern, Brake					Malaysia, Tahiti.
Bromegrass *Bromus sitchensis*	Stems	Ornament		Used as overlay on spruce root for white pattern by Tlingit of Alaska. (O.T. Mason)	Woods and banks near coast, Alaska to Ore.
Broom Sedge: *See* Grass, Broom Beard					

Broomcorn
    Sorghum bicolor
	Seed heads	Coiling:
		    core
					E. U.S.

Buckbrush: *See* Coralberry					

PLANT	PART	TECHNIQUE	SEASON	PREPARATION AND NOTES	RANGE, HABITAT
Buckthorn California Lilac, Soapbloom, Deerbrush *Ceanothus integerrimus*	Shoots	Coiling: core			Calif. Other species (over 50 in N. Amer.) on Pac. Coast; a few in e. N. Amer.
Bulrush Chairmaker's Bulrush *Scirpus americanus* Salt Marsh Bulrush *S. robustus* Tule *S lacustris, S. pacificus,* *S. paludosus*	Roots Stems	Coiling: stitching Twining Ornament	Fall	Use whole or split.	Shores and marshes of N. Amer.
Bunchgrass: *See* Grass, Broom Beard					
Butternut Walnut, White *Juglans cinerea*	Leaf stems	Wickerwork	Fall	Gather leaf stems when they drop in the fall. Soak to use.	Mixed hardwood forests of e. N. Amer.
Buttonball Tree: *See* Sycamore					
Calycanthus: *See* Allspice					
Cane River Cane *Arundinaria gigantea,* *A.g.* spp. *tecta* (*See also* Rattan)	Stems	Splintwork Plaiting		The split outer portion of stem is used by many southern Indians. Cut at base. Split and dry. Soak to use.	Se. U.S.
Cast-Iron Plant *Aspidistra elatior* 'Variegata'	Leaves Stems	Twining Coiling: core	Fall Winter	Cut leaf at base. Use green or dry to store. Soak to use.	Japan. House plant, gardens.
Catalpa *Catalpa* *bignonioides,* *C. speciosa*	Seedpods	Splintwork Coiling: core Ornament	Early spring Fall Winter	Gather pods as they fall. Store in bags or baskets. I've gathered them in early spring after they have lain under snow all winter. To use, soak in hot water for one hour. Open pod (if not already open); remove pith and seeds. Use whole or cut into thin strips.	*C. bignonioides:* Ga. to Fla. and Miss. *C. speciosa:* Cen. U.S. Widely nat. and cult. in e. U.S. moist; rich soils.
Catbrier: *See* Greenbrier					
Catclaw: *See* Sumac, Threeleaf					

PLANT	PART	TECHNIQUE	SEASON	PREPARATION AND NOTES	RANGE, HABITAT
Cattail *Typha angustifolia*	Stems	Coiling core	Late summer	Cut off at water level. Cut off top and split stem in half. Dry in sun. Soak to use and continue to split until thin enough. Remove pith.	Marshes, N. Amer.
Cattail *Typha latifolia*	Leaves	Plaiting Coiling: core stitching Twining Ornament	Early fall	Cut at water level. Separate leaves. Wash and dry. Tie into loose bundles and hang or store upright Soak in warm water to use, removing excess moisture.	Marshes, N. Amer.
Cedar, Eastern Red *Juniperus virginiana*	Inner bark	Splintwork Plaiting Coiling: stitching Rib baskets: weavers Ornament Twining	Spring Summer	Gather bark after tree is cut. Remove outer, shreddy bark. Cut, loop, and hang to dry. Soak to use. (Sap will make fingers sticky; use paint thinner to clean hands and tools.)	Widespread in e. U.S. from swamps. to dry, rocky outcrops.
Cedar, Northern White *Thuja occidentalis*	Roots	Coiling: core	Anytime	Split into thin strands.	Cen. and e. Canada, ne. U.S.; local in Appalachians.
Cedar, Post Incense Cedar *Calocedrus decurrens*	Trunk	Splintwork		Klamath Indians made round, V-shaped pack baskets from wood of the post cedar.	Cascade Mts. of Ore. and Sierra Nevada of Calif. s. to Baja Calif.
Cedar, Western Red Canoe Cedar *Thuja plicata*	Inner bark Roots	Plaiting Coiling: core stitching Twining Cordage			Areas of high precipitation in Pacific NW from se. Alaska along coast to nw. Calif., also se. B.C.
Century Plant: *See* Agave					
Cherry *Prunus* spp.	Inner bark	Wickerwork Splintwork Plaiting Twining	Spring Summer	Remove bark when green. Score length with knife. Make another cut about 1 inch away. Insert knife under strip and peel back.	Widespread.
Cladium Twig Rush *Cladium mariscoides*	Roots	Coiling: core stitching			Fresh or brackish swamps, marshes, or shores of e. N. Amer.
Clematis Virgin's Bower *Clematis virginiana*	Vine	Wickerwork Rib baskets: weavers	Spring Summer Fall	Use whole or split. This is the only vine that climbs by twining leaf stalks.	E. N. Amer. Other species cult. and escaped.
Cliffrose Quinine Bush *Cowania mexicana*	Bark	Twining Cordage Tying		Shreddy bark used for rope, sandals, and clothing.	E. Calif. to Colo. and N. Mex. Also grown as an ornamental.

PLANT	PART	TECHNIQUE	SEASON	PREPARATION AND NOTES	RANGE, HABITAT
Coconut: *See* Palm					
Coralberry Buckbrush, Indian Currant *Symphoricarpos* *orbiculatus*	Runners	Wickerwork Rib baskets: weavers	Spring Winter	To strip, boil for 3 hours. Rub with rough cloth. Coil and let dry. Soak 1 hour to use.	Open woods, thickets, and dry banks, N.Y. to Colo., s. to Fla. and Tex., n. Mexico.
Cordgrass Salt Marsh Grass, Slough Grass *Spartina* spp.	Leaves	Twining Cordage		Tough leaves were historically used to make cordage.	Marshes and shores of N. Amer.
Corn Indian Corn, Sweet Corn *Zea mays*	Husk	Coiling: core Twining Ornament Cordage	Summer	Cut stem end off cob. Remove husks. Spread to dry. Soak to use. Good for braiding. Garden varieties all useful.	Widely cult.

Cottonwood
Poplar
Populus angustifolia,
P. fremontii
	Trunk
	
	Shoots
	Roots
	Buds
		Splintwork
		Plaiting
		Rib baskets:
		  hoops
		  ribs
		  weavers
		Wickerwork
		Coiling:
		  core
		Cordage
			Spring
			Summer
				See pages 25 to 27.	*P. angustifolia:* Alberta. s. to n. Mexico.
					P. fremonti: sw. U.S. and n. Mexico.

Cottonwood, Black: *See* Poplar, Western Balsam					

Crocosmia
Montbretia
Crocosmia aurea **x** *pottsii*
	Leaves	Coiling:
		  core
		  stitching
		Twining
		Cordage
			Fall		S. Afr. Cult in warm climates and greenhouses.

Cycad *Cycas* spp.	Leaves	Coiling: core Twining		Some species of this palmlike plant may be hardy enough to resist frost.	Old World tropics. Cult. in greenhouses.
Daffodil *Narcissus* spp.	Leaves	Twining Coiling: core Cordage		Gather leaves after plants flower. Dry. Soak and wrap in towel to remove as much water as possible.	Eur., N. Afr. Widely cult.
Date: *See* Palm					

Daylily
Hemerocallis fulva
	Leaves	Coiling:
		  core
		  stitching
		Twining
			Late spring
			Fall
				Spread leaves to dry. Tie in bundles, tip end down. Soak to use. Wrap in towel.	Eur., Asia. Cult. and escaped in e. U.S.

Deergrass: *See* Epicampes					

PLANT	PART	TECHNIQUE	SEASON	PREPARATION AND NOTES	RANGE, HABITAT
Desert Spoon: *See* Sotol					
Devil's Claw: *See* Martynia					
Dogbane Indian Hemp *Apocynum* *androsaemifolium,* *A. cannabinum*	Stem fibers	Cordage Tying	Summer	Remove fibers as you would string celery. Gentle pounding or crushing may help to remove pulp from fibers. Twist into cordage.	*A. androsaemifolium:* N. Amer. *A. cannabinum:* U.S., Canada.
Dogwood, Flowering *Cornus florida*	Shoots Bark Wood	Wickerwork Rib baskets: rims weavers Carving awls and needles	Spring Summer	Use green, or dry and soak for several hours or overnight. *See* Tools, page 192.	E. U.S. Widely planted as ornamental
Dogwood, Red Osier *Cornus stolonifera*	Withes Bark	Wickerwork Rib baskets: hoops rims weavers Coiling: stitching Plaiting Ornament	Spring Summer	Use green, or dry and soak for several hours or overnight. Strip when green, if desired.	N. N. Amer.; local s. to Va. and N. Mex. Widely planted.
Dogwood, Silky *Cornus amomum*	Withes	Wickerwork Rib baskets	Spring Summer	Use green, or dry and soak for several hours or overnight.	Nfld. to Fla. and Tex.
Dracaena Cabbage Tree *Cordyline australis*	Leaves	Wickerwork Splintwork Twining Coiling	Anytime Spring is best		New Zealand.
Dracaena Dragon Tree *Dracaena draco*	Leaves	Plaiting Twining Ornament			Canary Islands. Frost-free climates and greenhouses.
Dune Grass, American *:* *See* Rye, Beach					
Elephant's Trunk: *See* Martynia					
Elm, American *Ulmus americana*	Shoots	Wickerwork Rib baskets: hoops rims weavers	Spring Summer	Prepare as for other shoots.	E. N. Amer. from s. Canada to Fla. and Tex. Virtually eliminated by Dutch elm disease.
Elm, Slippery Red Elm *Ulmus rubra*	Inner bark	Splintwork Plaiting	Spring Summer	Strip while green as for other barks.	Lowlands of ne. N. Amer. from s. Ont. to nw. Fla.

PLANT	PART	TECHNIQUE	SEASON	PREPARATION AND NOTES	RANGE, HABITAT
Elm, Winged Cork Elm *Ulmus alata*	Inner bark	Cordage			S. Midwest and se. U.S.
Epicampes Deergrass *Epicampes rigens,* *Muhlenbergia rigens*	Stem above top joint	Coiling: core			Deserts of se. Calif.

Eucalyptus
Blue Gum
Eucalyptus globulus
	Bark
	
	Branches
	Pods
		Plaiting
		Twining
		Cordage
		Coiling:
		  core
		  Ornament
				Large pieces of bark can be stitched together.	Australia and Tasmania. Nat. and widely cult. in Calif.

Fatsia: *See* Aralia, Japanese					
Fennel *Foeniculum vulgare*	Split stalks	Plaiting Twining	Spring Fall	Cut stalk at base and split. Also cult. as herb. Strong odor.	Old World. Widely nat. Also cult. as herb.
Fern, Brake Bracken *Pteridium aquilinum*	Rootstock Shoots	Ornament	Spring Fall	Crush with mallet or stone. Remove inner dark brown flat strands. Discard white strings, outer skin, and pulp.	Common, widespread.
Fern, Giant Chain *Woodwardia spinulosa*	Stalk	Twining Ornament	Spring Fall Winter	Remove leaflets and top. Pound stalk with rock. Twist to separate outer section and discard. Use the two light green strands inside stalk. Dry.	Mexico, Guatemala. Cult. in moist woodlands or greenhouses.

Fern, Golden-Back
Ceropteris triangularis,
Gymnogramma
triangularis,
Pityrogramma
triangularis
	Stems	Coiling:
		  core
		  stitching
			Fall	Black stem used as substitute for maidenhair fern.	B.C. to Baja Calif.

Fern, Maidenhair *Adiantum pedatum*	Frond Stems	Coiling: stitching Twining Ornament	Fall	Dry frond intact, then remove leaflets and store stem. Soak and split to use. Beautiful dark mahogany color (almost black). Check your state's list of protected plants before collecting any of this species.	Woods, N. Amer.

PLANT	PART	TECHNIQUE	SEASON	PREPARATION AND NOTES	RANGE, HABITAT
Fern, Sensitive *Onoclea sensibilis*	Stalk with spore cases	Wickerwork Ornament		Leave spore cases attached for unusual ornament.	Ne. and cen. U.S.
Fir, Douglas *Pseudotsuga menziesii*	Roots	Coiling: stitching Twining		Used by Pomo Indians. (O.T. Mason)	Pac. Northwest and Rockies s. to Mexico
Fireweed *Epilobium angustifolium*	Stalks	Coiling: stitching Twining	Late spring Fall	Cut at base or pull out of ground. Use green or dry, then soak. Stalks are hollow.	Recently cleared or burned areas of N. Amer. Aggressive spreader.
Flag: *See* Iris					
Flag, Sweet *Acorus calamus*	Leaves	Coiling: core stitching Twining	Late summer Fall	Cut at water line. Dry. Soak and wrap in towel to use.	Wet places and borders of quiet water, N. Hemisphere
Flax *Linum lewisii, L. perenne, L. usitatissimum*	Stem fibers	Coiling: stitching Cordage Twining	Summer	*L. usitatissimum,* the species used to spin into linen, is now grown mainly in Eur. and Asia. Cult. extensively in the U.S. before the advent of the cotton industry, it is grown commercially only in the Willamette Valley, Ore., and Montana for seed. Grown for fiber on a small scale by many spinners and weavers.	Chiefly N. Hemisphere. *L. usitatissimum* probably from Asia.
Flax, New Zealand New Zealand Hemp *Phormium tenax* 'Variegatum'	Leaves	Wickerwork Coiling: core stitching Twining Cordage		Use whole or split.	New Zealand. Grown for fiber or ornament, outside in warm climates or in pots.
Galleta *Hilaria jamesii*	Stems	Coiling: core stitching		O.T. Mason: Used by Moki Indians of n. Arizona.	Deserts, canyons, and dry plains, Wyo. and Utah to Tex. and Calif.
Gladiolus *Gladiolus* spp.	Leaves		After flowering	Pull dry leaves at base of plant. Dry. Soak as briefly as possible.	Gardens.
Goldenrod *Solidago* spp.	Stems	Ornament	Early spring Fall Winter	Soak dried stalk. Rub with fingers or cloth to remove thin outer layer. Use for beading in twining or coiling.	Widespread in N. Amer.

PLANT	PART	TECHNIQUE	SEASON	PREPARATION AND NOTES	RANGE, HABITAT

Grape
Vitis spp.
	Vines
	Bark
	Roots
	Fruit
		Wickerwork
		Rib baskets:
		  hoops
		  ribs
		  weavers
		Coiling:
		  core
		Ornament
			Anytime	Use whole or split. Use bark bunched for cores. Fruit for dyeing.	Numerous species throughout U.S.

Grass, Bear
  Squaw Grass
    Xerophyllum tenax
  See also Nolina
	Leaves	Coiling:
		  stitching
		  twining
		Ornament
			Spring
			Summer
				Leaves are 3 ft. long. Nip off at bottom of stalk. Dry for 3 days. Soak for 15 minutes to use. Long, white leaves shaded faint purple at one end.	Open woods and clearings B.C. to Wyo., and cen. Calif.

Grass, Esparto
  Spear Grass
    Stipa tenacissima
		Cordage
		Tying
				In Old World, grass used also for paper making.	Spain and N. Afr. Sometimes cult. for ornament.

Grass, Broom Beard:
  Bluestem, Bunchgrass,
  Broom Sedge
    Andropogon virginicus,
    Schizachyrium scoparium
	Stems
	Leaves
		Coiling:
		  core
		  stitching
		Twining
		Dyes
					Open ground and open woods e. and cen. N. Amer.

Grass, Pampas
  Cortaderia selloana
	Leaves	Coiling:
		  core
					S. Amer. Cult. as ornamental in warmer parts of U.S.

Grass Salt Marsh: *See* Cordgrass					

Grass, Sweet
  Holygrass, Seneca Grass,
  Vanilla Grass
    Hierochloe odorata
	Leaves	Coiling:
		  core
		Twining
			Summer
			Fall
				Cut and dry. Tie in bundles or braids to store.	Meadows of n. N. Amer., sw to N. Mex. and Ariz.

Grass, Sweet Vernal
  Anthoxanthum odoratum
	Leaves
	Stems
		Coiling:
		  core
			Summer
			Early fall
				Cut and dry. Tie in bundles to store.	Europe. Fields, waste places of e. N. Amer. and Pac. slope.

Grass, Tufted Hair
  Deschampsia caespitosa
	Stems	Coiling:
		  stitching
		Twining
				For white patterns.	N. and cen. N. Amer. Also cult. as ornamental.

Grass, Wire: *See* Rush, Soft					

Greenbrier
  Catbrier, Smilax
    Smilax spp.
	Vines	Wickerwork		Thorns must be removed.	Woods and thickets of N. Amer.

PLANT	PART	TECHNIQUE	SEASON	PREPARATION AND NOTES	RANGE, HABITAT

Hazelnut
Corylus cornuta
var. *californica*
	Shoots
	Bark
		Wickerwork
		Rib baskets:
		  ribs
		  weavers
		Twining
				Strip when green. Let dry.
				Soak 15 minutes before using.
				Other species may prove useful.
				Bark may be used for dyes.
					B.C. to Calif.

Hedge Apple: *See* Osage Orange					

Hemlock, Black
Tsuga mertensiana
	Roots	Coiling:
		  core
		  stitching
				The split roots were used by
				the Indians of Neah Bay, Wash.
					Mtns of se. Alaska
					to Calif. and of B.C.
					and Id.

Hemlock, Eastern
Tsuga canadensis
	Inner bark
	
	Roots
		Splintwork
		Plaiting
		Coiling:
		  stitching
		Twining
		Rib baskets:
		  weavers
		Ornament
		
		Wickerwork
		Coiling:
		  core
		  stitching
		Twining
		Ornament
			Spring
			Summer
			Fall
				See pages 22 to 23.
				
				Wash, dry, and store in loose
				bundles. Soak to use.
					Ne. N. Amer. from
					s. Canada to n. Ala.
					and w. to Minn.

Hemp: *See* Marijuana					
Hemp, Bowstring *Sansevieria zeylanica,* *S. longifolia*	Leaves	Twining Cordage Tying		Leaves yield a strong fiber.	Ceylon, Afr. Nat. in warm climates.
Hemp, Indian: *See* Dogbane					
Hemp, River Wild hemp *Sesbania exaltata,* *S. macrocarpa*	Stem fibers	Cordage Tying		Grows 12 feet high, purple- spotted, yellowish, pealike flowers; thin foot-long seedpods. Prepare like dogbane and nettle.	N.Y. to Fla., w. to s. Calif.
Hickory, Bitternut *Carya cordiformis*	Inner bark	Splintwork Plaiting Ornament	Spring Summer	*See* method for hemlock, pages 22 to 23. Used by Cherokees of N.C. for yellow patterns in their baskets.	Que. s. to Fla. and La.

Hickory, Shagbark
Carya ovata
	Trunk	Splintwork
		Plaiting
		Rib baskets:
		  ribs
		  rims
		  weavers
		  handles
			Spring
			Summer
			Fall
				See method for white oak,
				pages 25 to 27.
					Que., s. to Fla. and
					Tex.

Holygrass: *See* Grass, Sweet					

PLANT	PART	TECHNIQUE	SEASON	PREPARATION AND NOTES	RANGE, HABITAT

Honeysuckle
 Lonicera japonica
	Vines	Wickerwork
		 Coiling:
		   core
		 Rib baskets:
		   weavers
			Spring
			 Summer
				Remove leaves. Boil for 3 hours to strip, if desired. Coil and dry to store. Try different species.	E. Asia; nat. in N. Amer.; a weed in woods of middle Atlantic states.

Horsetail Scouring Rush *Equisetum palustre*	Rootstock	Twining Coiling: stitching Ornament		Split into strips. Dark purple-black patterns made from surface splints of rootstock.	Various species widespread. Marshes and meadows of N. Amer.
Indian Currant: *See* Coralberry					
Indian Millet: *See* Rice Grass					

Iris
 Flag
 Iris spp.
	Leaves	Coiling:
		   core
		   stitching
		 Twining
			Late summer
			 Fall
				Beautiful rust and tan colors if harvested before frost. Dry and store in bundles. Soak in warm water to use. Wrap in wet towel to keep mellowed.	Widespread. Many cult. for ornament.

Ivy, Boston *Parthenocissus tricuspidata*	Vine	Wickerwork	Summer	Use like virginia creeper or other vines.	China, Japan. Cult. as climber or ground cover.
Jasmine *Gelsemium* spp., *Jasminum* spp.	Vines Roots	Wickerwork			*Gelsemium*: Asia, e. N. Amer. *Jasminum*: Asia, Afr. Australia. Grown outdoors in warm regions or in greenhouses.
Juneberry: *See* Serviceberry					
Kelp, Bull *Nereocystis* spp.	Runners Leaves	Wickerwork Twining		Use immediately or dry and redampen but do not soak.	Gather on beaches.
Kudzu *Pueraria lobata*	Vines	Wickerwork		Originally introduced to U.S. for its tuberous roots and for fiber.	China, Japan. Borders of woods and fields of se. U.S., spreading north to Pa. and Tenn.
Lauhala: *See* Pandanus					
Lavender *Lavandula angustifolia*	Stems	Wickerwork Rib baskets: weavers			Medit. region. Widely cult. as herb and ornamental.
Leatherroot: *See* Scurf Pea					

PLANT	PART	TECHNIQUE	SEASON	PREPARATION AND NOTES	RANGE, HABITAT
Leatherwood Moosewood *Dirca palustris*	Entire bark Twigs	Wickerwork Splintwork Plaiting Cordage		Extremely tough bark, used much like basswood.	Rich woods, N.B. to Minn, s. to Fla.
Lilac California: *See* Buckthorn					
Lilac, Common Syringa *Syringa vulgaris*	Twigs	Wickerwork	Spring Summer		Se. Eur. Widely cult. in U.S. as ornamental.
Lily, Ginger *Hedychium* spp.	Leaves	Coiling Twining Plaiting			Gardens.
Lily, Southern Bugle: *See* Watsonia					
Lily-of-the-Nile Blue African Lily *Agapanthus africanus*	Flower stem	Twining		Hollow flower stems are 18 to 20 inches long. Split into quarters.	S. Afr. often grown as tub plant.
Lilyturf *Liriope muscari*	Leaves	Coiling: core	Winter	Dry the grass like foliage. Minimal soaking.	Japan, China. Ground cover in moist soil, warm regions.
Lima Bean *Phaseolus lunatus*	Entire plant	Coiling: core			S. Amer. tropics. Cult. as vegetable.
Linden, American: *See* Basswood					
Locust, Black False Acacia *Robinia pseudoacacia*	Roots	Coiling: core		Has a wide-spreading fibrous root system.	Cen. Appalachian and Ozark Mts. Widely planted for ornament and shelter belts.
Maguey: *See* Agave					
Mandevilla Chilean jasmine *Mandevilla* spp.	Runners	Wickerwork			Trop. Amer. Cult. outdoors in warm regions, in pots and greenhouses elsewhere.
Manna Grass *Glyceria elata,* *G. striata* (formerly *G. nervata*)	Stems	Ornament		Used by the Tlingit of Alaska.	Widespread in N. Amer s. to. N. Mexico.
Maple, Oregon *Acer macrophyllum*	Inner bark	Plaiting	Spring	Indians of Mendocino Co., Calif., made baskets woven so closely as to hold water.	Sw. B.C. to s. Calif.

PLANT	PART	TECHNIQUE	SEASON	PREPARATION AND NOTES	RANGE, HABITAT

Maple, Red
Swamp Maple,
Scarlet Maple
Acer rubrum
	Shoots	Wickerwork
		Rib baskets:
		  hoops
		  ribs
			Spring
			Summer
				Prepare as for other shoots..	S. Canada and
					ne. U.S.

	Trunk	Splintwork
		Plaiting
		Rib baskets:
		  hoops
		  ribs
		  weavers
				See method for white oak,
				pages 25 to 27.	

	Inner bark	Splintwork Plaiting Rib baskets: weavers		*See* method for hemlock bark, pages 22 to 23. Beautiful reddish color; inner bark of various other maple species used for dyes.	
Maple, Vine *Acer circinatum*	Runners	Wickerwork Splintwork			Pac. Coast from sw B.C. to n. Calif.
Marijuana Hemp *Cannabis sativa*	Inner bark	Cordage Tying Twining		Grown in the past for fibers in stems. Inner bark of very tough fibers. Note: Growing marijuana in the U.S. and Canada is now illegal.	Cen. Asia. Nat. widely in N. Amer.
Martynia Devil's Claw, Elephant's Trunk, Unicorn Plant *Proboscidea fragrans*, *P. louisianica*, *P. parviflora*	Seedpods	Coiling: stitching	Late fall	The outer green layer of the seedpod falls off at maturity, leaving a long, thin horn, which splits along its length as the pod dries. Soak the horn, which can be up to 13 in. long, and split it further by piercing the tip with an awl. Discard the white pith inside.	*P. fragrans*: Mexico. Grown as ornamental or for young fruit, which is pickled. *P. louisianica*: Del. and Ind. s. to N. Mex.
Melaleuca Bottlebrush, Swamp Tea Tree *Melaleuca quinquenervia*	Bark	Ornament		Use dry. Fragile. Soaking causes delamination. Gather fallen bark.	Australia. Cult. in s. Calif. and s. Fla.
Mesquite, Screw Bean *Prosopis pubescens*	Inner bark	Splintwork Plaiting			S. Nev. s. to Mexico.
Milkweed *Asclepias cordifolia*, *A. syriaca*	Stem fibers	Cordage Tying Coiling: core Twining	Summer	Same as for dogbane.	*A. cordifolia*: Cen. Calif. to s. Ore. *A. syriaca*: N.B. to Sask., s. to Ga. and Okla.
Millet Broomcorn Millet *Panicum miliaceum*	Stems	Wickerwork Coiling: core	Summer		Asia. Escaped from cult., in ne. U.S. and occasionally elsewhere.

PLANT	PART	TECHNIQUE	SEASON	PREPARATION AND NOTES	RANGE, HABITAT

Mock Orange
  Syringa
    Philadelphus lewisii,
    P. inodorus
	Twigs	Wickerwork			*P. inodorus:* Pa. to Ala.
					P. lewisii: w. N. Amer.

Montbretia: *See* Crocosmia					

Morning Glory, Common
  Ipomoea purpurea
Morning Glory, Small Red
  I. coccinea
	Vines	Wickerwork	Spring
			Summer
			Fall
				Vines can be used for small wickerwork baskets.	*I. purpurea:* Trop. Amer. Widespread, roadsides, etc
					I. coccinea: Trop. Amer. Waste places, e. and cen. U.S. sw. to Ariz.

Moss, Spanish
  Tillandsia usneoides
	Fibers	Coiling:
		  core
		Twining
		Ornament
		Cordage
				For cordage, use well-retted material found on ground. Coarse black fibers are durable; live, green plant is weak.	Hangs from tree branches, se. U.S. to Argentina.

Mother-in-Law's Tongue
  Snake Plant
    Sansevieria trifasciata
	Leaves	Cordage
		Tying
		Twining
			Anytime	Split leaves with knife or needle. Dry. Soak to use. For cordage, pound leaves to separate fibers.	Afr. Asia. House plant. Also outdoors, s. to Fla.

Mulberry, Paper *Broussonetia papyrifera*	Shoots Inner bark	Wickerwork	Spring	Use shoots whole or split as for basket willow. Soaking inner bark in water, then pounding yields tapa cloth.	E. Asia. Planted and nat. widely in e. U.S.
Mulberry, Red *Morus rubra*	Inner bark	Splintwork Plaiting Cordage Tying	Spring Summer	May be pounded and crushed to make pliable. (Choctaw)	Rich bottomland soils of e. N. Amer.
Mulberry, White *Morus alba*	Inner bark Root bark	Splintwork Plaiting Cordage Tying	Spring Summer	May be pounded and crushed to make pliable.	China. Widely cult. across U.S. and nat. in e., s., and Pac. states.

Myrtle
  Periwinkle
    Vinca minor
	Runners	Coiling:
		  core
		Twining
			Summer
			Fall
					Eur. Ground cover.

Nettle
  Laportea canadensis,
  Urtica breweri,
  U. canadensis,
  U. dioica, U. gracilis
  ssp. *holosericea,*
  U. lyallii, U. nivea
	Stalk fibers	Cordage
		Tying
			Fall	Dry in the fall. Soak to separate fibers from pulp and bark. Cordage is stronger than that made from cotton or hemp.	*L. canadensis:* e. N. Amer.
					U. dioica: Eur. and Asia. Widely nat.

Nolina
  Parry's Nolina, Bear Grass
    Nolina parryi
	Leaves	Twining
		Coiling:
		  core
				Leaves are 2 to 3 ft. long. Use whole or split.	S. Calif.

PLANT	PART	TECHNIQUE	SEASON	PREPARATION AND NOTES	RANGE, HABITAT
Nutmeg, California *Torreya californica*	Roots Bark	Coiling		Pomo Indians used the split root.	Mountains of cen. and n. Calif.
Oak, Basket *Quercus michauxii*	Trunk	Splintwork Plaiting Rib baskets: ribs weavers		*See* pages 25 to 27	Bottomlands of se. U.S. from N.J. to Fla. and e. Tex. and n. to s. Ill.
Oak, White *Quercus alba*	Trunk	Splintwork Plaiting, Rib baskets: hoops ribs weavers		*See* pages 25 to 27. Bark of various species used for dyes.	Me. to Fla. and Tex.
Oats *Avena fatua,* *A. sativa*	Stems	Coiling: core	Summer	Cut and dry. Tie into bundles for storage. Soak in warm water to use.	*A. fatua:* Eurasia. Rare in e. U.S., but common weed in Pac. states. Cult. for hay. *A. sativa:* Medit. Widely cult.
Orchid, Cymbidium *Cymbidium* spp.	Leaves	Plaiting Twining		Dry. Soak 15 to 30 minutes before using.	Trop. Asia, Australia. Cult. in greenhouses or outside in Calif.
Osage Orange Hedge Apple, Bois d'Arc *Maclura pomifera*	Roots Inner bark	Coiling: core stitching Cordage			Lowlands of s. cen. U.S.; planted throughout the U.S.
Palm, Cabbage Palmetto Carolina Palmetto *Sabal palmetto*	Leaf stalks Leaves	Splintwork Plaiting Coiling: stitching Ornament		Best fibers in young leaf stalk. Coarser fibers from mature leaves. Use green or dry. Wet briefly before using dried leaves.	Fla. n. along coast to s. N.C.
Palm, Coconut *Cocos nucifera*	Leaves	Splintwork Plaiting Coiling: stitching Ornament			Coast of s. Fla. and Keys.
Palm, Date *Phoenix canariensis,* *P. dactylifera*	Seed stalks	Wickerwork Twining Coiling: stitching Ornament			*P. canariensis:* Canary Islands *P. dactylifera:* Afr., Arabia. Both spp. planted in Fla., Calif., Ariz., and Tex.

PLANT	PART	TECHNIQUE	SEASON	PREPARATION AND NOTES	RANGE, HABITAT
Palm, Fan *Washingtonia filifera*	Leaves	Splintwork Plaiting Coiling: stitching Ornament		Split dried blades with fingernail or needle.	Near springs and streams, sw. Ariz., se. Calif and ne. Baja Calif.
Palm, Jelly *Butia capitata*	Leaves	Coiling: stitching		I used a frond of this species obtained from the New York Botanical Garden for stitching in coiled baskets. Many other palms are good for weaving.	Brazil. Planted in Fla. and Calif.
Pandanus Lauhala, Screw Pine *Pandanus odoratissimus,* *P. tectorius, P. utilis*	Leaves	Splintwork Plaiting		In Tahiti, sleeping mats are woven of the pandanus. Leaves may be 6 or 7 ft. long. Dried leaves can be used as is or lightly dampened.	Old World tropics. Grown in greenhouses in cold regions, outdoors in warm.
Papyrus Umbrella Plant *Cyperus alternifolius,* *C. papyrus*	Stems	Wickerwork	Anytime	Cut stem at base of plant. Flatten stem (try clothes wringer).Lightweight and good for large baskets.	N. Afr., Near East. Cult. in water gardens and as pot plant.
Peach *Prunus persica*	Twigs Shoots	Wickerwork			China. Cult. in temperate climates for fruit.
Periwinkle: *See* Myrtle					
Philodendron, Giant *Philodendron giganteum*	Leaf sheath Leaf stems Roots	Plaiting Twining Coiling	Anytime	Soak for 2 days.	

Phragmites
   Giant Reed
 Phragmites australis
	Seed heads
	 Stems
	 Leaves
		Coiling:
		   core
		 Ornament
			Winter
			 Spring
				See A.S. Hitchcock's *Manual of the Grasses of the U.S.* Gather dried tassels after seeds have been dispersed by wind. They will still be present before new growth starts in early spring. Indians and Mexicans used stems for cordage and carrying nets.	Widespread, but more abundant near coast.

Pine, Digger *Pinus sabiniana*	Roots	Twining Cordage Tying		Warm roots in hot, damp ashes and split before cooling. May be soaked in water also, then scraped. Some roots may be 50 or 60 ft. long.	Dry foothills of coast ranges and Sierra Nevada of Calif.

Pine, Jack
 Pinus banksiana
	Roots	Twining
		 Coiling:
		   core
		   stitching
				Use like spruce root.	Canadian Rockies e. to n. New Eng. and s. to Ind. and Minn.

PLANT	PART	TECHNIQUE	SEASON	PREPARATION AND NOTES	RANGE, HABITAT
Pine, Longleaf Georgia Pine, Longstraw Pine, Southern Yellow Pine *Pinus palustris*	Needles	Coiling: core	Spring Summer	Gather needles from tree or from the ground if they have not lain there long. Wash in mild detergent. Rinse, dry in shade, and tie in bundles to keep them straight. (*See* Osma G. Tod's *Earth Basketry.*)	Coastal Plain of se. U.S. w. to e. Tex.
Pine, Ponderosa Western Yellow Pine *Pinus ponderosa*	Roots Needles	Coiling: core stitching			S. B.C. to Tex. and Mexico.
Pine, Running Ground Pine *Lycopodium complanatum*	Runners	Wickerwork	Fall Winter	For novel effect, use the runners with the greenery intact. The tiny leaves of this club moss will shrivel up, but when you want to show off your basket soak it in warm water and the greenery will "come to life."	Dry woods of n. N. Amer.
Pine, Slash *Pinus elliottii*	Needles	Coiling: core	Late spring Summer	*See* Pine, Longleaf.	Coastal plain of se. U.S.
Pine, Sugar *Pinus lambertiana*	Roots	Coiling: stitching		Steam roots under sand with a fire above. Slender strands split from roots.	Mountains from w. Ore. s. through Sierra Nevada to S. Calif.
Pine, White *Pinus strobus*	Trunk Bark	Plaiting Splintwork			Ne. U.S.
Plane Tree, American: *See* Sycamore					
Plantain *Plantago* spp.	Stem	Wickerwork	Spring	Cut stem at base. Dry. Soak to use.	Widespread, mostly weedy.
Ponytail *Beaucarnea recurvata*	Leaves midvein	Twining Plaiting		Leaf edges can be sharp, but soften when wet. Green part of leaf can be removed to expose usable midvein.	Mexico. Cult. outdoors in warm, dry regions or indoors.
Poplar, Balsam Balm-of-Gilead *Populus balsamifera,* *P.* x *gileadensis*	Roots	Wickerwork Coiling: core stitching Twining		*P.* x *gileadensis* may be a hybrid of *P. balsamifera* and *P. deltoides.*	N. Amer.
Poplar, Western Balsam Black Cottonwood *Populus trichocarpa*	Roots	Cordage Twining			S. Alaska and Yukon, s. to Calif. and Baja.
Quinine Bush: *See* Cliffrose					

PLANT	PART	TECHNIQUE	SEASON	PREPARATION AND NOTES	RANGE, HABITAT
Rabbitbrush *Chrysothamnus laricinus,* *C. moquianus,* *C. nauseosus,* *C. tinctorius*	Branches	Wickerwork		Moki Indians made wicker plaques from this plant.	Dry, open places with sagebrush or open woodlands, W. Canada to Calif., Tex., and n. Mexico.
Raffia *Raphia pedunculata*	Leaves	Coiling: core stitching Twining Cordage		Commonly available as a basketry material from commercial suppliers.	Madagascar.
Raspberry *Rubus* spp.	Canes	Wickerwork Coiling: stitching	Fall	Remove thorns and leaves with heavy-gloved hands. Split cane.	Wild or cult. for fruit in n. and cen. N. Amer.
Rattan Reed, Cane *Calamus siphonospathus*	Inner bark Vines	Splintwork Plaiting Wickerwork Coiling: core stitching Rib baskets: hoops ribs weavers		Commonly available as a basketry material from commercial suppliers.	E. Asia.
Redbud, Eastern *Cercis canadensis* **Redbud, Western** *Cercis occidentalis*	Branches Bark	Coiling: stitching	Fall	Leave bark on. Split branches. Remove pith. Bark has dark red patterns	E. U.S. Widely planted for its spring flowers. N. Calif. e. to s. Utah and S. Ariz., often in oak and chaparral woodlands.
Redtop *Agrostis gigantea*	Stems	Coiling: core	Late spring Summer Fall	Dry. Soak a half hour in cold water. Wrap in towel.	Eurasia Cult. in cooler parts of U.S. for pastures and lawns.
Redtop, Tall *Triodia flava*	Stems	Coiling: core	Late spring Summer Fall	Dry. Soak a half hour in cold water. Wrap in towel.	Dry fields and roadsides of e. and cen. U.S.
Redwood *Sequoia sempervirens*	Inner bark	Plaiting Splintwork			Pac. Coast of sw Ore. and n. and cen. Calif.
Reed: *See* Rattan					
Reed, Giant: *See* Phragmites					
Reedgrass, Wood *Cinna latifolia*	Stem	Ornament		Tlingits of Alaska made overlay on spruce root for white pattern.	N. and cen. N. Amer.
Rice *Oryza sativa*	Stems	Coiling: core	Spring Fall	One of the world's most important food plants.	Se Asia. Cult. in Calif. and s. U.S.

PLANT	PART	TECHNIQUE	SEASON	PREPARATION AND NOTES	RANGE, HABITAT

Rice, Wild
   Indian Rice, Water Oats
   Zizania aquatica
	Stems	Coiling:
		   core
		   stitching
			Spring
			Fall
					Quiet waters, from s. Me. and s. Que. to se. Wis., to w. Fla., La., Id.

Ricegrass
   Indian Millet, Silk Grass
   Oryzopsis hymenoides
	Stems	Coiling:
		   core
			Spring
			Fall
				Oryzopsis means "likeness to rice."	W. N. Amer. from se. B.C. and Man. to Tex., Calif., and n. Mexico.

Rose
   Rosa spp.
	Canes	Wickerwork
		Rib baskets:
		   hoops
		   ribs
			Fall
			Winter
				Remove leaves and thorns. Boil to remove bark. Coil, dry to store. Some species are brittle but stringy enough to use for ribs.	Everywhere.

Rush
   Juncus acutus
Rush, Basket
   Juncus textalis
Rush, Soft
   Wire Grass
   Juncus effusus
	Stems	Coiling:
		   core
		   stitching
		Twining
		Ornament
			Fall	*See* O.T. Mason's *Aboriginal American Indian Basketry.* Soft rush used in Japan for weaving tatami.	Afr., Eurasia, N. Amer.

Rush, Scouring: *See* Horsetail					
Rush, Twig: *See* Cladium					

Rye
   Secale cereale
	Stems	Coiling:
		   core
		Ornament
		Plaiting
			Late
			summer
				Cut and dry. Tie into bundles for storage.	Widespread. Escaped from cult. into fields and waste places.

Rye, Beach Wild
   American Dune Grass
   Elymus arenarius
	Stems	Coiling:
		   core
		Twining
		Plaiting
				Split stems used for white patterns in spruce root baskets of Tlingit, s. Alaska coast.	Sand dunes along coast of N. Amer., also along Lakes Superior and Mich.

Sansevieria: *See* Mother-in-Law's Tongue					

Sassafras
   Sassafras albidum
	Roots
	
	Shoots
		Wickerwork
		Twining
		
		Wickerwork
		Rib baskets:
		   hoops
		   ribs
			Anytime
			
			Spring
			Summer
			Fall
					E. deciduous forests from Me. to Fla. and Tex.

Screwbean: *See* Mesquite, Screwbean					

Scurf Pea
   Leatherroot
   Psoralea argophylla,
   P. macrostachya
	Bark fibers
	Roots
		Cordage
		Tying
				Thread also made for sewing. Pleasant scent lingers for months.	*P. argophylla:* Dry prairies, cen. U.S.
					P. macrostachya: Calif.

PLANT	PART	TECHNIQUE	SEASON	PREPARATION AND NOTES	RANGE, HABITAT
Sedge *Carex* spp.	Roots	Twining Coiling	Anytime	Split root when fresh and remove outer covering. Split again, coil, and dry.	Widespread in wet areas.
	Leaves	Twining	Fall	Dry leaves; soak to use.	
Serviceberry Juneberry, Shadbush *Amelanchier alnifolia*	Branches	Wickerwork Rib baskets: hoops ribs			W. Ont. to Yukon, s. to Neb., Colo., Id., Ore.
Sequoia: *See* Redwood					
Smilax: *See* Greenbrier					
Snake Plant: *See* Mother-In-Law's Tongue					
Sotol Desert Spoon *Dasylirion simplex,* *D. wheeleri*	Leaves	Plaiting Splintwork		Remove coarse marginal teeth. Split leaves into fine strands. Many species, some becoming rare.	Sw. U.S. and Mexico.
Spider Plant *Chlorophytum comosum*	Leaves	Twining Coiling: core stitching			S. Afr. House plant.
Spruce, Black Swamp Spruce *Picea mariana*	Roots	Twining Coiling: core			N. N. Amer., s. to ne. U.S.
Spruce, Red Eastern Spruce, Yellow Spruce *Picea rubens*	Roots	Twining Coiling: core			Ne. N. Amer. and ridges of Appalachians.
Spruce, Sitka *Picea sitchensis*	Roots	Twining		Boil and split.	Pac. Coast from s. Alaska and B.C. to nw. Calif.
Spruce, White *Picea glauca*	Roots	Cordage Twining			N. N. Amer. s. to n. cen.U.S.
Squawgrass: *See* Grass, Bear					
Strawberry *Fragaria* spp.	Runners	Wickerwork	Spring Fall	Pretty red color—for very small baskets.	Widespread. Wild or cult.
Strawberry Shrub: *See* Allspice					

PLANT	PART	TECHNIQUE	SEASON	PREPARATION AND NOTES	RANGE, HABITAT
Sumac, Smooth *Rhus glabra*	Leaf stems	Wickerwork		Tapered leaf stems are up to 16 in. long	Widespread in e. and midwestern U.S.; local elsewhere.
Sumac, Staghorn Velvet Sumac *Rhus typhina*	Leaf stems	Wickerwork	Fall	Use whole leaf stems.	Ne. and cen. N. Amer.
Sumac, Threeleaf Catclaw *Rhus trilobata*	Branches Roots	Coiling: stitching	Early spring Fall	Use whole or split as for basket willow.	Ill. to Calif.
Sycamore, American Buttonball Tree, American Plane Tree *Platanus occidentalis*	Leaf stem	Ornament Spokes for miniatures	Fall	Gather when leaves fall. Cut off leaf. Soak for one hour to use. Flared end resembles small bell.	E. U.S.
Syringa: *See* Lilac, Mock Orange					
Ti *Cordyline terminalis*	Leaves	Cordage Twining		Very thin but strong leaves.	E. Asia. House plant.
Timothy *Phleum* spp.	Stems	Coiling: core	Late summer Fall	Cut at base. Dry. Soak and wrap in towel.	N. Amer., Eurasia. Cult as forage.
Tree-of-Heaven: *See* Ailanthus					
Trefoil, Prostrate Tick *Desmodium rotundifolium*	Runners	Coiling: stitching Twining Cordage	Summer Late summer	May be used green. Dry in coil and soak to use. Thin but strong.	Dry woods of e. N. Amer. from Fla. to Tex. to Ont. and Mich.
Tule: *See* Bulrush					
Umbrella Plant: *See* Papyrus					
Unicorn Plant: *See* Martynia					
Vinca Vine Band Plant *Vinca major* 'Variegata' *See also* Myrtle	Vine	Wickerwork		Light-colored vine useful for small baskets.	Eur. House plant; grown as annual in cold climates, as ground cover in South and West.
Virginia Creeper Woodbine *Parthenocissus quinquefolia*	Runners	Wickerwork Rib baskets: weavers	Summer	Remove leaves but not nodes and bumps, which give character and a lovely, rustic appearance. Work green if pliable enough or soak in warm water.	Ne. U.S. to Fla. and Mexico. Also cult. as ground cover.

PLANT	PART	TECHNIQUE	SEASON	PREPARATION AND NOTES	RANGE, HABITAT
Virgin's Bower: *See* Clematis					
Walnut, Black *Juglans nigra*	Leaf stems Inner bark	Wickerwork Plaiting	Fall Spring Summer	Stems are tapered, up to 24 in. long. Gather and let dry. Store, butt ends down, in paper bags or tie in bundles. Soak at least one hour to use.	E. U.S. except northern border. Grown for its lumber and edible nuts.
Walnut, White: *See* Butternut					
Watsonia Southern Bugle Lily *Watsonia* spp.	Leaves	Coiling: core stitching Plaiting Twining		Dry. Soak to use.	S. Afr., Madagascar Nat. in Australia. Gardens.
Wheat *Triticum* spp.	Stems	Coiling: core	Late summer	Same as for rye.	Medit. region and sw Asia. Widely cult. as cereal grain.
Willow, Basket Purple Willow *Salix purpurea* **Willow, Basket** *Salix viminalis, S. triandra*	Twigs Withes Bark Roots	Wickerwork Plaiting Rib baskets: weavers hoops ribs Plaiting Wrapping Cordage Coiling Twining	Spring Summer Fall	*S. purpurea* and *S. viminalis* introd. by pioneers from Europe. Harvest by cutting to the ground each year. Many native species also are suitable for basketry. A good account of willow cultivation, harvesting, preparation, and weaving is given in *Baskets and Basketry* by Dorothy Wright.	Eur., Asia. Escaped from cult., e. N. Amer. Also grown as an ornamental.
Willow, Black *Salix nigra*	Rods Roots	Wickerwork Rib baskets: weaver hoops ribs			E. and cen. U.S., n. Mexico.
Willow, Pussy *Salix discolor*	Withes	Wickerwork			Wet ground, n. and cen. N. Amer.
Willow, Sandbar Narrowleaf Willow *Salix exigua*	Twigs Bark	Wickerwork			N. and cen. N. Amer. along streams and lakes s. to n. Mexico.
Willow, Sitka *Salix sitchensis*	Twigs	Wickerwork			Pac. Coast from sw. Alaska to cen. Calif. and mts. in w. Mont. and cen. Alberta.
Willow, Upland *Salix humilis*	Inner bark	Cordage Tying			E. N. Amer.

PLANT	PART	TECHNIQUE	SEASON	PREPARATION AND NOTES	RANGE, HABITAT
Willow, Weeping *Salix babylonica*	Withes	Wickerwork Rib baskets: weavers	Spring	Gather before leaves appear.	China. Nat. in e. N. Amer. Also planted in w. states.

Wisteria
Wisteria floribunda,
W. sinensis
	Vines
	
	Bark
		Wickerwork
		Rib baskets:
		  hoops
		  ribs
		
		Coiling:
		  stitching
			Spring
			Summer
			Fall
				Use whole or split. Strip when
				green.
					Asia. Commonly
					cult. Hardy to
					zone 5.

Woodbine: *See* Virginia Creeper					
Woodwardia: *See* Fern, Giant Chain					

Wormwood
  White Sage,
  Western Mugwort
  Artemisia ludoviciana
	Stems	Twining		Granary baskets—Colo. desert
				and Calif.
					Dry soils, cen. and
					w. U.S. s. to Mexico.
					Now spread to
					e. seaboard.
					Var. *albula* cult.
					as ornamental.

Yew
  Taxus spp.
	Trunk
	Bark
		Splintwork
		Plaiting
		Twining
		Rib baskets:
		  weavers
				Wood of some species is close
				grained, hard, and springy
				(used for bows).
					N. Hemisphere.
					Many cult. forms.

Yucca, Aloe *Yucca aloifolia*	Leaves	Cordage Tying			S. U.S., W. Indies, Mexico.
Yucca, Banana *Yucca baccata*	Leaves Roots	Plaiting		Roots used to make red patterns.	Sw. U.S.

Yucca
  Joshua Tree
  Yucca brevifolia
	Roots	Wickerwork
		Plaiting
		Coiling:
		  stitches
		Ornament
					Calif. to Utah.

Yucca
  Silkgrass
  Yucca filamentosa
	Leaves	Coiling:
		  stitching
		Plaiting
					Sandy soil, coastal
					plain, N.C., s. to Fla.
					and Miss. Often cult.
					and est. northward.

Yucca
  Soapweed
  Yucca glauca
	Leaves	Plaiting			Dry plains and
					sandhills S. Dak. to
					N. Mex. Also cult.
					Hardy.

Techniques

I sat on the stump of an oak. In my jeans pocket I had only a small wire cutter. I was weaving a basket of bittersweet vines that had climbed up and around a nearby tree and then spilled over onto an adjacent stone wall.

I was alone (not a house or human in sight), yet I could hear the insistent voice of a wood pewee all the while I sat there.

The vines were rough on my hands—and strong—but the basket was beginning to take shape. The air was balmy and cool. A box turtle walked past my stump. The wood pewee continued his calling.

I wove.

I was serene and happy. I was ancient in that I felt more kinship than ever before with my ancestral sisters who somewhere, sometime, probably labored at the same craft (although for different reasons) and perhaps heard the same wood pewee.

My senses were alert to sounds and smells as my hands worked along the vines. I looked ahead to fall, when the plant would yield the beautiful red-orange berries I would arrange in a tall crock that sat by the wood stove.

Hours later, I contemplated the finished basket. It was large, heavy, and crudely woven, but it remains one of my favorite baskets to this day. The finished piece represents a day of pleasantly wandering thoughts when I walked into the woods empty-handed and returned home with a basket.

Chapter 3

Wickerwork

Every part of nature teaches that the passing away of one life is the making room for another.

—HENRY DAVID THOREAU

Wickerwork is the technique I usually teach to a rank beginner. It's always a thrill to see the satisfaction expressed in a student's face upon completing his or her first wickerwork basket. This chapter should be practiced and studied carefully, with attention to the Glossary on page 188, for the skills learned here will guide you through more challenging work.

Wicker, wickerweave, and wickerwork all refer to the weaving of material that is round in section, such as rods, shoots, vines, or reeds. Wickerweave specifically applies to the simple in-and-out weaving technique using one weaver. The term wickerwork will be used here for all types of basketry using round material, employing one or more weavers.

Most baskets consist of two working elements: the framework, or *spokes* (called the *stakes* in rectangular baskets), and the *weavers,* or those elements that are woven in and out of the spokes and that compose the fabric of the basket. The spokes should be sturdier and thicker than the weavers, especially for the base. In most cases, the *base* is woven first, then the *sides,* after which the *border* is woven using the remaining length of spoke material.

In determining the length of spokes for the basket you wish to make, add the diameter of the basket to twice the height—then add at least 12 inches more. This is an average, as the type of border will determine the remaining length needed after the sides are woven. Typically, a 6-inch-diameter, 6-inch-high basket will have spokes 30 inches long. The amount of weavers needed for the fabric of a basket is not as straightforward to determine as the amount of material for spokes. The amounts given in the projects here are very approximate; there are many variables. Take the suggestions here as a starting point, then let your first baskets be your own guide.

1. Beginning the Base

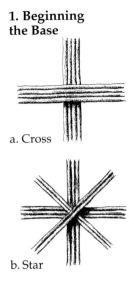

a. Cross

b. Star

Round Bases

A round base of round material may start in one of several ways. I will describe two beginnings most commonly used. The first one starts with two groups of spokes held in a cross (Figure 1a), the second with four groups of spokes held in a star formation (Figure 1b). Each group may consist of two or more spokes. One method is not necessarily preferable over the other, although experience with different materials may suggest which one to use in a particular situation. Basketmakers tend to use the base first taught them, which has much to do with why one base may be more prevalent in a given geographic area—or one school—than another.

A weaver (or weavers) is then woven in and out of each group, as close to the center as possible. (For clarity, some of the drawings show a separation between rows; however, each row should be worked close to the previous row.) After a number of rows (depending on the thickness of the material), the spokes of each group are separated, causing them to fan out like the spokes of a wheel, and the weaver (or weavers) continue to go around the separated spokes in the designated sequence. This separation of spokes is called the *breakdown*. When the base reaches the desired size, the basket is

upset or *turned*; that is, the spokes are bent into an upright position and the weaving is tightened to hold the spokes in place. Then the sides are woven.

There are many variations on these bases—in the number of spokes used to start, the number of spokes included in the breakdown process, and the weave or sequence in which the weavers are worked in and out of the spokes. Two round bases are fully described here, as well as a way to create an odd number of spokes on any base.

Japanese Base

This base is so named because it is woven in the Japanese weave, which is over two, under one. The entire base is worked with one weaver (Figure 2). The number of spokes cannot be a multiple of three, because that's the number of spokes in the Japanese weave pattern, and you need to alternate going over or under spokes in successive rounds (Figure 11, page 65). Arrange the spokes in an equilateral cross, positioning the vertical group under the horizontal group. Hold the cross in your left hand with your thumb on top. With your right hand, begin by laying a long weaver under Group A, over Group B, under Group C, over Group D, working clockwise. (You have not yet started the Japanese weave.) The beginning end of the

2. Japanese Base

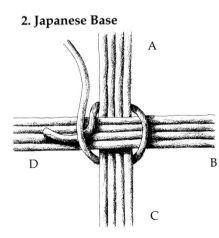

a. Starting the weaver

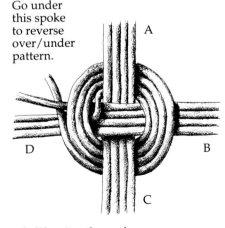

Go under this spoke to reverse over/under pattern.

b. Weaving the spoke groups

c. Beginning the Japanese weave

weaver can be bent and laid parallel to the spokes in Group D (Figure 2a). Subsequent rows will cover and secure it, or you can simply cut this end off after the base is woven. Weave around the groups three more times, or as many times as your design dictates. On the fourth round, go under the *last spoke* of Group D (Figure 2b.). This will reverse the over/under order as you now go over all of Group A, under Group B, over Group C, under Group D. Repeat for three more rounds. On the ninth round, at A (Figure 2c), begin the breakdown into the Japanese weave (over two, under one), separating the spokes as you continue to weave and spreading them apart as the rows progress. Keep the spokes as equidistant as possible.

Twining or Pairing Base

This base is worked with two weavers and any number of spokes (Figure 3). The first weaver is folded and the fold placed around Group A. Both ends are brought forward and woven in a twining pattern (Figure 9, page 64). See that the fold of the first weaver is off center so that the ends do not require a splice in the same place. Twine around each group for the designated number of rounds—usually two, three, or four. Then break down to two spokes for the designated number of rounds (Figure 3b)—or break down to two-one-two spokes if there are five spokes in each group. Weave a few more rows, and when there is enough space between each spoke, break down to single spokes and weave the remainder of the base.

Base with an Odd Number of Spokes

No matter how many whole spokes you start with, you will have an even number of working spoke ends. To make it an odd number, which is necessary for certain weaves, you must either add a spoke half the length of the others, or cut off half the length of one existing spoke. This spoke is called an *odd spoke* or a *half spoke*. Do this as soon as possible—sometime before or during the breakdown process.

If you are starting a base with one weaver, weave around the groups for four rounds. On the fifth round begin a twill weave (over two, under two, Figure 12, page 65). At the end of the fifth round, you can see that it will be necessary to add the

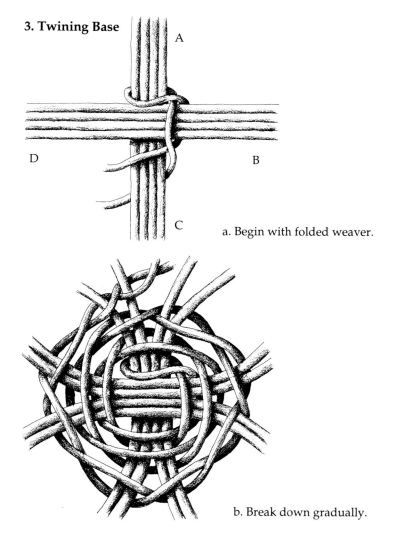

3. Twining Base

A

D

B

C

a. Begin with folded weaver.

b. Break down gradually.

odd spoke before you start the sixth round; otherwise you will be repeating the weave sequence over the same spokes. Insert the end of the odd spoke in the corner (Figure 4) and weave over it. The end of this may be left on the inside of the basket or brought up through the corner diagonally opposite and remain on the outside of the basket. Continue the twill weave, treating the odd spoke as though it were a pair. The entire base can be woven in the twill weave. Separate the pairs one or two rows before the upset, using a multiple-strand weave, such as twining or triple weave (discussed on page 64).

If you've worked the base in a twining or pairing weave, add the odd spoke after the first few rounds. Tuck the odd spoke into the weave at one of the corners of the original cross, or simply lay it under the base and twine around it as you start the breakdown. You'll have to hold it in place for a row or two until it is secure.

4. Odd Number of Spokes

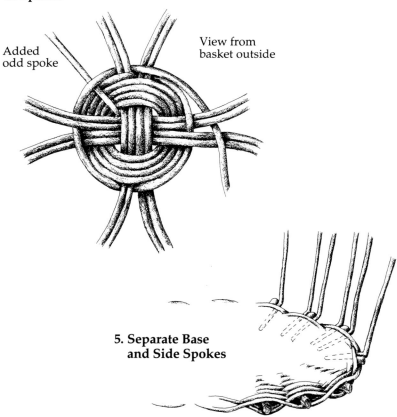

Added odd spoke

View from basket outside

5. Separate Base and Side Spokes

UPSETTING

Upsetting or turning the basket is best accomplished with a multiple-strand weave, which enables you to control the tension of the weavers and the position of the spokes. If you are using one weaver for the base, introduce one or more additional weavers just before upsetting by inserting the bent ends into the weave or simply by laying the ends behind the spokes as described for the triple weave in Figure 10, page 64. Weave one row of the multiple-strand weave on the flat base. Then pick the base up, and holding the outside of the basket toward you, push the spokes gently away from you. Now strive for a nicely rounded upsett by consistently increasing the tension of the weavers (starting at the first spoke) and by pushing the spokes away from you. It will take three or four rows for the spokes to turn up. You will soon learn the limitations of the material you are working with and will then be able to place your upsett precisely where you want it.

Separate Base and Side Spokes

Baskets may also be made with separate *base spokes* and *side spokes* as in Figure 5. You may need or want to do this if your spoke material is not long enough for the entire basket or if you want a very sturdy base or an abrupt upset. Keep in mind, too, that your spoke material is what is going to compose the basket's rim. Heavy spokes, advantageous in the base, may not be right for the type of rim you want.

After the base has been woven to the desired size, cut off the base spokes close to the last row. Then trim side spokes to a point and insert them 1 or 2 inches into the weave, one on each side of each base spoke. Pinched with your fingers or a pair of needle-nose pliers and bent upward, they will be held nicely in place by the next few rows of weaving.

Bi-spokes

If the material on hand does not seem sturdy enough for spokes, you can add what are called *bi-spokes* (or in rectangular baskets, *bi-stakes*). These are reinforcing spokes, added alongside existing spokes. Work them in as soon as there is space enough to insert them into the weave before upsetting the basket. The spokes can then be worked doubled for the remainder of the basket, including the border, or the bi-spokes can be cut off before the border is woven. This will give the side spokes the necessary support while allowing you to make any of the woven borders using only single spokes.

SQUARE OR RECTANGULAR BASES

To make a square or rectangular base with round material, you set up a number of *base sticks* (odd or even doesn't matter), parallel to each other, holding them in place with a clamp (Figure 6; see also Tools, page 190). The outside sticks should be a little thicker than the inside sticks, and therefore must be tapered so that the clamp will hold all sticks firmly. Fold a weaver and wrap it around the base stick on the left. Bring both ends forward and weave one row of twining (Figure 9, page 64) from left to right. Cut off one weaver and bend the cut end so that it lies alongside the outside base stick for about ½ inch. Wrap the long weaver around the outside stick and the tail of the short weaver, and weave the base in a randing weave (over one, under one, Figure 8, page 64). The first rows will lie on top of the short tail end so that it will be held firmly in place.

Now the tendency here is for the weaving to be pulled in, resulting in a tapered base. The clamp's holding plate will help to prevent this. After two or three rows, drop the plate down on the two outside sticks. The inside sticks are not held in the plate, which can be pushed up as the rows are woven. When the base is the desired size, insert an-

other weaver down into the weave at the left outside stick and twine to the right as you did at the beginning. Tuck one end down into the weave at the outside stick. Bring the other end *around* the outside stick and tuck it into the weave at the inside stick next to it.

After the base has been woven, the excess length of the base sticks is cut off. *Side stakes* are lashed to the base with a fine weaver and held in place by a flat splint or piece of bark (Figure 7). A foot border is woven with the lengths of stakes extending below the base, the same way you would any border (page 67). The sides and border are woven as in other baskets.

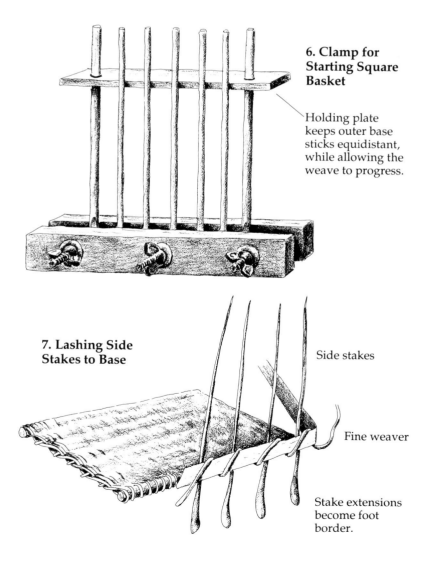

6. Clamp for Starting Square Basket

Holding plate keeps outer base sticks equidistant, while allowing the weave to progress.

7. Lashing Side Stakes to Base

Side stakes

Fine weaver

Stake extensions become foot border.

8. Randing

9. Twining or Pairing Weave

10. Triple Weave

a. Starting

b. Pattern

c. Alternate start

d. Ending

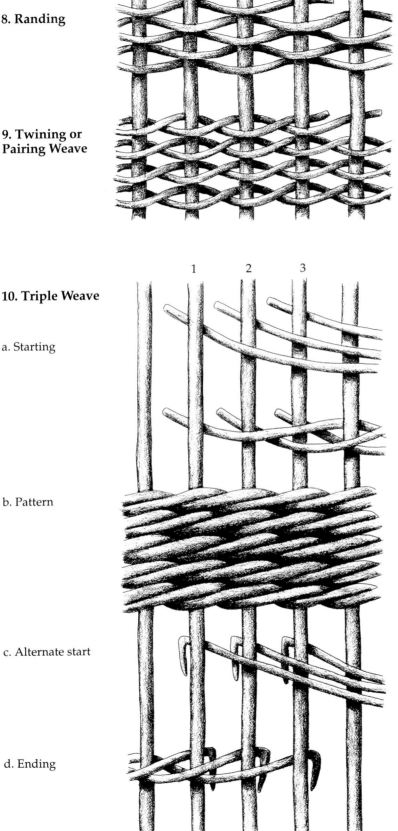

WEAVES

Here are the basic weaves for wickerwork. Many are used for other techniques of basketry as well.

Randing

One weaver; odd number of spokes (Figure 8). Lay one weaver behind a spoke and bring it forward.

Stroke: Front of one, behind one. Repeat stroke.

Twining or Pairing Weave

Two weavers; any number of spokes (Figure 9). Lay two weavers behind two consecutive spokes and bring forward. Always start each stroke with the weaver on the left and place it on top of the other weaver.

Stroke: Front of one, behind one, and out. Drop that weaver and repeat stroke with next weaver on the left.

Triple Weave or Three-Rod Wale

Three weavers, any number of spokes (Figure 10). Lay three weavers behind three consecutive spokes and bring forward. Always start each stroke with the weaver on the left and place it on top of the other two weavers.

Stroke: Front of two, behind one, and out. Drop that weaver and repeat stroke with weaver farthest on the left (Figure 10b).

Alternate Method of Starting: Bend and tuck end ½ inch into the weave at the left side of consecutive spokes (Figure 10c). Take each one behind that spoke and out to the front. Other multiple-strand weaves can also be started and ended by bending and tucking into the weave at consecutive spokes.

Ending: The triple weave is ended on the same spokes (1, 2, and 3) that were used to start the weave (Figure 10d). This ensures a level basket. Begin when a weaver reaches the space to the left of Spoke 1. Tuck that weaver to the right of and behind Spoke 1. Make the next stroke with the weaver now farthest on the left and tuck it behind Spoke 2. Make the next stroke with the remaining weaver and tuck it behind Spoke 3.

Beginnings and ends of weavers may be tapered with wire cutters or knife as in Figures 10c and 10d. To bend, pinch with needle-nose pliers or your fingernails. This will compress the fibers, helping them to bend without cracking or breaking.

Japanese Weave

One weaver; number of spokes must not be a multiple of three (Figure 11). Lay the weaver behind a spoke and bring it forward.

Stroke: Front of two, behind one. Repeat stroke.

Twill Weave

One weaver; odd number of spokes (Figure 12). Lay the weaver behind a spoke and bring it forward.

Stroke: Front of two, behind two. Repeat stroke.

Note: Basketmakers in some areas refer to Japanese weave as a variation of the twill weave. There are other variations, as well. This one may be called the two-two twill.

Arrow Weaves

An arrow consists of two rows of twining or triple weave (Figure 13). The first row (clockwise twist) is worked in the usual manner; i.e., the working strand is laid *on top* of the other strand(s), which makes the twist go *away* from you. In the second row (counterclockwise twist), the working strand is laid *under* the other strand(s), which makes the twist come *toward* you. You can work an arrow with other multiple-strand weaves as well.

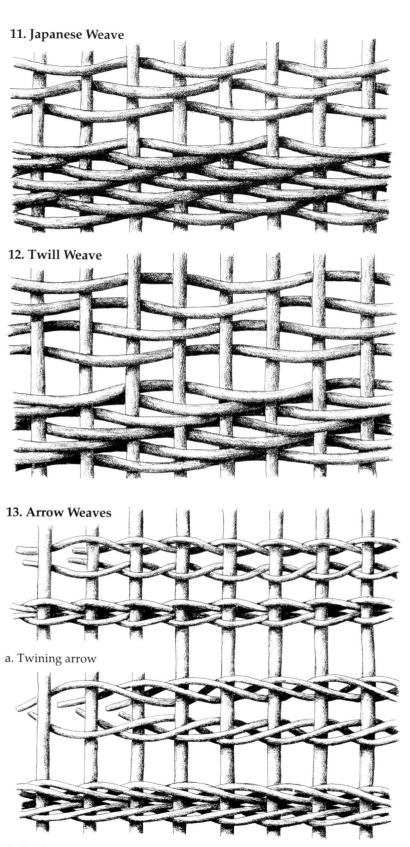

11. Japanese Weave

12. Twill Weave

13. Arrow Weaves

a. Twining arrow

b. Triple-weave arrow

14. Splices

(Old weavers are shown shaded)

a. Overlap behind spoke

b. Bend-and-tuck between spokes

c. Bend-and-tuck behind spoke with twining weave

d. Bend-and-tuck between spokes with twining weave

e. Interlocking overlap

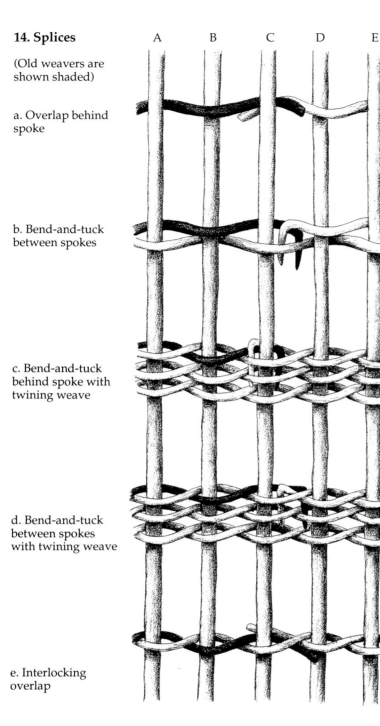

A   B   C   D   E

SPLICING

When you run out of a weaver, you introduce a new length. Here are five splice variations to choose from:

Figure 14a: Simply overlap the end of the old weaver (shaded) and the beginning of the new weaver behind the same Spoke C. (In some instances, it may be preferable to have the splice appear on the outside of the basket.)

Figure 14b: The old weaver is bent and tucked into the weave just to the left of Spoke D. The new weaver is bent and tucked into the weave to the right of Spoke C.

Figure 14c: The old weaver is bent and tucked behind and to the right of a spoke as at Spoke C. The new weaver is then bent and tucked into the weave behind and to the left of the same spoke.

Figure 14d: This splice is like Figure 14b, except it is shown with a twining weave.

Figure 14e: The old end is taken to the front of Spoke D. The new weaver is left on the inside behind Spoke C.

When working with multiple-strand weaves, the weaver to be spliced must be in the right-hand position. After making the splice, I do not make a stroke with that weaver, but rather drop it and pick up the weaver farthest to the left and make the stroke with that one. This ensures continuity of the weave pattern. Many beginning students make a mistake here, particularly when working with a triple weave.

The type of splice you use can depend on a number of factors. Your weavers may not be flexible enough for a bend-and-tuck splice, in which case you might use an overlap. The bend-and-tuck may be too pronounced, particularly for a multicolored basket, and again, a simpler overlap may be more appropriate. And there is the basket's function to consider. A yarn basket, for instance, ought not to have sharp ends inside.

BORDERS

Borders may be completed in one or more rounds. Soak spokes well before working a border. Some materials may have to be pinched with needle-nose pliers before bending. The type of border you weave will depend on the distance between spokes and their remaining length. As a guide, 4 inches of standing spokes remaining after the sides are woven will be enough to complete a simple trac border (Figure 15a) when the spokes are 1 inch apart. Thickness and stiffness of your material will also be factors.

Simple Trac Border

Work in one round (Figure 15a). Start anywhere. Bend each spoke, take it in front of one, behind one, and leave it on the inside. This border is often used as a foot border at the bottom of a basket.

Trac Border II

Work in one round (Figure 15b). Start anywhere. Be especially careful at the end to keep the proper sequence. Take each spoke in front of one, behind one, front of one, and in behind the next one. This can also be worked in front of two, behind two, front of two and in, particularly if spokes are close together.

Wrapped Border

Work in one round (Figure 15c). Start anywhere. Bend each spoke to the right and cut it off so that it reaches at least two spokes over. Use a fine, flexible weaver and lay the beginning on top of bent spokes so the wraps will cover it. If splicing is necessary, simply lay the new end and old end together and wrap over both. This is one of my favorite border treatments; it can be worked over one or more cores laid over the bent spokes. The additional core laid above the bent spokes and worked in a figure-eight wrap (photo at right) makes a neater and more finished rim. This border requires a very flexible wrapping.

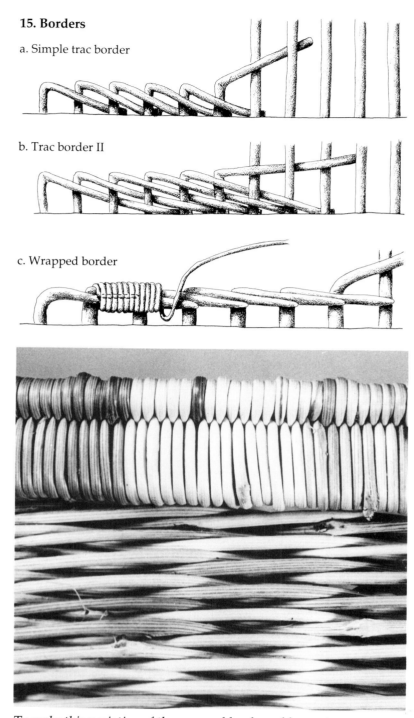

15. Borders

a. Simple trac border

b. Trac border II

c. Wrapped border

To make this variation of the wrapped border, add an extra core above the bent ends of the spokes and wrap both cores in a figure-eight pattern. The material here is stripped akebia.

15d. Closed border

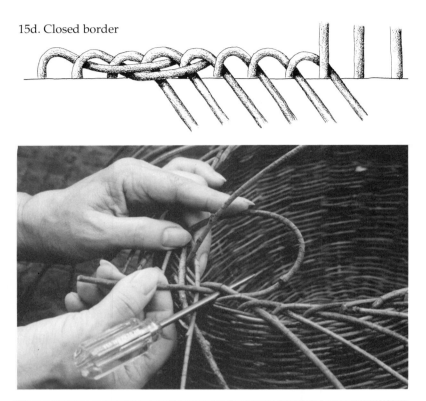

Closed Border

There are a number of variations on the closed border, depending on the path of the spokes and the number of rounds. A simple one is described below and illustrated in Figure 15d.

Work the simple version in two rounds. Start anywhere. Complete Round 1 before starting Round 2.

Round 1: Take each spoke behind the next spoke to the right and out. (The last spoke will go behind the first spoke, which is already bent down.)

Round 2: Take each spoke in front of two and in.

Round 3: (Optional) Front of one and down, as in Figure 15a. This makes an extra rim on the inside of the basket and helps to hide spoke ends as well as add reinforcement.

The photos at left depict a variation of the closed border worked in three rounds:

Round 1: Behind two (or more) and out.

Round 2: Front of three (or more) and in.

Round 3: Front of one and down.

Round 4 (Optional): Repeat Round 3.

Finishing the first round of a closed border (here the variation is behind two and out) may require an awl to open a space where the first worked spokes are already lying down.

Round two of this closed border completes the pattern by going in front of three and in.

Round three (in front of one and down) finishes at the beginning spoke, marked with a twist tie.

Projects: Getting Started

BY NOW, YOU HAVE SPENT a good many delightful hours in fields, woods, and roadsides gathering and preparing material, and have a good store of it in your shed, workshop, attic, or hall closet. You have studied the first section on techniques and are eager to make your first basket.

Choose a comfortable, well-lighted work area with prepared material, tools, and equipment at hand. In warm weather, a few tree stumps under the shade of a tree make an ideal workshop. Don't work in the sun. It tends to dry out the material and make it brittle. Have your soaking tub nearby, filled with warm water. (A little on the hot side is best, since it will soon cool down.) A small amount of glycerine in the water helps to make some fibers softer or more pliable. Make sure the material is soaked enough to be pliable before starting to weave.

Allow yourself ample time for your first session. If this is your initial endeavor, the first basket given here should take you approximately four hours to complete. Prolonged and repeated soakings may weaken some fibers. If you cannot finish the basket in one sitting, it would be better to let it dry out and resoak it the next time.

Use your left hand to hold the basket (or the spokes, at the beginning) and your right hand to make the stroke with the weaver. (If you are left-handed, make your first basket as directed here. After you have learned the technique, you can transpose the directions to suit yourself. Beginning left-handed students in my classes have had no trouble with this, and some have even continued as for right-handed weavers.) Weave from left to right. You will be working with the outside of the basket toward you. This way, upsetting the basket is easier, and you will be able to see the finished surface, which for some patterns is different on the inside surface.

Complete each stroke before repeating, and strive to keep the spacing even between spokes. Always end the basket at the first spoke. Mark it with a small rubber band or string tied to the tip. This will enable you to keep track of each round. Changes of weave or color also start and end at the first spoke in order to keep the patterns and basket straight and level.

Round Basket

Materials
- 10 stout vines, 36 inches long, for spokes
- 60 to 70 yards fine vines for weavers

THIS BASKET, 5 inches high and 6½ inches in diameter, is made entirely of unstripped akebia, although any other vine similar in flexibility and thickness may be used. I thoroughly enjoy working with akebia; it is easily controlled, yet effectively retains its character. But whatever vine you choose, the gentle, rounded shape of this basket is sure to please.

Construction

BASE: Arrange the ten spokes in a cross, as in Figure 1a. With a fine weaver, weave under and over groups of five for four rounds, beginning the Japanese base (Figure 2). Remember to mark your initial spoke. At the end of the fourth round go *under* the *last* spoke of that group. Now go over and under each group for four more rounds. On the ninth round begin the Japanese weave (over two, under one). Continue the Japanese weave until the base is 5 inches in diameter and end with the weaver behind the initial spoke. Add two more weavers to Spoke 2 and Spoke 3. Weave one round of triple weave (Figure 10). Then pick up the base, and holding the outside of the basket toward you, push the spokes away from you and upset the basket, page 62.

SIDES: Triple-weave the sides to about 4½ inches high, leaving 6 to 8 inches of spokes for the border. The basket turns slightly inward toward the top.

BORDER: Round 1: Take each spoke behind two and out (the closed border pictured on page 68).

Round 2: Take each spoke in front of three and in.

Round 3: Front of one and down.

Round 4: Repeat Round 3, placing this round as close to Round 3 as possible.

Akebia basket.

THIS LITTLE BASKET is composed of bittersweet spokes, honeysuckle weavers, and a band of walnut leaf stems. It is 3¼ inches high with a diameter of 6 inches at the top. For a taller basket, the sides may be worked almost entirely in a broad band of leaf stems. This can be particularly attractive, because the spiraling butt ends will have a larger field to play in.

Construction

BASE: Arrange your spokes in a cross, two groups of four. With a fine weaver, work under four, over four for four rounds, then go under one spoke to reverse the pattern and go over four, under four for four more rounds (Figure 2b). Now weave over two, under one until base measures 3 inches.

SIDES: Add one weaver and twine for a few rows to upset the spokes. After the spokes are upset, twine for 1½ inches (This is one of my very early baskets. I think a better balance would be achieved if the band of dark brown were placed a little closer to the top of the basket.) Soak the black walnut stems well and rand-weave (Figure 8) for 16 rows, using a new stem for each row and leaving both ends on the outside. Start each row one spoke to the right. This will create the spiral of the butt ends. Twine with honeysuckle for 1½ inches.

BORDER: Pinch and bend spokes to the right at the top of the weave and trim so that they reach two spokes over. Place split bittersweet on outside of bent spokes and wrap with honeysuckle (Figure 15c).

ROUND BANDED BASKET

Materials

- 8 spokes of stripped vines, ⅛ to 3/16 inch in diameter by 14 inches long
- 30 to 35 yards fine, stripped vine for weavers
- 16 leaf stems for weavers
- 1 piece stripped and split vine, ¼ inch by about 21 inches long, for rim

Basket of bittersweet, honeysuckle, and walnut leaf stems.

SQUARE BASKET

Materials

BASE:
- 6 woody shoots, ¼ inch by 8 inches, for center base sticks
- 2 woody shoots, ⅜ inch by 8 inches, for outside base sticks
- Unstripped vine, about 25 yards, for weavers

SIDES:
- 25 stems, about 12 inches long, for side stakes
- 1 piece of thin, flexible bark, ⅜ inch by 34 inches
- 1 long, thin piece vine for lashing
- Stripped vine for weavers, about 30 yards
- Approximately 75 leaf stems for weavers

RIM:
- 3 to 5 yards stripped vine

Equipment
- Clamp (Figure 6)

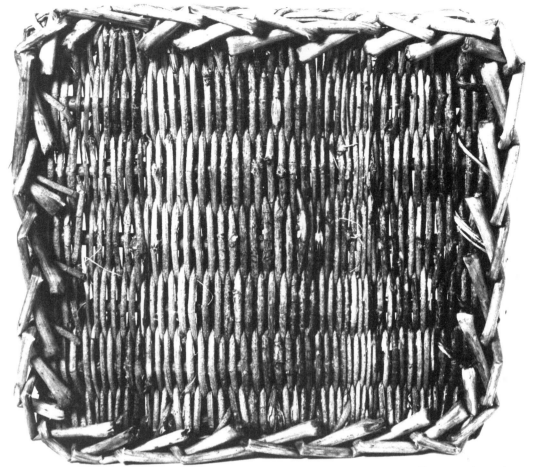

Bottom view of square basket.

THIS BASKET IS MADE of red osier dogwood for the base sticks, sumac for the side stakes, and akebia vine, unstripped for the base weavers and stripped for the side weavers. In addition, there are cedar bark and black walnut leaf stems The various materials make for a lively, structurally pronounced basket. Any woody shoots can be substituted for the osier and sumac. The distinguishing characteristic is the contrast between the light, stripped akebia and the dark walnut leaf stems. The basket is 7 inches square at the base and 5 inches high. The sides flare out slightly, making the basket 7½ inches square at the top. It is not a difficult basket to make. It can also be made rectangular.

Construction

BASE: Taper one end of each of the two outside sticks to ¼ inch so they will be the same thickness as the inside sticks. Place the seven sticks in the clamp and secure them so that the two outside sticks are 6¾ inches apart and the five inside sticks are equally spaced between them.

Fold a piece of unstripped akebia and place the fold around the left end stick close to the clamp. Weave the base, following the directions given on page 63, until the base is square. Finish the base by cutting off the excess length of the base sticks.

SIDES: Lay the piece of bark around the outside edge of the base, and lash around the base stick and bark with a long, thin piece of unstripped akebia. Lay in the side stakes as shown in Figure 7 with the butt ends extending down below the base about 3 inches. Because there is no heavy base stick on two sides of the base, the lashing must go around four or five rows of weaving (shown in the photo on the facing page).

Insert an extra stake on one side to create an odd number, necessary for randing. Allow bark to overlap a few inches where it meets and tuck the tail end of the akebia under the last three or four wraps and pull tight. Now weave a simple foot border with the butt ends of the sumac (Figure 15a).

Starting at the center of one side, lay three ends of stripped akebia behind three stakes and triple-weave for 1 inch (Figure 10). Then rand-weave for 2½ inches using black walnut stems, laying them in butt end first and leaving both butt and tip ends on the outside of the basket in a simple overlap splice (Figure 14a). These will occur randomly, rather than in a spiral. Finish the side by triple-weaving three rows with stripped akebia.

BORDER: Soak stake tops well, pinch them with needle-nose pliers, and bend them to the right. Cut stake ends off so that they reach just three stakes over. Wrap with stripped akebia (Figure 15c).

Basket of red osier dogwood, sumac, akebia, cedar bark, and walnut leaf stems.

Sumac Rim Basket

Materials

BASE:
- 10 woody shoots, 3/16 inch by 8 inches
- 8 to 10 yards stripped vine weavers
- 8 to 10 yards unstripped vine for weavers

Basket of red osier dogwood and stripped and unstripped akebia, with a border of sumac leaf stems.

THE BOLD VERTICAL STRIPES and distinctive rim of this basket come from using two special materials: akebia and sumac leaf stems. Unstripped akebia is darker and coarser than stripped akebia. The stripes are the result of twining the two around an even number of stakes. A similar contrast might be had from dyeing any stripped vine. Perhaps more distinctive is the rim, which features the flared ends of long sumac leaf stems woven from the side stakes. The basket measures 7½ inches in diameter at the base, 6 inches in height, and 10 inches in diameter at the top.

Construction

BASE: Using ten red osier base sticks and a long, fine piece of stripped akebia, work a Japanese base as in Figure 2. Continue until the base measures 4¾ inches in diameter,

making certain that the base sticks are equidistant. Now use unstripped akebia and continue in the same weave until the base is 7 inches in diameter.

SIDE: Cut the base sticks off close to the weave (see Figure 5). Bend each of the 40 well-soaked sumac side stakes exactly 10 inches from the *butt* end (the butt is a finished end; it will not be trimmed later). Cut the other end off 1½ inches beyond the bend and insert it into the weave, one on each side of a base stick. This will be easier if you place the woven base on the table. Mark the end of one of the side stakes with a small rubber band or string as Stake 1. Now hold the base in your lap and push the stakes away from you.

Place three pieces of unstripped akebia behind Stakes 1, 2, and 3 and triple-weave (Figure 10) for two rounds to upset the

SIDES:
• 40 large leaf stems for side stakes (Sumac is necessary for the distinctive border)
• 38 to 40 yards stripped vine for weavers
• 38 to 40 yards unstripped vine for weavers
• At least 18 to 20 yards fine leaf stems for weavers

stakes. This will not be difficult because the stakes are already pinched and bent. Then work 2¾ inches of twining using one stripped and one unstripped akebia to create the striped pattern.

Now work one arrow (two rows) of triple weave with stripped akebia (Figure 13b). Work ¾ inch of rand weave with sumac, leaving both butt end and tip on the outside of the basket. Work each row independently; that is, after the first row, start the next row on another spoke. You will probably use two or three sumac stems for every row. This will enable you to space the butt ends randomly.

Work another arrow of triple weave, then work ¾ inch of twining, again using one unstripped and one stripped akebia. Finally work two more rows of triple weave with unstripped akebia, ending at your initial spoke, as in Figure 10d.

BORDER: Soak butt ends again. Pinch and bend them ½ inch above the last row of weave. Note that the following method is opposite of what's usual, ending with the second round protruding, rather than being tucked to the inside:

Round 1: Front of one and in (Figure 15a).

Round 2: Behind two and out. Do not trim butt ends.

SHALLOW BASKET

Materials

- 6 base spokes, ¼ inch by 28 inches
- 24 side spokes, ¼ inch by 14 inches
- 45 to 50 yards fine weavers (smaller in diameter than the spokes)
- Approximately 12 yards of ¼-inch bark strips for border

Unstripped bittersweet basket, woven green.

I WORKED THIS BASKET entirely of fresh-cut, unstripped bittersweet vines. As the basket dried, it became lighter in weight, and the weave opened up. Remember that material worked green will shrink in diameter as it dries, sometimes as much as 50%. This may or may not be desirable. If you wish to minimize shrinkage, allow the material to dry thoroughly, then soak it before using. I like the light, airy weave shown here; in such a wide, shallow, bowl-shaped basket, it's ideal for holding fruit. The nodes of bittersweet contribute to the rustic appearance.

The base is 6 inches at the start of a gradual upsett, and the sides flare out to a diameter of 15½ inches at the rim. It is 5½ inches high.

Construction

BASE: Cross the six spokes in two groups of three, as in Figure 1a. With a thin weaver, work over three, under three for four rounds. On the fifth round, go over one spoke only of the next group and under two of the same group. Continue over and under each of the four groups to complete four more rounds. Now add one weaver and twine (Figure 9) around single spokes for two rounds. Insert side spokes into the weave alongside every spoke and twine over the doubled spokes for two more rounds. Break down to single spokes and continue to twine.

SIDES: When the base is 6 inches in diameter, start the upsett and continue to flare out to a large shallow shape. Twine the entire basket.

BORDER: Bend the spokes to the right and wrap with bark (Figure 15c).

A HANDLE CAN BE WORKED into a wicker-work basket by extending the spokes and continuing the weave from one side of the basket to the other. This basket is made entirely of unstripped wisteria. The bark and nodes prevent the handle from slipping out. The basket measures 10 inches in diameter by 13 inches high.

You need an even number of spokes for a balanced basket. Determine how many spokes you wish to include in the handle (three or four on each side is good for most baskets), and make them long enough to shape the handle and be inserted as far as possible down into the opposite side. The spokes not included in the handle are simply pinched, bent, and tucked between the neighboring spokes to the right. The last one on the right will be bent and inserted to the left. The weaving continues up the handle from both sides, meeting in the middle.

Instead of burying the handle spokes in the opposite side, you could begin with them long enough to bend them at the height of the side and weave them into a continuous border. Include the non-handle spokes in this border.

HANDLED BASKET

Materials

- 60 to 70 yards of unstripped vine

Unstripped wisteria basket.

Weaves in Wickerwork

Name of Weave	No. of Spokes	No. of Weavers	Color of Weavers	Stroke	Result
Rand Weave In-and-Out Weave Plain Weave	Odd[1]	One		Front of one, behind one, and out.	
Double (or more) Weave Slewing	Odd	Two (or more) used as one		Front of one, behind one, and out.	
Twining Pairing	Any number	Two		Front of one, behind one, and out. Repeat stroke with left-hand weaver.	
Twining Pairing	Even	Two		Same as above.	
Twining Pairing	Odd	Two		Same as above.	
Triple Weave[2] Three-Rod Wale Three-Rod Coil	Any number	Three		Front of two, behind one, and out. Repeat with each left-hand weaver.	
Triple Weave Three-Rod Wale Three-Rod Coil	Any number divisible by 3 plus 2	Three		Same as above. Result is spiral.	
Triple Weave Three-Rod Wale Three-Rod Coil	Any number divisible by 3 plus 1	Three		Same as above. Result is mottled.	
Triple Weave Three-Rod Wale Three-Rod Coil	Any number divisible by 3	Three		Same as above. Result is vertical stripes.	

[1] Weaves ordinarily worked over an odd number of spokes may be also worked over an even number if you change the stroke at the beginning of each round.

[2] Four- and five-rod weaves can be used similarly to three-rod wale: The stroke for four-rod would be front of three, behind one, and out. The stroke for five-rod can be front of three, behind two, and out, repeating with each left-hand weaver. An alternate stroke for five-strand weave can be front of four, behind one, and out, repeating with each left-hand weaver.

Name of Weave	No. of Spokes	No. of Weavers	Color of Weavers	Stroke	Result
Chasing	Even	Two		Front of one, behind one, and out. (One weaver is worked ahead of other.)	
Chasing	Even	Two		Same as above.	
Japanese Weave[3] Rib Randing	Any number not divisible by three	One		Front of two behind one, and out.	
Twill Weave Colonial Weave Basket Weave	Odd	One		Front of two, behind two, and out.	
French Randing[4] French Slewing	Any number	Same number of weavers as of spokes	Any color	Front of one, behind one, and out. To repeat, add each new weaver to left.	
Arrow Weave Chain Weave	Any number	Two		First row: same as twining. Second row: reverse.[5]	
Arrow Weave Chain Weave	Any number	Three		First row: same as triple weave. Second row: reverse.[5]	
Fitching Openwork	Any number	Two		Same as twining, but work with spaces between rows.	
Fitching with Arrow or Chain	Any number	Two		Same as arrow or chain, but work with spaces between rows.	
Fitching with Cross Warp	Any number	Two		Same as twining, but spokes are crossed between rows.	

[3] Some call this a variation of twill weave.

[4] Good for use with short rods.

[5] Arrows or chains consist of two rows: First row is worked in normal manner. Second row is reversed: i.e., the weaver making stroke goes *under* ends of other weavers instead of *over*. Colors can also be used in arrows or chains, producing various effects. Countertwining: Similar results can be achieved by reversing *direction* of weavers in second row: i.e., work from right to left instead of left to right as in first row.

Chapter 4

Splintwork

Go forth under the open sky, and list
To Nature's teachings.

—WILLIAM CULLEN BRYANT

*S*plintwork refers to basketry techniques that use flat strips of materials. Some "splints" may already be flat strips, as in cattail and palm. Others must be split out of the wood or bark of trees and shrubs (see pages 19 to 29).

Splintwork is a versatile category of basketmaking. It lends itself well to various forms of decoration by dyeing (weavers, spokes, or both), varying the weave, stamping or imprinting the materials with designs carved into a stamping block, and painting. It can also be combined with other types of basketry. Surface curls add still another form of embellishment (see page 155).

As in wickerwork, two elements are required: the stakes (or spokes) and the weavers. The weavers should be thinner (and usually narrower) than the stakes. You weave the base first. Then you turn up the stakes or spokes and weave the sides. Finally, you bend the tops of half the stakes or spokes (the other half are cut off), tuck them into the weave, and lash a rim into place.

Splintwork typically involves one of two weaves: a plain, checkerboard weave (over one, under one) or a twill (over two, under two). Combinations and variations of these two can be used to create interesting designs and textures (see the chart on page 93).

In square or rectangular splintwork baskets, the sides may be worked with a continuous weaver, in which case there must be an odd number of stakes; or you can use a separate weaver for each row, in which case there must be an even number of stakes. By contrast, round splintwork baskets are generally worked with a continuous weaver over an odd number of spokes. (As is often the case, there are exceptions: some round—or square—splintwork baskets are worked over an even number with a continuous weaver by going over two stakes once every round, thus changing the stroke.) You can create an odd number of spokes in a round basket by splitting one of the existing spokes down the middle for about half of its length. In a square basket you can split one of the existing stakes down to the completed base. If possible, this stake should be a little wider than the others to start with.

If you wish to attach a handle to a square or rectangular basket, make the number of stakes on that side odd, so that the handle may be centered. For example, a square base may be seven stakes by seven stakes, or a rectangular basket six stakes by nine stakes, the handle being attached to the center stakes of the nine-stake sides.

16. Weaves for Rectangular Bases

a. Plain

b. Twill

BASES

Bases are of two sorts: rectangular and round. Rectangular bases are simple to make; everybody remembers making square baskets out of strips of construction paper in elementary school. Round bases are a little more challenging, and they tend to be stronger because radial spokes support one another. Here's how each is made:

Square or Rectangular Base

The drawings at left show the placement of the splints in square or rectangular baskets. Figure 16a is a plain weave; Figure 16b shows a twill weave. Notice the diagonal effect the latter creates.

The base can be woven with the rough side of your material up or down, but when you upset the base, the rough side should become the inside of the basket. (In making a shallow tray or flat mat you may want the rough side facing down.)

To construct the base, lay the horizontal splints on the table parallel to each other with about a ½-inch space between them. Place the edge of your left hand (thumb up) across them at their centers. With your right hand, lay in the first vertical splint in the center of the base, close to your left hand. Lay in half the remaining splints to the right of the first one. Now turn the base around 180° and lay in the remaining splints on the other side of the first splint. Close in the spaces until there is about ¼ inch between splints in both directions. (This spacing will vary with the type, width, and thickness of material used as well as the weave and the function of the basket.) When closing the splints, start from the center splint and bring each succeeding splint close to it until you reach the outside edge of the base. Repeat this step on all sides, from the center out, until the base is centered and evenly spaced. Now you are ready to turn up the stakes in preparation for weaving the sides.

Round Base

A round basket can be worked with 8 or 16 spokes. The two constructions start the same way; the extra eight spokes needed for a larger base are added after beginning to weave.

Taper the middle of the spokes to allow the weaving to come as close to the center as possible. Figure 17a shows the shape to aim for in a ½-inch-wide spoke; adjust the taper proportionally for wider or narrower spokes. If you wish to weave with a continuous strand, you will have to create an odd number of spokes. To do this, select one spoke that is wider for half of its length. (If all the other spokes are ½ inch wide, this spoke half may be ¾ inch wide, tapering toward the center.) Split the wide half almost to the center as shown in Figure 17b.

Eight spokes will now be laid rough side down in a star formation in the following manner: Lay the split spoke down vertically, with the split end up. Lay the second spoke on top of the first, horizontally. Lay Spokes 3 and 4 across the first two, as shown in Figure 18a. Continuing to center the spokes in the spaces, lay Spokes 5 and 6 into place, then Spokes 7 and 8, as shown in Figure 18b.

17. Shaping Spokes

a. Taper center for a tighter weave.

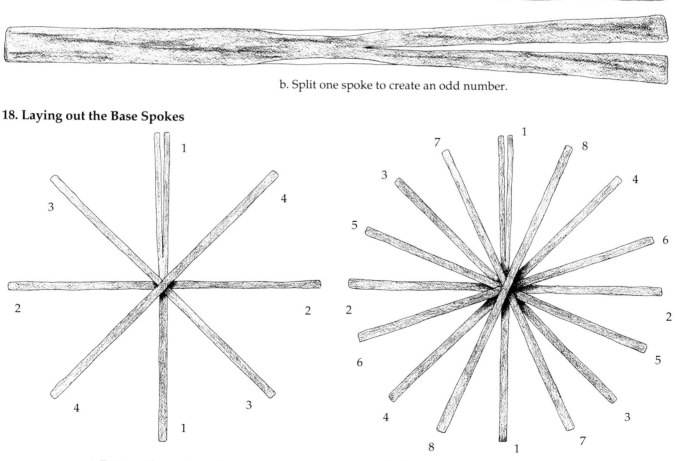

b. Split one spoke to create an odd number.

18. Laying out the Base Spokes

a. Begin with star formation.

b. Continue until all eight spokes are arranged.

19. Weaving the Base

a. Beginning the weave

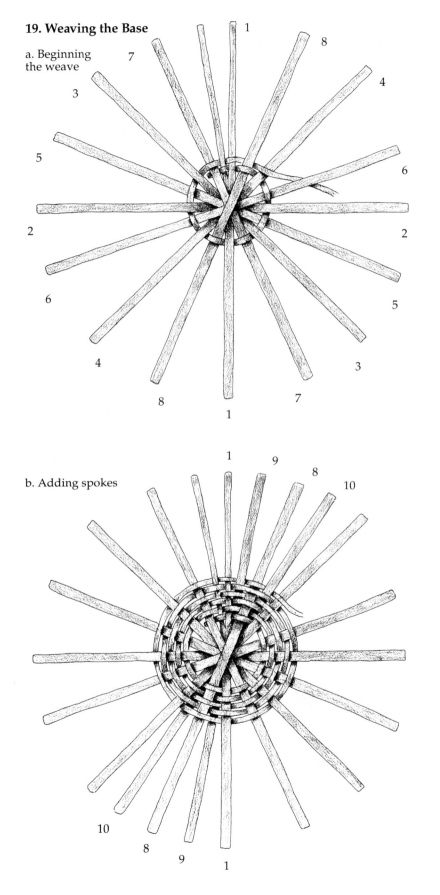

b. Adding spokes

In starting the weave, the first yard or so of the first weaver may be made extra-thin and extra-narrow, to help you make the rows nice and round close to the center. Place the end of the weaver under Spoke 7, which is the spoke just to the left of the split spoke. Weave over the left half of the split spoke, under the right half, and over and under each consecutive spoke (Figure 19a). Make the first row perfectly round before proceeding to the next row. Keep each row as close to the preceding row as possible. Weave until there is enough space between the spokes to accept the side weavers; or, at this point, if you wish a larger basket, add eight more spokes the same length as the first eight.

Fit these additional spokes in the spaces between the first set of spokes. Keep in mind that the weaver must continue to be placed very close to the preceding row, so as you begin to fit the additional spokes, allow for the thickness of the weaver as well as its width.

If you find it difficult to place the rows close together as you attempt to add new spokes, weave one or two more rows on the original eight spokes and then start adding. Begin when the weaver is over the right half of the split spoke. Lay a new spoke under the base and to the right of the split spoke (Figure 19b shows the first two added spokes). Weave under the new spoke and add another spoke to the space between the next two existing spokes. Weave under that new spoke and so on. In other words, you will be weaving under a new spoke, then over an old spoke until, at the end of that round, all the new spokes have been woven in.

Be certain that the other ends of the new spokes are between the proper spokes on the opposite side of the base from which you are working, because it's easy for them to get misplaced. For instance, as you add Spoke 9 at the right side of the split spoke, the other end of Spoke 9 should appear between Spoke 1 and Spoke 8 at the opposite side of the base. Use a spring type clothespin to clip it to one of the adjacent spokes. You will need eight clothespins. After you have woven halfway around, you can remove the pins one at a time until the round is completed.

It is possible to add new spokes without the aid of clips, but I suggest for your first basket that you use some type of clip or tape to hold the spokes in place. Continue to weave until there is enough space between spokes to accept the weavers that will be used for the sides.

A round base can also be made on an even number of spokes by using a separate weaver for each row. Stagger the overlapping of the ends so they are not all in the same place. For example, if you start and end the first row at Spoke 1, start and end the second row on the opposite side. The third may be added at Spoke 2, and so forth.

UPSETTING

If the splints are rigid, it may be necessary to score them in order to turn them up without splintering. Score lightly with a knife on the inside of the basket; however this rule also varies, as I have seen basketmakers score on the outside. Some materials turn up better if the fibers are severed on the outside. If I have the choice, I score on the inside where it won't show.

If you wish to keep an even number of stakes in a square or rectangular basket, remember to use a separate weaver for each row. Begin and end each weaver on alternate sides of the basket, so that the joints do not all occur on one side. If you intend to use a continuous weaver, you need to create an odd number of stakes by cutting one down the middle to the base. This can be a corner stake or a middle stake.

In upsetting square or rectangular baskets, I find it much easier if I weave a temporary row of twining (with string or yarn)

Starting and upsetting a splint basket is made easier by working the mat on a grid board.

Finishing nails through spaces at the corners hold the mat in place and allow the basket to be lifted off later.

around the base. This holds the base together while putting in the first few rows. Another method of upsetting is to place the base, rough side up, on a working board. Any piece of scrap wood will do. If the board is marked with a grid, it will help in keeping the basket square. Temporarily secure the base to the working board with small finishing nails outside the weave, one at each corner and one or two at each side. If using an odd number of stakes, weave several rows starting with a tapered weaver at the split spoke and weave around the nails. Remove the basket from the board and continue weaving the sides.

To upset a round basket, work the round base with the outside (smooth side) up—or facing you. Now pick up the base and push the spokes away from you, keeping the rough side on the inside of the basket. Weave a few rows to keep the spokes turned up, very slightly increasing the tension of the weave while holding the spokes in place. Keep the rows close together. Once the spokes have been upset, do not continue increasing the tension; too much tension will cause the spokes to be pulled in and the rows of weaving to separate. If this happens, undo the weave and try again. Relax. Loosen up a little.

SIDES

The sides of most splintwork baskets are kept straight. Occasionally you'll see some shaping, especially at the top of the basket. You can narrow the spokes as they go up, which will allow the sides to be brought in, or you can widen the spokes, and the basket will flare out. The last few rows, however, should be straight-sided, or it will be difficult to add the rim.

When the basket is the desired height, and if it is a spiral or continuous weave on an odd number of spokes, taper the top of the weaver of the last row so that the step-up will not be so noticeable. End simply by cutting off the weaver just past the split spoke. Now let the basket dry out for a few days away from direct heat. Some shrinkage will occur, and the rows can be pushed down tight again.

Splicing

As Figure 20 indicates, a splice involves overlapping weavers for a distance of four spokes (or stakes). The old weaver (shaded) ends on the outside of one spoke. The new weaver then starts behind the third spoke to the left. In this way, both ends are hidden on the outside as well as the inside.

RIMS

To prepare a basket for tucking the stakes and adding the rim, first cut all the stakes to the same length, 2½ inches above the last row. Resoak the stakes, then:

1. Cut off every other stake (those that are on the inside of the last row of weave) at the top edge of the last weaver.

2. Trim the remaining stake ends neatly—in any one of the three ways shown in Figure 21a, facing page.

3. Lightly score the trimmed stakes on the inside of the basket and tuck them into the last several rows of weave on the inside of the basket (Figure 21b). Use a small screwdriver to help you guide these stake ends into the weave. They should be trimmed to a length so that each end is hidden beneath a weaver.

Usually, the top of a splintwork basket consists of a rim (outside) and a rim liner (inside). The last row (or two) of weave is sandwiched in between them. Select a thick splint for the rim; the rim liner may be as thick or a little thinner. Each should be long enough to go around the top of the basket and overlap the ends by about 2 inches. Shape the ends so that the overlap is not bulky by shaving or trimming the face of one end and the underside of the other. You can also scrape and smooth the outside edges so that they are slightly rounded.

Place the end of the rim on the outside of the basket 1 or 2 inches to the left of the split spoke. (On a basket with an even number of spokes, start anywhere.) Place one end of the rim liner on the inside of the basket a few inches or so to the left of the rim end. This will stagger the overlaps and enable you to adjust the lengths when you reach the end. The joints can also be positioned on opposite sides of the basket, in which case you'll have to trim the rim liner to size before the lashing begins. A few spring-type clothespins will hold everything in place while lashing.

To lash the rim together, use a long, thin, narrow splint. At the split spoke (or beginning of the round), insert the lashing splint between the rim and rim liner so that 1 inch of the tail protrudes up between them. Before tightening the first two stitches of the rim lashing, tuck the 1-inch tail down to lie hidden horizontally between the rim and rim liner (Figure 21c).

Working from left to right, lash the rim and rim liner to the last row of weave between the stakes. If necessary, use the awl to open up a space for the lashing splint. When you have lashed around the basket and reached the first stitch, reverse directions and lash all the way around again. If you do not prefer to cross-lash, simply double over the first stitch, and then end.

To end, tuck the end of the lashing splint down into three rows of weave on the inside of the basket, then up through two rows and up between the rim and rim liner. Cut off the lash close to the rim.

To maintain a level rim on a basket with a spiral weave, it will probably be necessary to pierce holes and lash through the weaver of the last row exposed below the rim. Place the rim on the basket, level all the way around, and temporarily clip it in place. You will notice that as the weaver slopes up, it disappears behind the rim. With an awl, pierce holes through this weaver along the lower edge of the rim. Position these holes so you can lash through them into the spoke spaces behind. Now lash the rim in place.

20. Splicing Weavers

(Old weaver is shown shaded)

Overlap splices four spokes so that both the beginning and end of the weavers are concealed.

21. Weaving the Rim   a. Three alternative stake tapers

b. Tucking in the tapered spokes
(View is from inside basket)

c. Lashing the rim

Start here between rim and rim liner.

HANDLES

If you wish to attach a handle, you must do so after the spoke ends are tucked down into the weave and before the rim is lashed on. Make a handle as follows:

Select a heavy splint, as wide as the spokes and about ¾ inch thick. With a sharp knife, cut a notch 2 inches from each end on the inside of the handle as wide as and a little deeper than the rim liner. One half inch from the notch, carve a taper toward the end, also on the inside (Figure 22). The tapered end may be narrowed also, so that you have a flat, blunt point. Now carve away some of the thickness between notches, particularly at the corners or where the handle will bend the most.

To bend the handle, first soak it in hot water for an hour or more. Carefully flex the handle to shape, so that it will fit the top of the basket, and tie it with heavy cord until completely dry. You can also use a board sawn to a U shape on which to clamp the soaked and carved handle until dry. Then complete any further carving, shaping, and rounding of edges on the inside where the handle will be held.

Wood at times has a mind of its own, and often it bends where you least expect or want it to. Therefore, I sometimes bend my handle splint before carving the notches. Once I have bent it so that it works with the basket, I let the handle dry and then carve the notches and edges.

Insert the completed handle into the weave on the inside of the basket. Place the rim and rim liner so that the rim liner fits into the handle notches. Now you can lash the rim, securing the handle at the same time.

Splintwork baskets may also have the handle on the outside of the basket with the notches cut to fit either the rim or rim liner (Figure 23a). Another handle may be made to swing back and forth by attaching to loops woven into the basket (Figure 23b).

22. Carved Handle Shape

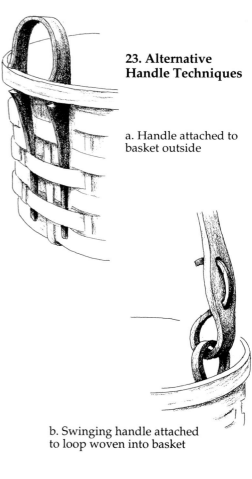

23. Alternative Handle Techniques

a. Handle attached to basket outside

b. Swinging handle attached to loop woven into basket

Basket Projects

THIS BASKET MEASURES 6 inches high and 8 inches square at the rim. The dark reddish-brown of the maple bark makes a striking contrast with the white oak stakes and rim. Many other combinations of splint and bark will also yield pleasing contrasts. This basket has a rugged appearance and is quite sturdy.

Construction

BASE: Plain-weave a 6-inch base (as shown in Figure 16a).

SIDES: Use one weaver for each row, starting each successive row on opposite sides of the basket. Work a plain weave for the sides.

RIM: Start the rim and rim liner on opposite sides of the basket. Single-lash them to the last row of weave.

Materials

- 14 splints, ½ inch by 26 inches
- 10 bark weavers, ½ inch by 32 inches
- 2 splints for rim and rim liner, 1¼ inch by about 30 inches
- 1 long, thin splint for lashing, about 75 inches

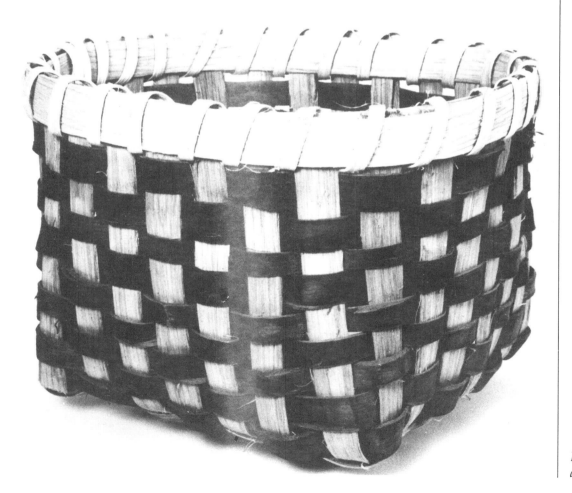

Basket of oak splint and maple bark.

LOW RECTANGULAR BASKET

Materials

- 15 splints, ½ inch by 17 inches, for stakes
- Approximately 12 splints, ³⁄₁₆ inch by 28 inches, for weavers
- 2 thicker splints, ⅜ to ½ inch wide by 28 inches long, for rim and rim liner
- 1 very thin splint, ⅛ inch by about 50 inches long, for lashing the rim

THIS BASKET, for which I used ash splint, has an oval opening, 7 inches by 9 inches. Alternatively, it could be shaped to have a rectangular opening, by bending corners into the rim. The base is 4½ inches by 6½ inches. The height is 3 inches.

I enjoyed making this basket in a workshop given by Carol Hart. It was hard work, though fascinating, to pound and split the ash into almost paper-thin splints.

Other splints that will work well in a basket of this type include oak, hickory, and maple, all hardwoods known for their strength.

Construction

BASE: Plain-weave a rectangular base 4½ inches by 6½ inches.

SIDES: Use one weaver for each row. Start each row on alternating sides of the basket. Work plain weave for the sides.

RIM: Trim and insert stakes into the weave. Start rim a few inches ahead of rim liner. Single-lash to last row of weave.

White ash basket.

*Round basket
of cedar bark.*

ROUND BARK BASKET

Materials
- 7 bark splints, ⅝ inch by 20 inches
- 1 bark splint, 1 inch by 20 inches
- ¼-inch-wide weavers for sides
- 2 heavier bark splints, ½ inch by 24 inches, for rim
- Approximately 70 inches thin, ¼-inch-wide splint for lashing

THIS ROUND BARK basket measures 6¾ inches in diameter and is 5 inches high. I like working with cedar bark. It's easy and fun to strip the bark from the log. Because the material isn't sturdy enough for very large baskets, a small basket is most appropriate. Other suitable, relatively thin barks include willow and cherry.

Construction
Trim the 1-inch wide splint so that it is ⅝ inch wide for one half of its length. Split the other half down the middle to create the odd number necessary.

BASE: Arrange spokes as in Figure 18 and weave until base is 5½ inches in diameter.

SIDES: Turn splints up and weave with a continuous weaver until sides are 5 inches high.

RIM: Trim and insert splints into the weave. Start rim a few inches ahead of rim liner. Lash all the way around once. Insert lashing into first stitch and reverse directions for a cross lashing.

SMALL SQUARE BARK BASKET

Materials

- 4 yards bark strips, ¼ inch wide, for spokes
- 4 yards bark strips, ⅛ inch wide, for weavers

THIS BASKET MEASURES 2½ inches square at the base and 3¼ inches high. The base is a checker-weave. Each row has a separate weaver, ⅛ inch wide. Like most of my other square-based baskets, this one is round at the rim. This transition—square base to round rim—is intriguing and, to me, attractive. On the other hand, the sides may be shaped squarish by pinching the corners as you weave. After the rim has been attached, it too may be squared off by pinching.

Gently increasing the tension on the weavers of this small basket caused it to taper in slightly at the top. If you wish to do this, be certain to leave some spaces between stakes; you need room to tuck the ends of the stakes down into the weave.

Construction

Follow directions as for the square splint and bark basket on page 89.

Basket of red maple inner bark.

WEAVES IN SPLINTWORK

NAME OF WEAVE	NO. OF SPOKES	NO. OF WEAVERS	COLOR OF WEAVERS	STROKE	RESULT
Plain Weave **Checker Weave** **In-and-Out Weave**	Odd	One		Front of one, behind one, and out.	
Twill Weave **Colonial Weave**	Odd	One		Front of two, behind two, and out.	
Wrapping	Any number	One		Wrap around each stake.	
Diagonal Wrapping	Odd	One		Wrap around every other stake.	

Weaving with splints in a spiral manner with one continuous weaver requires an odd number of spokes (unless you change the stroke at the beginning of each row). You can weave an even number of spokes by using a separate weaver for each row. Various patterns can be achieved with either an odd or an even number of spokes by:

1. Changing the stroke of some rows

2. Using colored weavers

3. Using colored spokes

4. Using weavers of different widths

5. Using spokes of different widths

6. Using any of the previous combinations

Chapter 5

Plaiting

The term *plaiting* has been used broadly to mean *splintwork* (because plaiting is usually done with flat elements) and also *weaving* (because plaiting is fundamentally the interlacing of like elements). What distinguishes plaiting for me is that all the elements in a plaited form are the same in terms of *function*. There is no distinction between the warp (spokes or stakes) and weft (weavers). Plaiting is not really limited to flat elements, to elements of the same size or shape, or to simple weaves. Braided hair, for instance, which begins with bundles of round strands, is plaiting in its most familiar form. Shereen LaPlantz, in her book *Plaiting, the Woven Form* (unfortunately out of print), reveals an incredible array of shapes that can result from even the most humble plaited beginnings.

Plaiting techniques may be grouped as straight plaiting, diagonal plaiting, and hexagonal plaiting (Figure 24). You are already familiar with simple forms of straight plaiting from the previous chapter; splintwork mats are straight-plaited. Hexagonal plaiting is a three-element weave too complex to be covered here. I will concentrate on that very versatile form: diagonal plaiting. At the end of the chapter you will learn to make long plaited strips.

24. Plaiting techniques

a. Straight plaiting

b. Diagonal plaiting

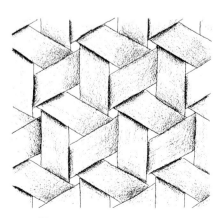

c. Hexagonal plaiting

A diagonal plaited basket can start in the same way as a splintwork basket (Figure 16, page 82). Here the similarity ends. In a splintwork basket, the elements in the woven base are turned up and become the stakes or framework upon which the weavers are woven. In a diagonal plaited basket, all elements that formed the base are woven together to form the sides of the basket (no elements are added). The weave may be a simple over one, under one, or over and under multiple strands.

Diagonal plaited baskets can evolve into countless shapes, even with a very simple base, by the control and placement of the corners. The more I learn of plaiting, the more interesting it becomes.

BASE

The sample basket illustrated here begins with a square base of twelve splints: two groups of six which are plain-woven together. An even number of elements is necessary if you want to place the corners in the center of each side. Keep the spacing between all elements the same in all directions. From this square base you can produce a round basket or, if you crease the corners, a square one. Learn this simple form well and you will soon see how to apply it to larger sizes and various shapes.

25. Weaving the Sides

a. Base with temporary row of twining

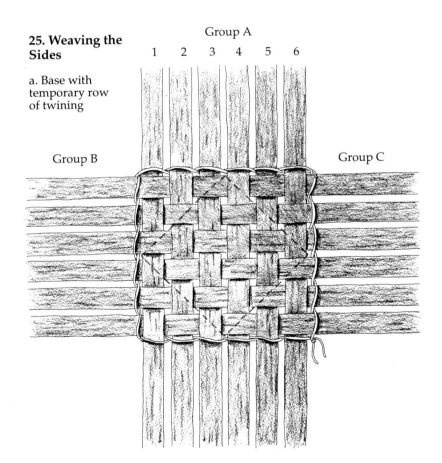

Group A

1 2 3 4 5 6

Group B

Group C

b. Begin weaving from the center of a group.

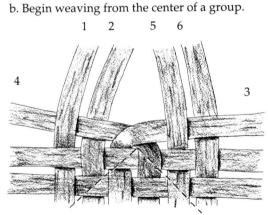

1 2   5 6

4

3

c. The center of a group becomes a corner.

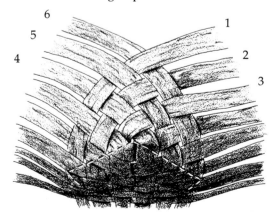

6

5

4

1

2

3

SIDES

Turning up the sides of a diagonal plaited basket surprises most first-time makers. The corners become the middle of the sides, and vice versa. In Figure 25a, the square (dashed line) in the center of the base will be the actual base of the plaited basket, the lines showing exactly where the basket turns up. The triangles on each side of the square will become the sides. Weave a temporary row of twining around the flat woven square (not the dashed lines) to hold it in place.

Now working with the six splints of Group A of the plaited mat, divide them in half so that three are in your left hand and three are in your right hand. Cross the two center splints and weave diagonally toward Groups B and C. Splint 3 will be woven to the right, over #4, under #5, and over #6; and Splint 4 will be woven to the left, over #2, and under #1 (Figure 25b). Weave Splint 5 to the left, under #2 and over #1. Weave Splint 2 to the right, under #6. Continue with Splint 1 going toward the right and Splint 6 going toward the left (Figure 25c). Hold the weave in place at the top with a clothespin. Repeat the same process with the other three groups, forming the basic structure. You will see that the basket has been turned up and the sides started. (You will not be holding the basket on the table but in your hands, so that the elements may be pushed away from you.)

Blend one group into the next by continuing the same weave sequence. (Continue to use clothespins whenever necessary.) Each strand is woven over one, under one, around the entire basket. The sides will become one continuous round of weaving. After the sides have been woven, the top of each splint is turned down and woven into the sides to form the rim.

26. Weaving a Straight Rim

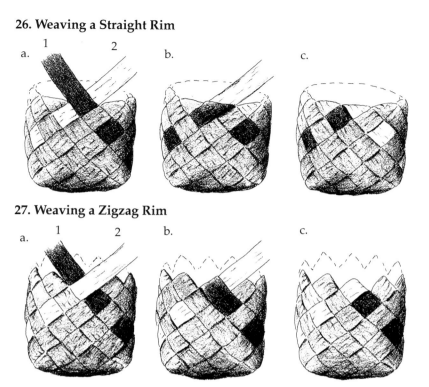

27. Weaving a Zigzag Rim

RIM

Work with a pair of crossed splints, as shown in Figures 26a and 27a. (For clarity, only two standing splints are shown in the drawings.)

Straight Rim

Turn Splint 1 down at a right angle and weave it into the next few splints of the weave (Figure 26b). Fold Splint 2 over Splint 1 at a right angle and weave it into the next few splints of the weave (Figure 26c). The result is a straight or level rim.

This rim may be reinforced and bound further as in a splintwork basket.

Zigzag Rim

Fold Splint 1 over onto itself and weave it down through the next few splints (Figure 27b). Then fold Splint 2 over the first splint and weave it down over itself and into the weave (Figure 27c). Continue all the way around, always working with a pair of crossed splints. This results in a toothed or zigzag rim.

Basket Projects

Materials

- 12 bark splints, ½ inch by 22 inches

TWO WILLOW-BARK BASKETS are shown here. The one below has a straight rim and the one on the facing page has a toothed rim. Both baskets are 4 inches square at the base and 3½ inches high. Whenever I look at these baskets, I recall the magnificent clump of willow where I gathered the material for

them growing by the railroad tracks of a nearby town. The willow and surrounding shrubs and weeds have since been cleared away to make room for a new road.

As you gather willow, you will find that the bark slips off very easily. The dark green on the outside and light tan on the inside

Diagonal plaited basket of willow bark, straight rim.

will both turn reddish brown as the basket dries and ages. Both of these baskets were worked while the willow bark was fresh and green.

At the rim, you can see the difference in color and texture where the inside of the turned-down strips appear on the outside of the basket. With longer strips you could, after turning down at the rim, continue to weave all the way back to the bottom and across the base. In that case, you would not see the outer green skin of bark at all. If you want the green to show on both inside and outside, start the basket with the inside of the splints facing out.

Construction

Follow directions given on pages 96 to 97. After completing the square base and starting the diagonal plaiting for the sides, you will soon develop a rhythm, weaving the splints in and out. One hand will go away from you and the other will come toward you. Remember to keep the tension and spacing even, and to maintain the weave sequence as one side blends into another.

Diagonal plaited basket of willow bark, toothed rim.

ELBOW BASKET

Materials

Palm leaf:

- 12 strips, ½ inch by 16 inches, for initial mat
- 22 strips, ¼ inch by 10 inches, for weavers
- 4 strips, ½ inch by 10 inches, for rim and rim liner
- 2 strips, ⅛ inch by 24 inches, for rim lashing
- 2 strips, ¼ inch by 20 inches, for handle

ONE OF MY FAVORITE forms of plaited basketry is the elbow basket. Learning to make it is a simple matter, but whoever figured it out the first time (it's traditional in various cultures) was a genius. I especially enjoy the reaction of my students when they make this form. The elbow basket is a combination of diagonal plaiting and straight plaiting. These can be augmented with splintwork techniques or twining at the top.

A friend's Florida vacation proved beneficial to me as well as to him. He brought back the palmetto leaves I used in this small basket. Palmetto is thin, yet strong, well suited to plaiting techniques. It is possible to slit this material into extremely narrow strips by running a needle down the length of the leaves. Many other palm leaves can be prepared similarly.

This basket, originally designed for drying herbs, has no base to stand on, so it needs a handle for hanging. This is a perfect opportunity to employ a plaited strip. The basket measures 5½ inches from point to rim, 7½ inches from point to handle, and 7½ inches across.

Construction

Step 1: Plait a square mat using the twelve 16-inch strips. Locate the mat toward one end, so that half the length of the elements of both groups is unwoven (Figure 28a). Temporarily twine the perimeter of the mat to hold it in place. This mat will be the back of the basket.

Step 2: Bring the long ends of Group A up and over the mat toward the opposite ends of Group A holding them in your right hand. Bring the long ends of Group B up and over the mat toward the opposite ends of Group B and hold them in your left hand (Figure 28b). Now keeping the continuity of the mat's weave sequence, plait the long ends of both groups over and under each other, starting at the lower corner. This part will form the front of the basket and should be the same size as the back (Figure 28c). Gently coaxing each splint into place will likely leave a gap at the bottom of the elbow. As you shift the splints sideways to close this gap, evening the spacing throughout the basket, you will also extend the unwoven ends that will form the arms of the basket.

Step 3: Now weave the long ends of each group with ¼-inch-wide weavers (Figure 28d). You will actually be weaving two little baskets here: one on the ends of Group A and one on the ends of Group B.

In this project, I finished these top sections in a twill weave (see page 82)—eleven rows on each group. You can make the weavers the same width as the original elements, or you can use splintwork techniques—narrower weavers, or a combination of narrow and wide. Use a separate weaver for each row. As another alternative, you can twine around these group ends. Depending on the material used, you may want to split the ends in half to make your twining stitches smaller.

After completing these groups, cut every other end flush and tuck the rest down into the weave in preparation for adding the rim and handle.

Step 5: Insert and plait the handle as follows: Fold the two handle splints around the last woven row, so that the four strands point toward the opposite rim in equal lengths. Plait the four splints as described in Figure 40a, page 107. When you reach the other rim, wrap the four ends around the last woven row and weave them in and out horizontally for a few strokes. They will be hidden under the rim.

Step 6: Now add the rim and rim liner, as you would for splintwork, Figure 21, page 87 .

28. Elbow Basket

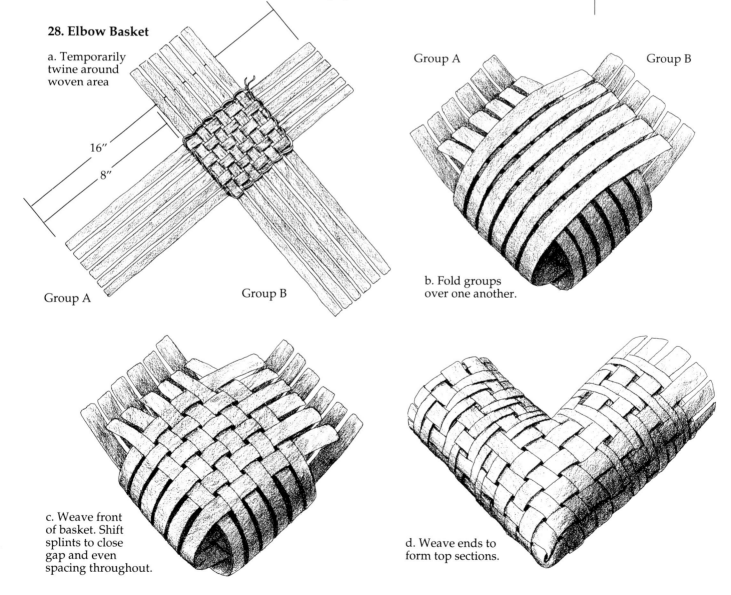

a. Temporarily twine around woven area

16″

8″

Group A

Group B

Group A

Group B

b. Fold groups over one another.

c. Weave front of basket. Shift splints to close gap and even spacing throughout.

d. Weave ends to form top sections.

**LONG
PLAITED
STRIPS**

Plaits, from left to right: Cattail (five-strand flat), cattail (four-strand flat), black willow bark (four-strand round from flat material), daffodil (four-strand round), Siberian iris (three-strand), iris (four-strand flat plait, version II), dyed and natural corn husk (eight-strand round), corn husk (four-strand round with hemlock-bark arrow).

Key to plaiting
abbreviations:
R = right
L = left
O = over
U = under
> = change
    direction
    to right
< = change
    direction
    to left

LET'S LEARN TO MAKE long, continuous strips by plaiting three or more elements. These strips can be used as weavers in splint and wickerwork baskets. They can also be sewn together, as in braided rugs, or used for rims, handles, cords, ropes, and embellishments. You can even plait the plaits.

29. Three-Strand Plait

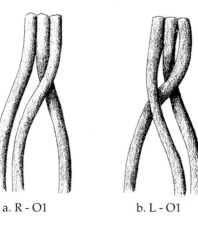

a. R - O1   b. L - O1

Flat Plaits from Round Material

Most of us are familiar with three-strand plaiting used to braid hair. From Figure 29, you can see that each outside strand is worked alternately over the center strand. Any plait having an odd number of elements can be worked using this simple concept, except that the center will actually consist of more than one strand. For instance, in a five-strand plait the right outside strand goes over two, then the left outside strand goes over two (Figure 30). In a seven-strand plait, each outside strand goes over three, etc. The more strands, the wider the plait.

30. Five-Strand Plait I

R - O2; L - O2

31. Five-Strand Plait II

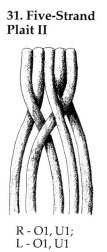

R - O1, U1;
L - O1, U1

You will find it helpful to practice these plaits with thick yarn or cord taped to a working surface. Work them loosely, so you can see what happens. When you have learned them well, try some natural materials: grasses, iris or daylily leaves, corn husks, cattail, and other soft fibers. In working with short lengths such as corn husks, start with strands of uneven length. When one runs out, overlap it with a new length for several strokes. Trim any protruding ends when the plait is completed.

Now look at the five-strand plait again. Let's call the outside strands the working strands. You can see that besides going over two (Figure 30), the working strand can alternatively go over one, under one (Figure 31). As the number of strands used for each plait increases, so too, does the number of options. For further variety, use light and dark colors for your strands, placing color wherever you wish. You'll likely be as fascinated as I was with the possible variations.

You can also make plaits having an even number of strands. In a four-strand plait, R will go over one and L will go over two (Figure 32a). In a six-strand plait, R will go over two and L will go over three (Figure 32b). In these and other plaits from even-numbered strands, this sequence theoretically results in one edge being thicker than the other; however, in most cases, the difference is hardly noticeable.

Another option for plaits from even-numbered strands is for one working strand to begin with an over stroke and the opposite working strand to begin with an under stroke. This produces an evenly woven plait of over one, under one (Figure 33).

Starting one strand with an over stroke and the other with an under stroke is also possible with odd numbers of strands. Either the working strand or one of the other strands will be going over or under two strands: in the center of the plait, somewhere near the center of the plait, or at one edge of the plait. This can produce very interesting results. It may also cause the plait to twist, somewhat like a macrame sennit of half knots. This can happen with even-numbered plaits, too. If using fine grass or straw, you may eliminate the twist by dampening and pressing the plait or wrapping it on a spool. The twists can be lovely, though. Whether you want them or not depends on the intended use of your plait.

In this group, it doesn't really matter whether you start on the right or left, but to be consistent, because it does make a difference with some of the plaits described later, I specify right and left in the drawings, as well as over and under. You will no doubt discover other options or invent some of your own. Be sure to allow the working strand to return to a vertical position at the end of its sequence, so that it can be counted in the stroke made with the next working strand.

32. Even-Strand Plait I

a. Four Strands:
R - O1; L - O2

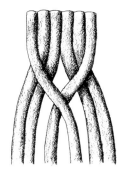

b. Six Strands:
R - O1; L - O3

33. Even-Strand Plait II

a. Four Strands:
R - O1; L - U1, O1

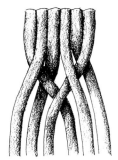

b. Six Strands:
R - O1, U1;
L - U1, O1, U1

34. Beginning Flat Plaits from Flat Material

A five-strand flat plait from flat material begins as a woven diamond (top) and proceeds quickly, using the weight of a heavy board (right) to secure the plait's beginning.

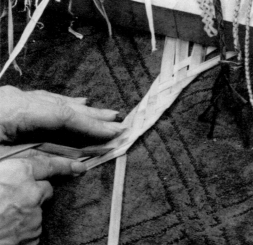

Flat Plaits from Flat Material

In this group the working strand will have to be folded, forming the plait's side edge, as it is worked diagonally downward to the other side. This will produce a flat plait with straight edges, and both sides of the strands will be visible. If your material has a right side and a wrong side, you may not prefer this kind of plait.

To practice, use strips of paper, ½-inch wide masking tape folded in half lengthwise, or any ribbonlike material, then try yucca, cattail, barks, splints, or any other flat, natural material. My favorites are cattail and inner barks the thinner the better.

Start these plaits by interweaving the strands in a diamond-shaped grid, as in Figure 34 and the photo, top, so that the two groups come down diagonally to the right and to the left. If you are using an odd number of strands, one group will have one more than the other. Figure 35 shows three-, four-, and five-strand plaits, so that you can see how the flat splint is folded at the side edges: on the over stroke the splint is folded toward you, and on the under stroke the splint is folded away from you. (In plaits of numerous strands, *over* and *under* refer to the first strand a working strand encounters.) Six-, seven-, and eight-strand plaits are made the same way.

This group does not offer as many options as flat plaits from round materials. They all start with a right-side working strand, which in the diamond-shaped grid is an under-stroke strand.

Also useful to know are flat plaits from flat material that are traditionally associated with straw hats. One, a four-strand plait, is worked in a combination of diagonal and horizontal strokes and produces zigzag edges. Start by drawing a 45° angle on a sheet of paper with the point at the top—like a tepee.

35. Flat Plaits from Flat Materials

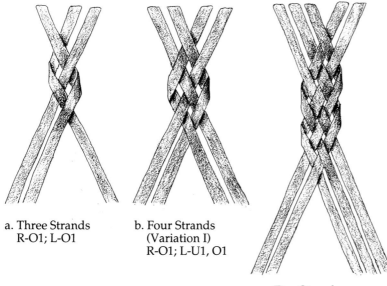

a. Three Strands
R-O1; L-O1

b. Four Strands
(Variation I)
R-O1; L-U1, O1

c. Five Strands
R-O1, U1; L-O1, U1

36. Four-Strand Flat Plait II

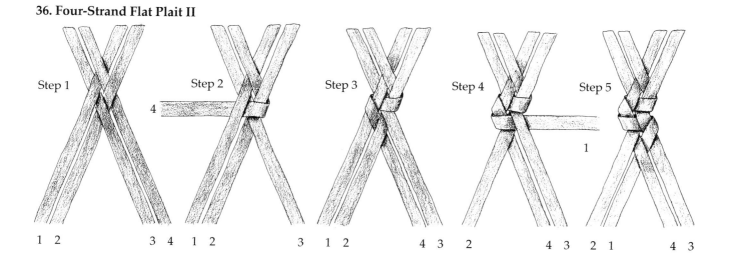

Step 1   Step 2   Step 3   Step 4   Step 5

37. Alternative Beginning for Four-Strand Flat Plait II

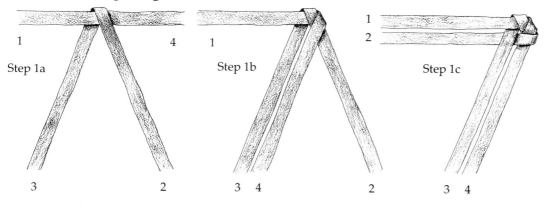

Step 1a   Step 1b   Step 1c

Step 1: Lay two strips next to each other on the left side of the tepee and two on the right side and interweave them toward the top (Figure 36). Tape them at the top to secure them. Number them on both sides of the strips, 1 through 4, as shown.

Step 2: Lay Strip 4 *horizontally* to the left and weave over two strands, under one strand.

Step 3: Lay Strip 4 *diagonally* down to the right alongside Strip 3, weaving over one, under one.

Step 4: Lay Strip 1 horizontally toward the right and weave over two, under one.

Step 5: Lay Strip 1 diagonally down to the left alongside Strip 2, weaving over one, under one.

With Strip 3 repeat Steps 2 and 3.

With Strip 2 repeat Steps 4 and 5.

Simply put, each strand makes a horizontal then a diagonal stroke.

This plait can alternatively be started by following these directions (Figure 37):

Step 1a: Fold one strip to make a tepee. Place another strip through the top. Number them as shown.

Step 1b: Lay Strip 4 *diagonally* down to the left alongside Strip 3.

Step 1c: Lay Strip 2 *horizontally* to the left alongside Strip 1 and weave over one, under one. Your teepee is now tipped over. Turn it so it is standing straight up again.

Revert to Steps 2 through 5 of Figure 36.

Work a four-strand round plait of round material from the bottom up, securing the end of a holding cord under your foot.

38. Four-Strand Plait III

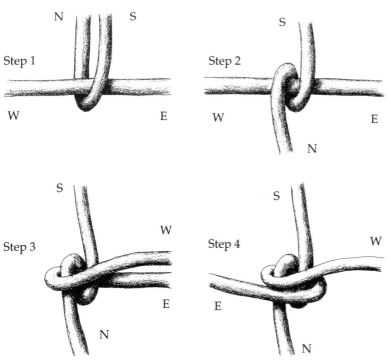

Round Plaits from Round Material

For this group use the same material as for the first group, flat plaits from round material. I like to work the four-strand plait from the bottom up, as shown in the photos at left. You can tie the ends to your foot or the rung of your chair. This might be considered more of a square plait because of the tight folding back and forth of four elements over each other. Some plaiters call this group solid plaits.

I learned this four-strand plait many years ago from a man at the county fair who was plaiting it into the top of a beautiful Belgian show horse's mane. To practice, use something very soft and flexible like thick yarn or raffia (the man was using long strips of cheesecloth). Believe me, you will not need the horse!

Begin with four separate pieces knotted together or two long strands, one folded over the middle of the other. We will call the strand ends North, South, East, and West. Use two colors: one color for North and South and another color for East and West. In a nutshell, North and South exchange places, then East and West exchange places—but you must be consistent about how they cross. Here it is step by step (Figure 38 is a bird's-eye view):

Step 1: South goes North (to the right or East side of North).

Step 2: North goes South.

Step 3: West goes East (over or North of East, not below it).

Step 4: East goes West.

Repeat each step.

I finally worked it out in my mind so I would remember by saying: South goes East of North (then North goes South). West goes over (or North) of East (then East goes West).

I further shortened it simply by saying: Southeast and Westover. It may also help you to remember by noticing that South (Step 1) and West (Step 3) always end up in the Northeast quadrant.

Figure 39 shows a four-strand plait that is the same as the horse's-mane plait, but worked from the top down. The working strand on the right goes to the left under two strands, then changes direction and goes over one strand to the right. The left strand goes to the right under two strands, changes direction and goes over one strand to the left again. Remember that the working strand must return to a vertical position at the end of its sequence. You can work variations on this technique using six or eight strands. Incorporating light and dark strands in different places will produce interesting effects.

Round Plaits from Flat Material

A four-, six-, or eight-strand plait can be worked using flat material. This actually produces a tubular structure. I worked the handle in the elbow basket described on pages 100 to 101 using this four-strand plait and palmetto splints.

To begin, arrange the splints in a diamond-shaped grid and tape the tops to a working surface. Work from the top diagonally downward. Examine the three grids of Figure 40 carefully. All three plaits start with the *right* strand. The grids for the four- and six-strand plaits show that the right strand is an *over* strand. The grid for the eight-strand plait shows that the right strand is an *under* strand. This is purely mathematical and if you follow the sequence exactly as given, it will come out right.

These beautiful plaits take practice, but are well worth it. To further challenge and delight you, try the six- and eight-strand round plaits using round material.

39. Four-Strand Round Plait from Round Materials

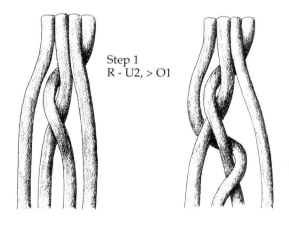

Step 1
R - U2, > O1

Step 2
L - U2, < O1

40. Round Plaits from Flat Materials

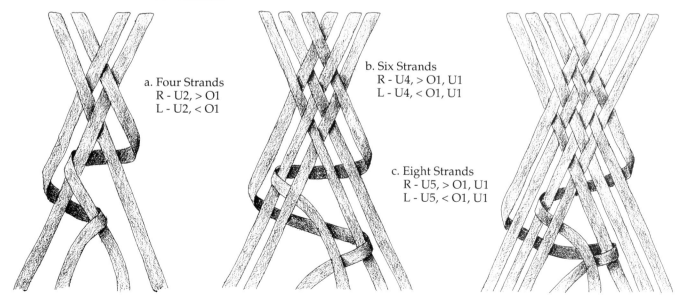

a. Four Strands
R - U2, > O1
L - U2, < O1

b. Six Strands
R - U4, > O1, U1
L - U4, < O1, U1

c. Eight Strands
R - U5, > O1, U1
L - U5, < O1, U1

Chapter 6

Twining

I will pick tender blossoms to twine in her hair,
Blushing roses so red and the lily so fair,
Lovely myrtle so bright like the emerald dew,
Modest buttercup yellow, forget-me-not blue.

—A.P. CARTER

In twining, one element (the spokes) is wrapped by two elements (the weavers), which also twist around one another. Twining may be the oldest type of basketry known. While this distinction has also been claimed of coiling, it seems to me that the idea of holding two twigs together by twisting a strand of grass or rush between them is more basic than the idea of bundling grasses together and sewing them into a coil. Furthermore, in coiling a tool is needed—either an awl of some type or a needle. However, does it really matter to today's basketmaker which came first? Both techniques are versatile, beautiful, and when designing your own basket, inspiring.

Twined baskets employ one of the weaves also used in wickerwork: the twining or pairing weave, described in Figure 9, page 64. Some terms in twining are the same as in wickerwork, and references will be made to some of the diagrams in that chapter. Wickerwork, however, is quite different in that it depends on the rigidity of the material to maintain shape, strength, and spacing between spokes. The spokes in a twined basket can be made of stout materials, such as those used in wickerwork. But more commonly, twined baskets employ softer materials woven close together with minimal

space between the weavers. The material is soft and pliant enough to draw the spokes in to form a tightly woven fabric. If such soft material were used with spacing between the spokes, the basket would be structurally and visually weak. Flat materials (such as soft inner barks) and roots (split into flat ribbons or used whole) have also commonly been twined.

Another characteristic of twined baskets is that because the spokes are so close together, there are typically a large number of strokes or stitches to the inch. It therefore takes longer to weave a twined basket than to weave a wickerwork basket of the same size. Smaller stitches also mean design possibilities different from those of wickerwork.

Although twining is generally thought of as being a two-strand structure, bands of three-strand weaves are found in twined baskets. These do not usually compose the entire basket.

The weave in some old twined baskets of northwestern North America, particularly those of the Attu and the Tlingit Indians and hats made by the Haida Indians, are so fine as to resemble grosgrain ribbon or cloth. Other baskets employing this weave have been woven tight enough to hold wa-

41. Double Square Base I

a. Begin mat with a plain weave; make two of these.

b. Orient the two as a cross and twine around the perimeter of the woven square.

c. Add spokes at the corners and in the spaces as you twine until the square has becomes round.

ter. Beautiful designs are possible using various twining techniques, some of which will be described in this chapter.

Shaping can be accomplished in several ways. Twisting the weavers an extra half turn (a full twist) between spokes adds bulk and causes the shape to flare out. Twining around two (or more) spokes instead of one brings the shape in. Cutting out some of the spokes or tapering them as they reach the top will also cause the sides to taper in, as adding spokes will expand the shape. Varying the thickness of the weavers may also result in a change of shape. Many twined

baskets are straight-sided which makes them easy to decorate by coloring the weavers or by adding weavers or ornament.

BASES

Because the spacing between spokes in a twined basket is so close, spokes must be added to round bases (which begin as square starts) as they grow in diameter. When the base is the desired size, you maintain the same spacing between spokes, which causes them to turn up. Other forms, as the rectangular base (Figure 43, page 111), or checkerwork base described for splintwork (Figure 16a, page 82), may have all the spokes laid in at the beginning.

Double Square Base I

This base, a start for a round basket, may be worked with spokes that are somewhat rigid, such as honeysuckle, akebia, willow, black walnut leaf stems, and sumac. Four base spokes are laid out and woven together at their centers with a simple over one, under one weave using one weaver (Figure 41a). The beginning of the weaver may be folded back for about ½ inch so that subsequent rows cover it, or it may be left loose for a few inches and woven in later. The weaving continues until the base is perfectly square. Push each row very tightly down on to the previous row (shown woven loosely for clarity). Make a second, identical mat using four more base spokes.

Now you have two groups of spokes with a square woven at the center of each. Position the two groups at right angles to form a cross, with one square placed directly on top of the other so that the weavers are at the same corner (Figure 41b). Working clockwise, use the two weavers to twine around each spoke, tracing the entire square and binding the squares together. (If you have not folded back your beginning ends, but have left them loose, you can work them in for a few strokes when you begin the twining and trim the ends later.)

On the next row, add two spokes to each corner by first tapering one end of each, laying that end on the inside of the base, and twining around (Figure 41C). A little masking tape over the ends of the added spokes will hold them in place temporarily.

As you proceed with the weaving, adding more spokes in each corner, the square will become round. As the diameter increases and spaces open up, continue to add spokes, keeping the spacing even. Once the weaving is at least ½ inch beyond the first twined row, you can add spokes by opening up a space with an awl and inserting the tapered ends into the weave along existing spokes. This will hide the ends. If you wish to expose the ends for a decorative effect, do not insert them into the weave, but leave the end on the outside of the basket as you twine each new spoke into the structure.

Double Square Base II
This base is similar to the first version of the double square base, except that the centers of each group of spokes are not first woven together in a square. One group of unwoven spokes is laid at right angles over another group, and twining begins with a folded weaver over a cor-

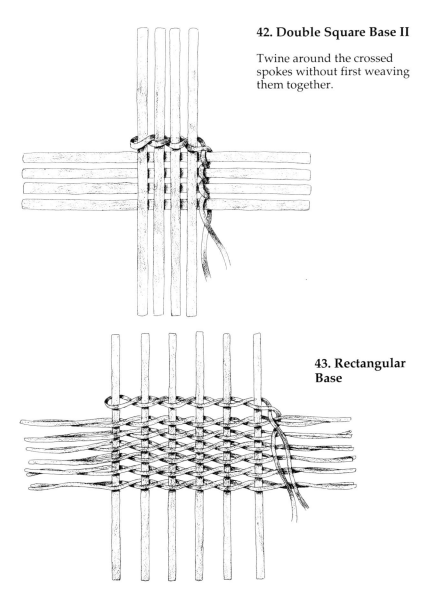

42. Double Square Base II

Twine around the crossed spokes without first weaving them together.

43. Rectangular Base

ner spoke (Figure 42). This beginning is less common than the first, but often used in openwork baskets, in which the spokes are rigid and the rows of twining aren't pushed close together (Figure 47, page 114).

Rectangular Base
In this base, separate weaving strands are twined across the center of a group of spokes. Then the ends of the weaving strands are turned up and become the spokes or warp for two of the sides of the basket (Figure 43).

Checkerboard Base

This base (pictured below) employs a splint-work technique, a simple over one, under one pattern, around which the sides are twined. It lends itself to square as well as rectangular bases.

A twined basket can begin from a simple checkerboard mat. Here both mat and weavers are cattail leaves.

The checkerboard base in a finished basket: the spokes are yucca leaves, the weavers are iris. Details for this project appear on page 119.

Spider Base

This base is worked with soft or flexible material such as cattail or iris leaves. Place eight to ten prepared (dried and dampened) leaves side by side on a table. Lay a short length of waxed linen or other thin, strong fiber across them in the center. Fold each leaf over onto itself (Figure 44a) and temporarily tie each pair of leaf ends together with a scrap of leaf, yarn, or string. Now tie the linen in a knot, drawing the leaves together at the folds and fanning out the ends in a circle. Pull the linen tightly and tie (Figure 44b).

Now select a long leaf as a weaver, fold it, and place the fold around one of the doubled leaves to begin the twining. Mark this spoke so you can finish the basket on the same spoke. Twine two or three rounds over the doubled spokes as close to the tied center as possible. (If you are using very long leaves such as iris or cattail for a weaver, you can secure the spokes at their folded centers with a long piece of leaf instead of linen, and use it to continue the twining.)

Remove the temporary ties from the ends and spread the spokes out singly. Now add a new spoke over each existing spoke and twine over both. If your material is very fine, you can weave the entire basket with doubled spokes, or if it's strong enough, you can separate the doubled spokes, after the end of the additional spoke is secure, and weave over single spokes. This process of adding new spokes and separating them continues until the base is large enough to upset. Trim the ends of the added leaves later; or as you add each new leaf, thread it down into the weave with a crochet hook.

SPLICING

When splicing soft material, overlap the old and the new ends for a few inches and weave them together as one (Figure 45). Trim off scraggly ends later. Splice heavier or more rigid material as described in splicing wickerwork, Figure 14, page 66.

44. Spider Base

a. Fold soft material over a waxed linen cord.

b. Draw the folded material together and fan the spokes out.

Remove temporary ties
after a few rounds.

Begin
twining.

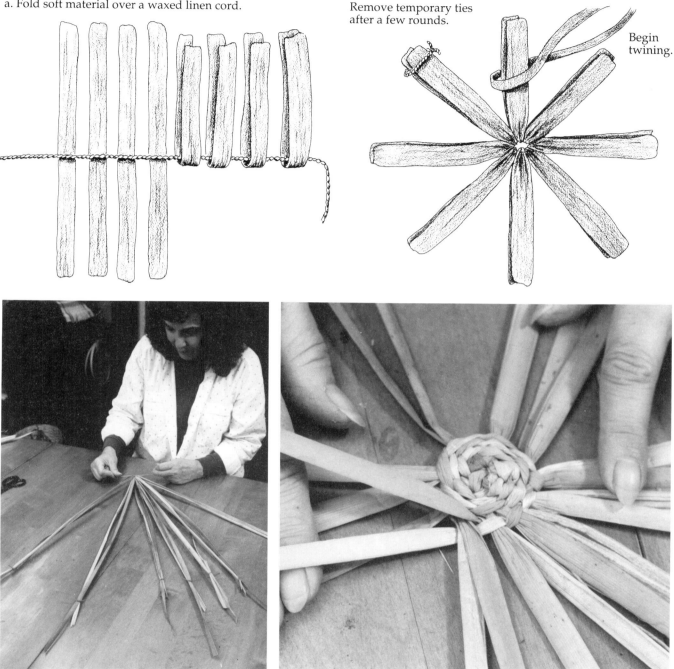

To begin a spider base, lay a waxed linen cord across your materials (in the photos above, cattail leaves), fold each length over onto itself, and tie the ends together with a scrap of yarn. When you draw the cord tight, the leaves will form radiating spokes. Begin twining with a separate, folded weaver and twine around the doubled leaf spokes. At right, after only a few rounds, five new spokes have been added.

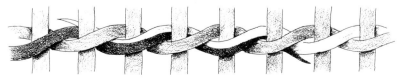

45. Splicing

(Old weaver is shown shaded)

46. Plain Twining Weaves

a. Basic

b. Alternating color

c. Doubled warp

d. Occasional doubled warp, diagonally shifted

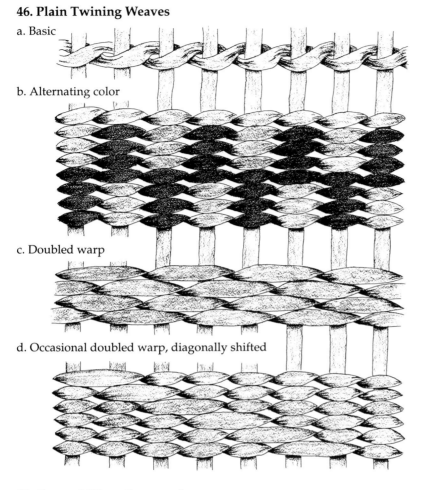

47. Crossed-Warp Openwork

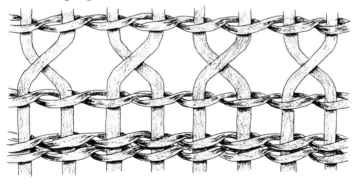

48. Beading

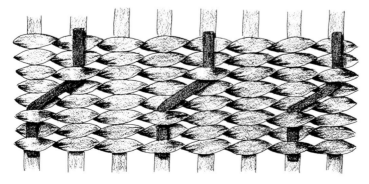

WEAVES

Twining is very pleasant and relaxing in its repetitiveness. Though time-consuming to weave, the resulting fabric of closely spaced, small stitches gives a feeling of peacefulness and composure.

Plain Twine

The movement of the weavers, to produce this weave (Figure 46a), has already been described in Figure 9 of Wickerwork (page 64). This simple pattern is capable of considerable variety. Figure 46b shows plain twine using a different color for each weaver. You can alternate the position of dark and light weavers by giving one extra half twist where you wish to make the change. Figure 46c is plain twining over two spokes. Figure 46d is plain twining over occasional pairs of spokes, diagonally shifted. Variations in weave as well as color can be found in the chart at the end of this chapter (page 121).

Openwork (Fitching)

Twined baskets with rigid spokes may have spaces between rows. Twined openwork (or open twined work) may also have crossed spokes, where two spokes exchange places and the twining continues over the cross spokes, as in Figure 47.

Beading

In this decorative treatment, a third element is held on the surface over the spokes, either vertically or diagonally (or both), and occasionally caught with twining stitches (Figure 48). This third element can be a contrasting color or texture; it can be attached at regular or irregular intervals; it can even be a different color on each side, and be twisted between spokes to show alternating faces.

Overlay (Double-Faced Weaver)

This weave employs two flat weavers of different color, one overlaid over the other. To change color, the doubled strand is twisted, causing the alternate color to appear on the right side of the work (Figure 49).

False Embroidery (Overlay)

A third element is laced up and around the surface weaver (Figure 50).

Frapped Twining

A third element is laced up and around both weavers at the twists (Figure 51).

Wrapped Twining

A rigid crosspiece is held horizontally behind (or sometimes in front of) the spokes by a flexible weaver, laced around both the spoke and the rigid crosspiece (Figure 52).

Lattice Twining (Tee Twining)

A rigid crosspiece is laid over the spokes and two flexible strands are twined around both (Figure 53).

Three-Strand Twining

This is the same as the triple weave, described in Wickerwork (page 64). Each weaver, in turn, goes in front of two spokes, then behind one spoke (Figure 54).

Three-Strand Braid

This is almost the same as three-strand twining, except for the following: After each strand is taken in front of two spokes, and before going in back of the next spoke, it is taken in between the other two weavers, instead of over them (Figure 55).

49. Overlay Twist to change color.

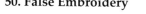

50. False Embroidery

51. Frapped Twining

52. Wrapped Twining

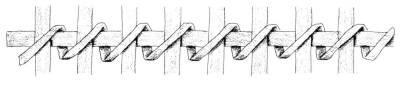

53. Lattice Twining

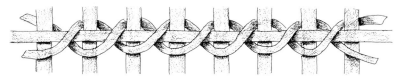

54. Three-Strand Twining

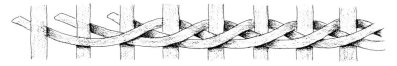

55. Three-Strand Braid

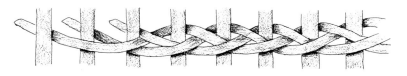

BORDERS

Some basketmakers find borders in twined baskets a problem because there are so many spokes to deal with. Here is a simple treatment for twined baskets with rigid spokes: When the basket has reached the desired height, simply cut off the spokes ¼ to ½ inch above the weave. You will see many historical twined baskets in museums with this treatment, and they do seem to hold up well.

56. Woven Border

Round 1

Round 2

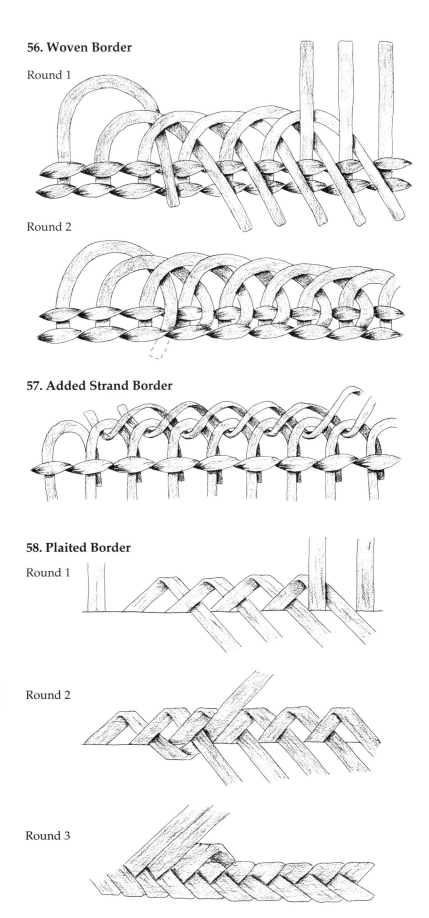

57. Added Strand Border

58. Plaited Border

Round 1

Round 2

Round 3

Wrapped Border

This border (Figure 15c, page 67) works well if each spoke consists of more than one strand. Some of the strands can be cut off or threaded down into the weave in order to minimize bulk. You can then wrap the remaining spokes .

Woven Border

This border (Figure 56) is worked in two rounds:

Round 1: Working from left to right, take each spoke behind two and out.

Round 2: Take each spoke under the last row of weave and in. The ends remain on the inside of the basket.

Added Strand Border

I really like this border (Figure 57). It is worked with two added elements of flat material that cover the exposed parts of the spokes.

Step 1: Bend each spoke down to align with one spoke to the right and insert it there into the last row or two of weaving. Bring the end out on the inside of the basket. Do not pull down tight.

Step 2: Insert two flat elements under the bights (or curves) of two adjacent turned-down spokes. Lace each one alternately around every other bight. As you lace each bight with the flat weaver, pull that spoke end down tight, then lace the next bight. Trim the spoke end.

Plaited Border

The plaited border (Figure 58) is suitable for flat, soft material such as cattail or soft, thin bark. It is worked in three rounds.

Round 1: Behind one spoke and out.

Round 2: Under one turned-down spoke and up.

Round 3: Over the top and down into the inside of the basket. With hook or needle, thread each end into the weave one spoke to the right for several rows.

Trim ends.

Basket Projects

THE SPOKES OF THIS BASKET are corn husks, which have ample strength in a small basket—this one is 4½ inches in diameter and 2 inches high. The husks provide a light-colored rim which contrasts nicely with other weaving materials. Here I've used iris leaves left whole, but other soft materials would work as well.

Construction

Using eight pieces of corn husks, knot pairs together at the narrow ends to form four 18-inch-long spokes. Work a double-square base as shown in Figure 42, except make it two spokes over two spokes. Mark the initial spoke. Twine three rows. Add one spoke to each spoke. Separate and twine around single spokes (there are now 16). Twine six rows. Add one spoke to each spoke. Separate and twine around each single spoke (32 spokes). Twine six rows. Add one spoke to each spoke. Twine around single spokes (64 spokes). Twine four rows. Start to upset basket. Weave to a height of 2 inches (about 20 rows). The woven border is worked as in Figure 56.

Materials

- 64 husk spokes
- 1 handful leaf weavers
- Waxed linen thread

Twined basket of iris and corn husk.

BOWL BASKET

Materials
- 6 rigid spokes, 14 inches long, for starting
- Approximately 70 additional spokes, 7 inches long
- Leaf weavers

Honeysuckle and iris bowl basket.

THE HONEYSUCKLE I USED for the spokes of this basket give it a little more rigidity than softer materials. Adding spokes can be tricky because the stripped vines are slippery and tend to slip out while weaving. This bowl-shaped basket measures 7 inches in diameter at the rim and is 3½ inches high.

Construction
Work the square base as in Figure 41. Add spokes as needed to maintain the desired shape. The basket has a band of lattice twining (Figure 53) just before turning up the sides. It also has a decorative band of triple weave (page 64) on the side. The border is wrapped (Figure 15c, page 67).

*Twined basket of
yucca and iris leaves.*

**SMALL-
MOUTH
TWINED
BASKET**

Materials
- 20 sturdy leaves,
  16 inches long
- Soft leaves for
  weavers

YUCCA IS AN EXCEPTIONALLY strong, fibrous plant and is useful for many basketry techniques. It forms the spokes of this basket, which is 4 inches square by 5 inches high.

Construction

The base of yucca is a simple plain-woven mat, ten leaves by ten leaves (see photo, page 112). Cut the protruding ends of the yucca leaves down the middle all the way to the base to double the number of spokes. Then twine between these divided spokes with the leaf weavers (I used iris). Maintaining tension on the weavers as you gently

push spokes away from you, the basket will upset. When the basket is 3 inches high, twine over two spokes at a time, bringing the shape in. The natural taper of the leaves also contributes to the basket's taper, especially at the rim. The yucca leaves will have to be trimmed at the base ends to match this taper at the tips. You could do this to all the leaves at the start, but I prefer to wait and first get a feel for the shape of the basket.

Work the border the same way as the corn-husk border (page 117), except return the ends to the outside of the basket four rows down and trim to ½ inch.

SMALL TWINED BASKET

Materials

- 1 handful of whole, soft leaves for both spokes and weavers

MY STUDENTS HAVE enjoyed making this diminutive basket, 2¼ inches in diameter by 2⅛ inches high. Both spokes and weavers are made of iris leaves, but other soft leaves, such as daylily, would work as well.

Construction

Start a spider base (Figure 44) with seven leaves. Twine three rows over the folded and doubled spokes. Separate the spokes and twine for five more rows. Add a spoke to each existing spoke, making a total of 28 single spokes. Twine a few more rows before turning the basket up. When you've twined to a height of 1 inch, add a band of lattice twining. Weave another inch in plain twining and work a wrapped border.

Small basket of twined iris leaves.

WEAVES IN TWINING

NAME OF WEAVE	NO. OF SPOKES	NO. OF WEAVERS	COLOR OF WEAVERS	STROKE	RESULT
Twining Pairing	Any number	Two		Front of one, behind one, and out. Repeat stroke with left-hand weaver.	
Twining Pairing	Even	Two		Same as above.	
Twining Pairing	Odd[1]	Two		Same as above.	
Triple Weave Three-Strand Twining	Any number	Three		Front of two, behind one, and out. Repeat with each left-hand weaver.	
Triple Weave Three-Strand Twining	Any number divisible by 3 plus 2	Three		Same as above. Result is spiral.	
Triple Weave Three-Strand Twining	Any number divisible by 3 plus 1	Three		Same as above. Result is mottled.	
Triple Weave Three-Strand Twining	Any number divisible by 3	Three		Same as above. Result is vertical stripes.	

[1] Weaves ordinarily worked over an odd number of spokes may also be worked over an even number if you change the stroke at the beginning of each round.

Chapter 7

Coiling

The cowslip startles in meadows green,
The buttercup catches the sun in its chalice,
And there's never a leaf or a blade too mean
To be some happy creature's palace.

—JAMES RUSSELL LOWELL

Coiled baskets seem to be universal. Even countries having climates too cold or too dry to support tree growth usually have some type of grass that can be bunched and wrapped into coils. Some of the finest, most beautiful baskets in the world are made in the coiling technique. Outstanding are those made by the Pomo and Washoe Indians of California. Tightly wrapped, with many stitches to the inch, these gems are often decorated with feathers and beads.

A coiled basket is constructed similarly to a coiled clay pot, in which one continuous, round length of material is wound around or on top of itself in an expanding or ascending spiral. The spiral can also be decreased to create closed forms. Coiling lends itself well to a wide variety of shapes, designs, and expressions, from crude and rustic to the very finest. It is adaptable to many plants and to various parts of plants, including roots, leaves, stems, midribs, splints, bark, husks, pods, and seed heads.

The chart on the next page shows natural material used by various cultures or individual basketmakers. It should spark your imagination for ideas in combining plants in coiling techniques. These and other plants suitable for coiling appear in the Harvest Calendar, beginning on page 31.

Two basic elements are used in coiled work: the *foundation,* or *core,* which may consist of one or more strands, rods, or splints, and the *stitching* or *wrapping,* which surrounds the core and binds one row to the next. The stitching can completely conceal the core or leave it exposed, contrasting with it in color and texture. The core material should be firm and strong, yet flexible enough to bend around the curves. The stitching material must be flexible, yet strong enough to hold the coils together.

Coiled basketry techniques may be divided into three categories, each applying to a part of the basket: the *center* (or *start*), the *stitches,* and the *rim.* The coil is continuous, of course, but I'll refer to two coils in explaining the various procedures: the *top coil,* or the coil currently being wrapped and attached, and the *bottom coil,* or the wrapped coil preceding the top coil. Coils are also commonly referred to as *rows.*

An awl or a blunt needle is necessary to make an opening through which to thread the stitching material. Needles made of wood work well; the round point finds its way between the fibers rather than piercing its way through, as sharp steel does. While wood needles may be a little thick for very fine baskets, they are useful for much fiber-

COILING AROUND THE WORLD

CULTURE	CORE MATERIAL	STITCHING MATERIAL
Pomo California	Willow rod	Sedge root, with designs of redbud splints, decorated with shells, beads, feathers
Salish Washington	Cedar or spruce root	Outer portion of cedar or spruce root, with imbrication of cherry bark, cedar bast, grass stems dyed with Oregon grape
Hopi Arizona	Split yucca (harder part)	Yucca (leafy portion)
Shoshonean Upper Great Plains	Grass stems	Sumac splints
Mission So. California	Grass stems	Martynia pods, sumac
Washoe California	Willow	White: mountain willow; Black: brake fern stems; Red: redbud bark
Havasupai Arizona	Willow splints	Willow splints
Pima Arizona	Split cattail stems, wheat straw	Willow, martynia pods, willow bark, mesquite bark
Navajo Southwestern U.S.	Sumac	Sumac
Papago Arizona	Yucca, bear grass, horse hair	Yucca, horse hair
Coushatta Louisiana, Texas	Pine needles, Spanish moss	Raffia
Seminole Florida	Palmetto fiber, grass	Colored cotton thread
Chippewa/Otawa Michigan	Birch bark, sweet grass	Black cotton thread
Gullah South Carolina	Pine needles, sweet grass	Palmetto leaf
Appalachia	Rye straw	Oak splints
Africa	Palm leaf midribs	Palm leaf
Shetland Islands	Straw	Twine
Chukchi Kamchatka, Russia	Sealskin bottom, straw core	Sinew thread

Detail of coiled Navajo basket.

work. Plastic needles break too easily. Wood needles may break also, though not often if you are careful, and since you can learn how to make your own wood needles as shown on page 192, you can make several to have in reserve in case you break one. Sometimes stitching material is stiff enough to use, when sharpened to a point, as its own needle. You can also make a needle with the tip of a *Yucca filamentosa* leaf (see page 193).

A coiled basket is more generally (and successfully) worked with the outside of the basket facing you, except in the case of a shallow, open shape in which the inside of the basket is more visible. After making a flat round mat for the bottom (Figure 59a), you can shape the sides by laying one coil on top of the preceding coil (Figure 59b) and by increasing or decreasing the diameter of each coil.

CENTERS OR STARTS

The center should be worked very small and the center hole completely filled in. Subsequent rows may gradually become thicker until they are the desired size. Sometimes softer material is used for the beginning to make the coil as tight as possible; then a more rigid piece is added by cutting off the old foundation at the last wrap and inserting the tapered end of the firmer material into the center of the soft core.

I stitch from right to left (except for some of the rim finishes), but if you prefer, stitching from left to right works, too. Put a marker of colored string at the end of the first round. The marked point will establish the beginning and end of each row as well as each change of design or color.

59. Coiling

a. Stitching the mat

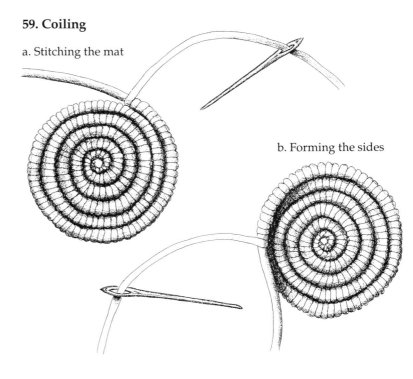

b. Forming the sides

Knot Start

This simple start is suitable for a very flexible multiple-strand core, such as grasses or long, thin leaves. Make an overhand knot at one end of the core strands. Insert the stitching material into the center of the knot, pull the knot snug, and wrap until the foundation is completely covered (Figure 60).

Alternatively, you can make the knot in the center of the grass bundle. Then gather together both ends of the bundle and stitch around it entirely to form the first coil.

Single-Rod-Foundation Start

With a knife, taper about 1½ inches of a flexible rod to a gradual point. Wrap the last inch of this taper with the stitching material, laying the end of the stitching strand along the core so that it is held in place by the wrap. Wrap tightly all the way to the point. Now shape the tapered rod into a circle by bringing the point end up to meet the core where you started wrapping. Make it as tight and small as possible. Wrap around the circle formed, taking stitches through

60. Knot Start

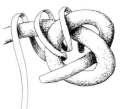

61. Single-Rod-Foundation Start

a. Taper foundation rod.

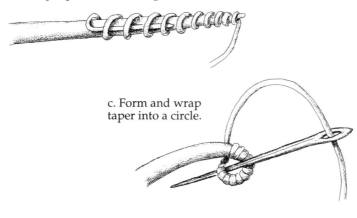

b. Wrap taper with stitching material.

c. Form and wrap taper into a circle.

62. Variation on the Single-Rod Start

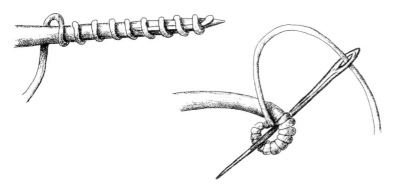

63. Oval Base

a. Bend rod and wrap the bend.

b. Wrap the two rod sections together using figure-eight stitches.

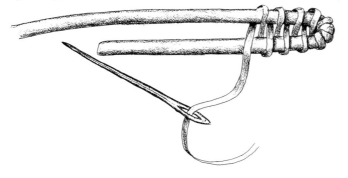

the center and around the unwrapped portion of foundation. Mark your starting point and, using any of the stitches described beginning on page 127, wrap the new coil to the preceding one (Figure 61).

A variation of this center begins by wrapping away from the point as shown in Figure 62. Bring the point around, catching and securing the tapered end in the subsequent wraps.

Oval Base

Bend a well-soaked rod about 6 to 8 inches from one end. Make several wraps at the bend, securing the start of the stitching material under the wraps (Figure 63). Work a figure-eight stitch (page 127) from right to left, as shown. Keep the rods as close together as possible, making the wraps firm and snug. When you reach the end of the left-hand side, bend the long end of the rod around and continue stitching. Make a few extra wraps at the bend to cover the rod. Continue as for other coiled bases.

Multiple-strand foundations may be worked exactly the same way as a single-rod foundation.

STITCHING OR WRAPPING

I prefer to work with the needle entering the work from front to back (or from outside to inside). There are exceptions: I sometimes find that pine needle coiling techniques, slant-stitching an exposed core, and the Apache stitch are better to work from the back. Working from the front makes it easier to see where the needle must enter. Several stabs are typically necessary working the other way, and this can weaken some fibers. Using an awl, it's even more difficult, particularly in a closed shape.

The lazy squaw and the figure eight are the two basic stitches from which most other stitches are derived. Many variations and combinations are possible.

Lazy Squaw Stitch

This stitch (Figure 64) is also called short-and-long stitch. Wrapping toward you, cover the top coil (short stitch) then wrap around the top and bottom coils (long stitch). Sometimes more than one wrap is taken around the top coil before wrapping around the two coils—and sometimes more than one wrap is taken around both coils.

Figure-Eight Stitch

This stitch (Figure 65) is also called the Navajo stitch. Wrap the top coil, then bring the stitching material between the top coil and the bottom coil, go around the bottom coil, then the top coil in a figure-eight pattern. The connecting stitches do not show on this stitch, as the wraps never span two coils. This is a very firm weave.

Peruvian Stitch

When the long stitch of the lazy squaw is continuously made to one side of the long stitch in the preceding row, it will result in a series that slants or spirals around the basket (Figure 66).

Mariposa Stitch

Work a lazy squaw stitch, this time from back to front. Wrap around the long stitch—horizontally—between both coils. A variation, the Samoan (or lace) stitch is the same as the mariposa, except that the long stitch is wrapped two or more times. The effect is to hold one coil away from the next coil, giving a lacy or open look (Figure 67).

Apache Stitch

Wrap the top coil away from you as in the figure eight, then stitch only the stitching material of the bottom coil rather than the entire coil. This stitch can be applied to every stitch of the bottom coil, or you can make two or more wraps over the top coil before catching the stitch of the bottom coil (Figure 68).

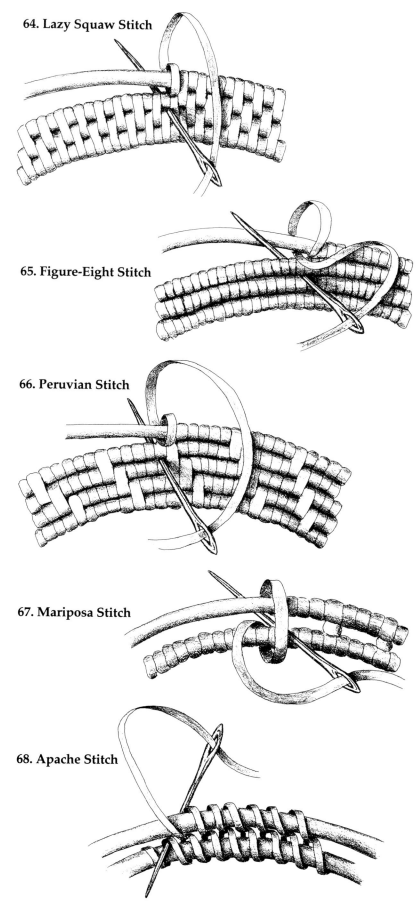

64. Lazy Squaw Stitch

65. Figure-Eight Stitch

66. Peruvian Stitch

67. Mariposa Stitch

68. Apache Stitch

EXPOSED-CORE STITCHES

Pine needle basketry is probably the best known type of exposed-core basketry, although many other materials are used in exposed cores. Pine needles were used by Native Americans for centuries, but a particular flavor of pine needle coiled work developed during the Civil War in the southeastern states. Ladies were coiling "straw" hats from pine needles and began using colored thread and raffia to stitch with. The form, called Tenerife, evolved, incorporating fancy patterns from Europe, embroidered on wire frames and attached to the coils. The center of many of these was a small ring covered with a double buttonhole stitch using raffia which was then laced back and forth across the inner part of the ring to form spokes, as in a wheel. (see facing page). Various patterns were woven in and out of the wheel spokes. Then the first coil of pine needles was attached to the buttonhole stitch on the outside edge of the ring. Various-sized rings, stars, and other shapes, covered with raffia, were added to the work. This made a very fancy basket. I tend to favor the plainer ones, the beauty of the material and the stitches giving decoration enough. There are times, however, when a small circle of vine, wire, or cord is an attractive start for a coiled basket.

The stitching material for pine needle baskets and other exposed-core work may be raffia, linen thread, fine bark strips, palm leaves, or tough, long grasses. Raffia is the best choice for working the stitches described here. Wrap dry raffia in a wet towel for an hour or more. Insert the base of a leaf in the needle's eye. Pine needles should be wrapped in wet towels for 15 minutes or more and kept in the towel while waiting to be worked.

The following stitches, generally used in pine needle basketry, are also used with other exposed cores—in rye straw baskets, for instance. There are many combinations and fancy variations of these stitches, and terms differ from one source to another. Pay particular attention when splicing the stitching material, so that the ends are well concealed. As the work progresses, the stitches will become farther apart, especially on the base of the basket. New rows of stitches must be added between old stitches to keep the weaving tight and secure (Figure 69 and photo, left).

Bottom of coiled basket of cattail and cedar bark. Notice where new stitches have been added as the base grew larger.

69. Additional Stitches

New stitches added between old stitches to fill larger diameter.

FILLING A STARTER RING

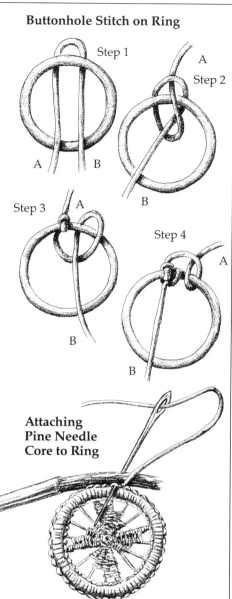

This pretty little ring is fun to make, especially if you enjoy embroidery and other forms of intricate needle work. Smooth "bone" rings 1 to 2 inches in diameter can be purchased in the curtain section of department stores. You completely cover the ring with a series of buttonhole stitches using raffia. Then the first coil of the basket is easily and neatly started by stitching to the wrapped ring.

Use the longest strand of raffia you can find. Do not thread it onto a needle yet, as this part of the work is done with the fingers.

Step 1: Fold the raffia in the center and place it in the ring as shown with the loop under the top of the ring. The two strands thus created are labeled A and B.

Step 2: Cross B over A. Bring A *up* through top loop and make it snug.

Step 3: Bring B to the right, in front of, then behind the ring and through the loop made. Pull B *down* to make it snug.

Step 4: Bring A to the right, spanning the B stitch just made, and bring it behind, then in front of the ring and through the loop made. Pull A *up* to make it snug.

Continue around with each strand spanning the stitch made by the other.

When the ring is filled, thread B into a needle and go through the bight (loop) of the first inside stitch from front to back. Then bring the needle up through the bight of the last inside stitch and pull snugly to close the gap. Do the same thing with A and this completes the ring wrap. Strand B can now be used to weave a spoked wheel or a grid on the inside of the ring. Use strand A to attach the first pine needle coil to the ring.

If it becomes necessary to add a new length to the inside strand, make a square knot at the back of the ring, leaving a few inches extending beyond the knot. Bring these ends straight up and through the bight of the outside stitch. Later, these can be hidden inside the first coil of pine needles. With the added length you can now fill in the inside of the ring.

To make a wheel, bring the strand to the point directly opposite the starting point and insert it into the bight on the inside of the ring. Now bring it back across the ring and insert it just a few stitches either to the right or left of the starting point. Continue back and forth around the ring until there are enough spokes for the size of your ring—six to eight for a 1-inch ring is good. If your choice of design for filling in calls for an odd number of spokes, bring the needle to the center of the wheel and wrap it around several strands of the hub and go back to the rim. The spacing on the last spoke will have to be adjusted accordingly. You can then weave over one, under one around the ring.

To fill the ring with a grid, bring the needle straight down, move over one or two stitches, and bring the needle straight up. Fill the ring with parallel threads, and then weave in an out across the warp. The photo below will give you some ideas for filling in the ring.

Attaching Pine Needle Core to Ring

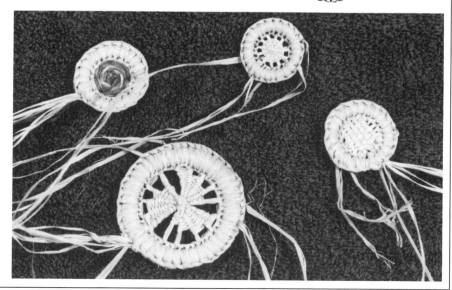

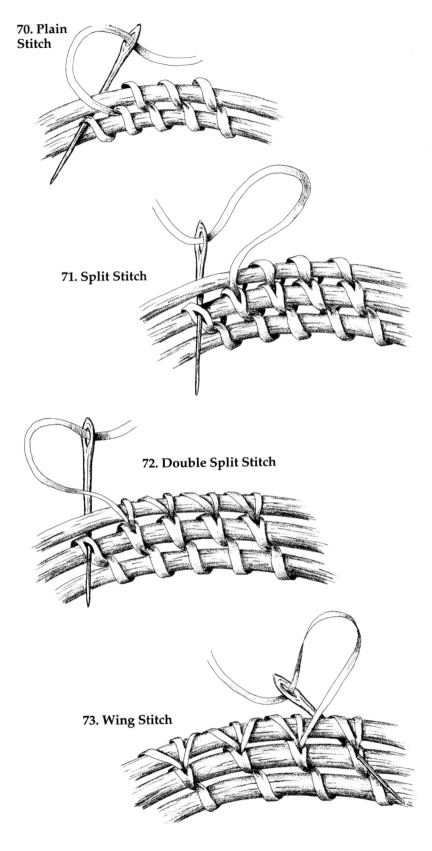

70. Plain Stitch

71. Split Stitch

72. Double Split Stitch

73. Wing Stitch

Plain Stitch

This is similar to the Apache stitch, except that instead of the stitch going through only the stitching of the coil below, this stitch includes part of the core bundle, too. In pine needle basketry the plain stitch is the basis for all other stitches (Figure 70).

Split Stitch

Work two rows in the plain stitch. On the third row pierce thorough the center of the stitching material, taking with it a portion of the core. Repeat this for the remainder of the split-stitch portion (Figure 71).

Double Split Stitch

Work two rows and pierce the first stitch of the third row as in the split stitch, then go around the top coil and into that same hole. This stitch will lie straight up. Now from behind, pierce the next stitch on the left. This second stitch will slant toward the left. On subsequent rows, split only the straight stitch and not the slant stitch (Figure 72).

Wing Stitch

Work the double split stitch for one row, from right to left in the usual manner. At the end, insert the needle into the first stitch of the completed row and make a stitch to the right. Continue working from left to right on that same row. Each row is worked twice (Figure 73).

Fern Stitch

Work two rows in the plain stitch. At the beginning of the third round insert the needle from behind the coil into the space slightly to the right of the first stitch of the preceding row (Figure 74a). Now spanning two rows (the top and bottom), go around to the back and insert the needle to the front just to the left but very close to the same stitch. Continue by inserting the needle into the next stitch to the left (Figure 74b) and return to the top row. On the fourth round, work two long stitches over the new top and bottom rows—between the two long stitches of the third round (Figure 74c). This will form a V-within-a-V. Continue working each round over one coil already worked and the new coil.

SPLICING STITCHING MATERIAL

The simplest way to splice stitching material over a concealed core is to lay the new end along the core and wrap the new end with the old end for several wraps. Then lay the old end along the core, bring up the new strand and continue wrapping it over the old end and core (Figure 75).

When splicing over exposed cores, you can use any of the following methods:

Weaver's Knot

Bring the end of the old strand between coils and form a loop. Wrap the end of the new strand around the loop and then bring it through the top of the loop, as shown in Figure 76. Pull both ends slowly to tighten, bringing the knot within an inch or so of the ends to lie hidden between coils, or on the inside of the basket, or in the center of a multiple-strand core.

Between-Coils Splice

Lay the ends of both the old and new stitching material on the top of the bottom coil (Figure 77), and stitch over them as though they were part of the coil, being careful to keep the ends from slipping to the sides of the coil. This way, they will be hidden between coils. It may be possible to thread the ends of both new and old strands under the stitches of the bottom row.

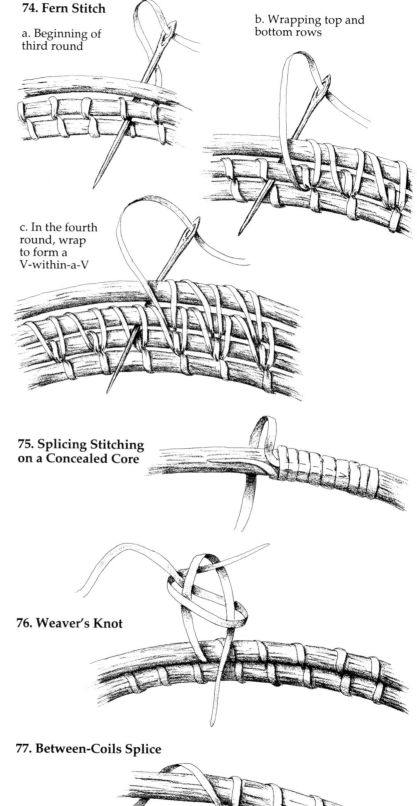

74. Fern Stitch

a. Beginning of third round

b. Wrapping top and bottom rows

c. In the fourth round, wrap to form a V-within-a-V

75. Splicing Stitching on a Concealed Core

76. Weaver's Knot

77. Between-Coils Splice

78. Splicing Single-Rod Foundation

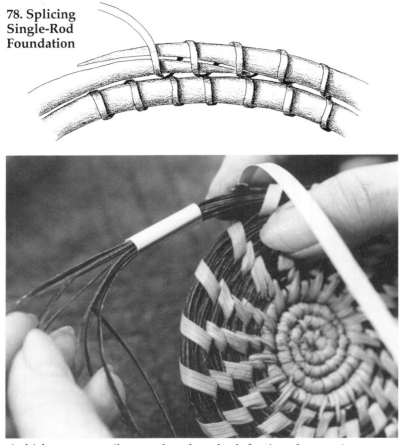

A thickness gauge (here, a short length of plastic soda straw) ensures even thickness when extending multiple-strand foundation material. The gauge stays just ahead of your stitching. When it gets loose, add more material. The basket being made is of split catalpa pods (for the foundation) and split palm leaves (for stitching).

79. Beading or Overlay

SPLICING CORE MATERIAL

The technique for splicing core material depends on whether it's a single-rod or a multiple-strand foundation. In a single-rod foundation (Figure 78), taper one side of the old piece for about 1 inch. Taper the opposite side of the new piece so that they meet to form one continuous thickness. Hold the two together and continue stitching.

In a multiple-strand foundation, new pieces are added gradually. Keep the foundation strands at unequal lengths. As one length is used up, insert a new piece into the middle of the bundle. You can keep multiple-strand foundations a constant thickness by keeping a gauge around the bundle just ahead of where you are stitching (see photo at left). The gauge may be a short section of plastic drinking straw, cow's horn, leather or any type of ring. When the gauge becomes loose, simply add more foundation material to the center of the bundle.

DECORATION

Coiling presents its own range of decorating possibilities, including changing color and adding other weaving elements or ornaments. Many are not applicable to other basketry techniques.

Adding Color

An additional stitching strand (or strands) of another color may be carried along with the core. When you want to change color, stitch with the new color and include the old color with the core.

Beading or Overlay

A flat strip is laid over a coil. The wrapping proceeds alternately over the flat strip for a few wraps, then under the strip for a few wraps (Figure 79). The intervals usually form a regular pattern.

80. Imbrication

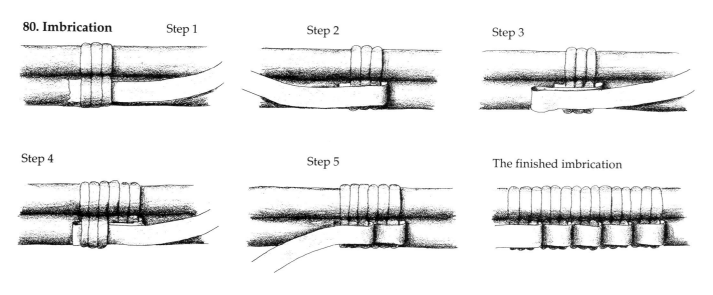

Step 1   Step 2   Step 3

Step 4   Step 5   The finished imbrication

Imbrication

Imbrication is a series of pleats made by folding an overlaid strip back and forth as you coil. You need a very thin, flat strip for imbrication; a thick piece will cause too much bulk at the folds. The strip is usually wide enough to completely cover the coil. Plants materials that lend themselves to imbrication include split rye stalks, bear grass, rush, and corn husk, as well as some very thin inner barks.

You may imbricate the top row as you are coiling it, or you may imbricate the bottom row which has already been wrapped. If you imbricate the top row, you will have to use the Apache Stitch on the next row so you won't cover the imbrication.

If you plan to imbricate the entire basket (or more than one row), I think it's best to imbricate the bottom row. This way you can use the figure-eight stitch. In effect, each row will be wrapped twice. Keep this in mind when you decide on the thickness of the material you are using.

The steps in Figure 80 describe imbrication on the bottom row using the figure-eight stitch. Remember that the bottom row has already been wrapped; for clarity the wraps have been omitted in the drawings.

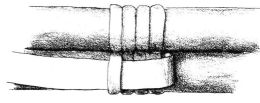

81. Extra Imbrication Wrap

Wrap between steps 2 and 3, Figure 80

Step 1. Lay strip over coil with short end to left. Take three stitches—you may make more than three for a wider pleat or only one or two for a narrow one.

Step 2. Fold strip to left, covering the three stitches.

Step 3. Fold strip to right.

Step 4. Take three more stitches close to the first three.

Step 5. Fold strip to left.

Repeat Steps 3, 4, and 5.

Some sources show one extra wrap taken between Steps 2 and 3, which can help to hold the pleat in place. Place this extra wrap next to the third stitch, before folding the strip to the right (Figure 81). Then wrap with the next three stitches. Be careful with the first of these stitches (in Step 4, Figure 80) to wrap right over or a little to the right of the extra wrap. You don't want this wrap to show when the pleat is folded to the left.

82. Adding a New Imbrication Strip

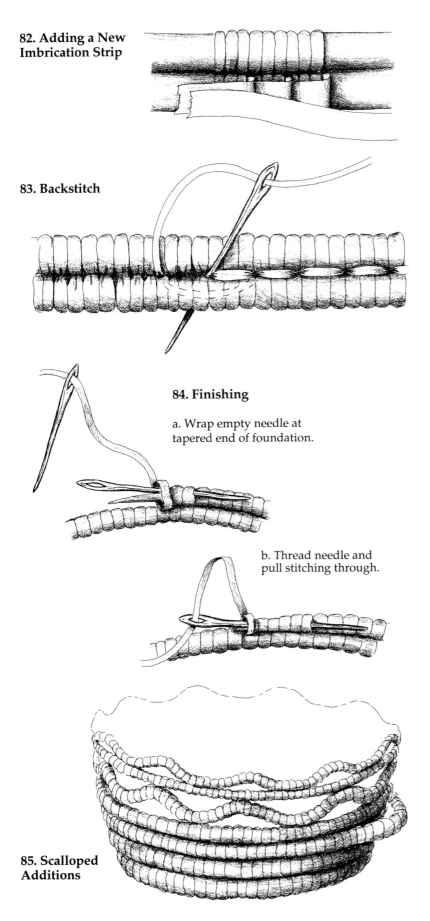

83. Backstitch

84. Finishing

a. Wrap empty needle at tapered end of foundation.

b. Thread needle and pull stitching through.

85. Scalloped Additions

To add a new imbrication strip (Figure 82), lay the new end over the old at the left before the wrap is taken in Step 4. Since this splice is well concealed and simple to do, you can use the technique to change color in your design or to incorporate short strips, such as corn husk.

Backstitch

Horizontal backstitching between coils may be worked over the vertical connecting stitches. Beads, shells or other ornaments are sometimes added. Keep the backstitching snug, so that the cord and the beads are nestled between the basket coils (Figure 83).

FINISHING AND RIMS

When the basket reaches the desired size, gradually taper the end of the foundation material for a few inches and continue stitching. Wrap an unthreaded needle along with the core for the last several wraps, leaving the eye and the point exposed (Figure 84). Now you can thread the stitching material into the empty needle, pull it through the last several wraps, and trim.

The basket may now be considered finished—or another decorative round added, and here are some lovely alternatives. Except for the scalloped rim, these finishes are worked right over the already-wrapped top coil, from left to right.

Scalloped Rim

The core or foundation is wrapped to the bottom coil at one point, lifted up to form a scallop, then wrapped to the bottom coil again farther on (Figure 85). A scalloped row may also be worked on the sides of the basket.

Small handles may be made this way by allowing the coil to extend beyond the basket, bringing it back to the body of the basket and stitching over it again. This creates a little space in the body of the basket.

Herringbone Rim

Step 1. Thread the wrapping strip between the last two coils with the long end coming toward you and the short end pointing down in front of the coil. (Figure 86).

Step 2. Make a wrap slanting toward the left, going over the beginning end and then behind the coil.

Step 3. Come through and go up, slanting to the right.

Step 4. Come down behind the coil to the right of the other wraps.

Step 5. Bring the strip up and toward the left next to the last left-slanted wrap, leaving a space between.

Step 6. Bring the strip behind the coil and up into the space just made.

Repeat Steps 3, 4, 5, and 6.

Blanket or Buttonhole Stitch

This stitch seems to work best with soft materials because it has to make a very tight bend (Figure 87).

Step 1. Thread strip between the last two coils with the long end coming toward you.

Step 2. Go up and behind the top coil, then between the last two coils toward you again, leaving the strip loose at the top of the coil to form a loop.

Step 3. Go up and then . . .

Step 4. Go into the loop from behind. Pull to tighten

Repeat Steps 2, 3, and 4.

86. Herringbone Stitch

Step 1
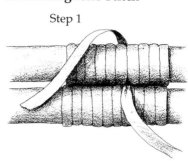

Step 2

Note: For clarity, wrapping between coils is not shown.

Step 3
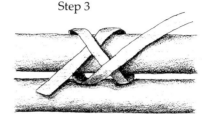

Step 4

Step 5

Step 6
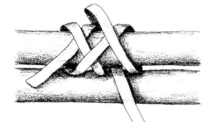

Top view

87. Blanket or Buttonhole Stitch

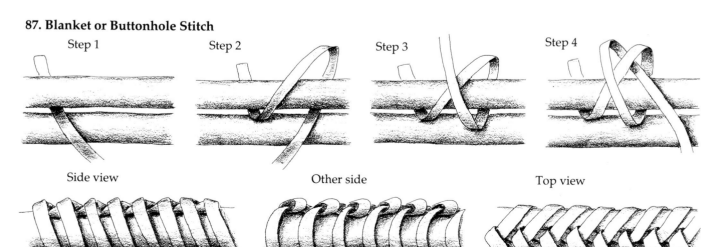

Step 1   Step 2   Step 3   Step 4

Side view   Other side   Top view

Looped Braided Edge
or Single Cordovan

This rim (Figure 88) is similar to the buttonhole, but for some reason, it seems more manageable. Though the difference is slight, the result has a more finished appearance. It also makes a nice ending possible. It can be done with a thin, flexible splint (or leather strip), as well as with soft, round material. It should be worked on the far side of the basket so the slanted stitches will appear on the outside.

88. Looped Braided Edge (Single Cordovan)

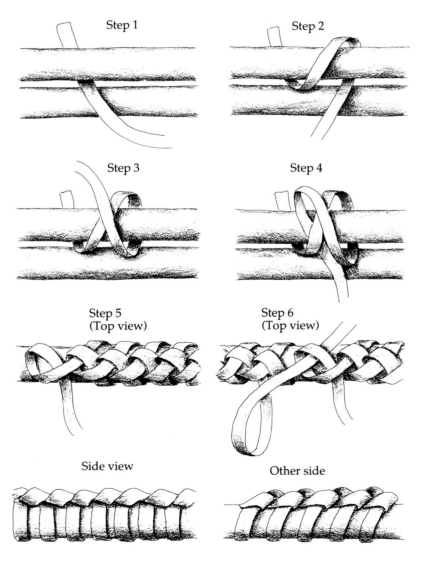

Step 1

Step 2

Step 3

Step 4

Step 5
(Top view)

Step 6
(Top view)

Side view

Other side

Step 1. Thread the strip between the last two coils with the long end coming toward you.

Step 2. Bring the strip up in front of the last coil, behind it, then between the last two coils toward you again.

Step 3. Go up and then . . .

Step 4. Instead of going through the loop, as in the buttonhole, go under the first upward wrap.

Repeat Steps 2, 3 and 4 until you come to first stitch.

Step 5. Carefully remove first wrap of first stitch until loop remains (hold loop in place).

Step 6. Bring last stitch up through loop of first stitch and bring around coil in its proper place. This will fill in the gap made by the removal of the first stitch. Bury both ends in the coil.

Double Cordovan

I used this stitch (Figure 89) in my days as a leathercrafter. Again, a thin flexible strip of bark, leaf or splint works best. It can be worked with soft, round material, but I think it's much prettier with flat. If you work on the far side of the basket, the slanted stitches on the side of the coil will appear on the outside. This finish makes more of a slant than the single cordovan, and the braid covers a wider edge.

Step 1. Thread the strip between the last two coils with the long end coming toward you.

Step 2. Go in front of the last coil, behind it, then between the last two coils toward you again.

Step 3. Go up and then . . .

Step 4. Go under the first upward wrap, as in the single cordovan.

Step 5. Bring strip up to the right, down behind the coil, then toward you between coils.

Step 6. Now bring the strip up and behind the previous wraps (you will be coming under two strands where they cross).

89. Double Cordovan

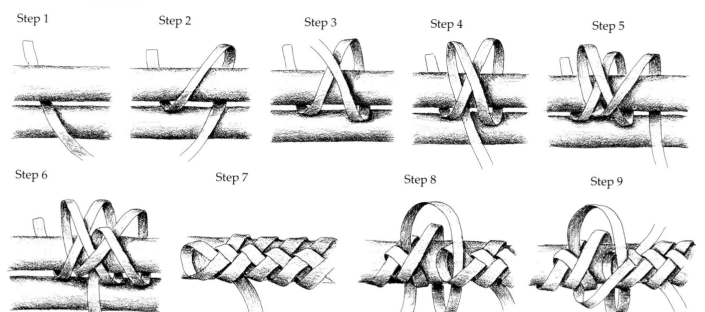

Step 1   Step 2   Step 3   Step 4   Step 5

Step 6   Step 7   Step 8   Step 9

Repeat Steps 5 and 6 until you come to first stitch.

Step 7. Carefully remove wrap of first stitch until loop remains.

Step 8. Make one or two more stitches with the end splint until you are very close to the loop made by the first stitch. End with the splint coming toward you, as in Step 5. Now lace up through the loop—then down behind the last stitch.

Step 9. Lace through the loop and down around the coil-making sure the stitch is in its proper place. All of the gaps made by the removal of the first stitch should now be filled. Bury both ends in the coil.

Study all finishes from both sides. You may want the slanted stitches on the inside of a wide, shallow basket or tray. You will notice that the top view of the double cordovan and the herringbone look the same. However, from the side you will see that the double cordovan has an actual braid at the top of the coil, while the herringbone simply crisscrosses at that point.

A small basket of iris leaves showing a double cordovan stitch at the rim. Note also the row of imbrication.

Basket Projects

TAPERED COILED BASKET

Materials

- 12 to 15 cattail leaves
- 12 to 15 yards bark strips

THE LINES OF CEDAR BARK stitching, contrasting with the cattail leaf core of this small basket, compose its visual as well as structural strength. The base is 5½ inches in diameter and the height is 2¾ inches.

Twist together several strands of cattail to form the core. Work with cattail just slightly damp. Try wrapping it in a very wet towel and leave it overnight. Because cattail absorbs and retains a large amount of water in its pithy center, it must be squeezed out before using. The basket is stitched with narrow strips of cedar bark.

Construction

Start the base as in Figure 62. Then use the lazy squaw stitch (Figure 64) with the stitches spaced to expose the core. When the base is 5½ inches in diameter, turn up the basket by decreasing the diameter of the next coil and attaching it on top of, rather than next to, the previous coil. To make the sides slant in, continue slightly decreasing the diameter of each coil as you work up the basket.

Coiled basket of cattail leaves and cedar bark.

Coiled basket of iris leaves with overlay of corn husks.

Materials
- Small bunch leaves
- A few husks

GENTLE SHAPING AND CLEAN LINES are always pleasing. The natural beauty of iris leaves is shown to advantage here by the simple shape and figure-eight stitches. This basket is 5 inches in diameter and 2¾ inches high.

Iris leaves, whole and bunched, form the core. More iris leaves, split when necessary, are used for the stitching strands. After soaking the leaves, wrap them in towels to remove as much water as possible, yet leaving them pliable. You may keep them in the towels several hours or even overnight. Alternatively, don't soak them, but wrap them in a very wet towel until they have absorbed enough moisture to be workable.

Construction

Start the base as in Figure 62 except here you have a multiple-strand core. Tapering will occur naturally with soft, pointed leaves. Start with a few leaves for the first round or so and gradually add leaves until you reach the desired coil thickness. In this basket the base started with five coils to the inch and gradually increased in thickness until it was four coils to the inch for the remainder of the base as well as the sides.

Use the figure-eight stitch throughout the basket. When the base is 5 inches in diameter, turn it up and shape the sides to curve slightly inward. The basket can be decorated, as shown, in an overlay of corn husk, using the beading technique described on page 132, Figure 79.

Chapter 8

Rib Baskets

For there is hope for a tree, if it be cut down, that it will sprout again, and that its tender branch will not cease. Though its root grow old in the earth, and its stock die in the ground; Yet at the scent of water it will bud, and bring forth boughs like a plant.

—JOB 14: 7–9

Rib or frame baskets are indigenous to many countries. They are different from other types of baskets, which are built up incrementally, in that the basic framework or skeleton of the rib basket is determined at the very beginning. Once the general shape and structure has been built, it doesn't change.

The nomenclature of rib baskets is as interesting as the baskets themselves. Some names pertain to function, as in egg, hen, potato, key, fish, and pigeon; others to shape, as melon, gizzard, fanny, and hip; while still others relate to construction, as in hoop, rib, and frame.

Rib baskets may be grouped by the number of hoops they have. (A *hoop* is a complete ring; a *rib* is an element of the warp that is not continuous.) Some have one hoop and multiple ribs (Figure 90a); others have two hoops and multiple ribs (Figure 90b); still others have more than two hoops and multiple ribs (Figure 90c). In a one-hoop basket, several ribs are lashed directly to the hoop to form the basic framework. In a two-hoop basket, the hoops are lashed together to form the frame. In a basket made with more than two hoops, no lashing is necessary; the basket is started by weaving at the top through several hoops.

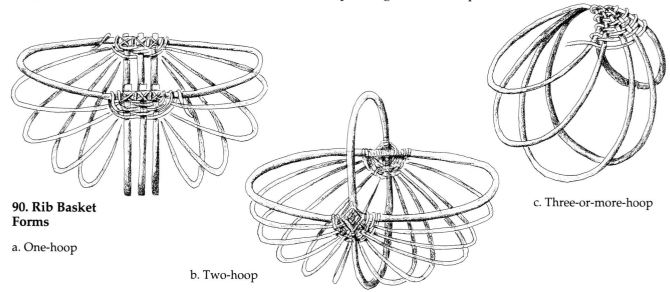

90. Rib Basket Forms

a. One-hoop

b. Two-hoop

c. Three-or-more-hoop

In most cases, the ribs are added as the basket is woven. The weaving continues from both sides and meets in the center.

Hoops and ribs should be made from strong, springy material, such as splints of oak, ash, maple, or hickory and rods of willow, red osier dogwood, grapevine, or other small saplings or branches used whole or split. Weavers may be any of the above as well as softer material such as fine vines, roots, bark, and thin withes. Flat and round materials can be mixed in the same basket. The weave is almost always a simple over-under weave.

MAKING THE HOOPS

91. Scarf Joints

a.

b.

c.

d.

e.

Select a stout vine, rod, or splint of even thickness. Soak it well, even (as with oak, for instance) overnight. Bend it into a circle and secure it by tying, taping, clamping, or nailing around it on a board and allow it to dry thoroughly. I put soaked hoops in a large, straight-sided soup pot and leave them until well dried. That way I can make and dry several hoops at one time.

Now shape the overlapping ends to make a scarf joint. There are a number of configurations. On round rods I find the slant cuts (Figures 91a through 91c) work well. With thick, flat material, either the straight cut (Figures 91d and 91e) or slant cut can be used.

92. Lashing Scarf Joints

a.

b.

Old rib baskets have been photographed and documented having scarf joints tied with string, cordage, or copper wire. Others are drilled and pegged, and still others are nailed and clinched. I generally carve small notches in two or three places where I tie waxed linen thread with a square knot (Figure 92a). On round-rod hoops, I sometimes make notches at the beginning and at the end of the joint and completely cover the joint with close wrapping, making a half hitch on each wrap (Figure 92b).

LASHINGS

Here are two popular lashings, along with a few variations, that are used to hold the hoops together. The God's eye (Figure 93) is a fourfold lashing, and the X-lashing is threefold.

If I'm using flat splints for hoops with flat material for weaving and lashing, I generally notch and tie the hoops with waxed linen to hold them in place. Then I begin lashing right over the ties. I don't notch and tie when using round material for the hoops and lashing, but start right in with the lashing, temporarily keeping the opposite intersection in place with tape or clamps. This is my own preference, so discover what works best for you.

Mark the hoops at the halfway point so that your basket will be well balanced. Place the two hoops at right angles to one another and lash them at both intersections. You can conceal each of the scarf-joints under a lashing, or you can position the handle joint on the bottom of the basket.

93. Two Hoops Lashed Together with the God's Eye

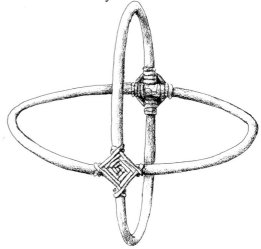

94. The God's Eye   a. Basic lashing sequence

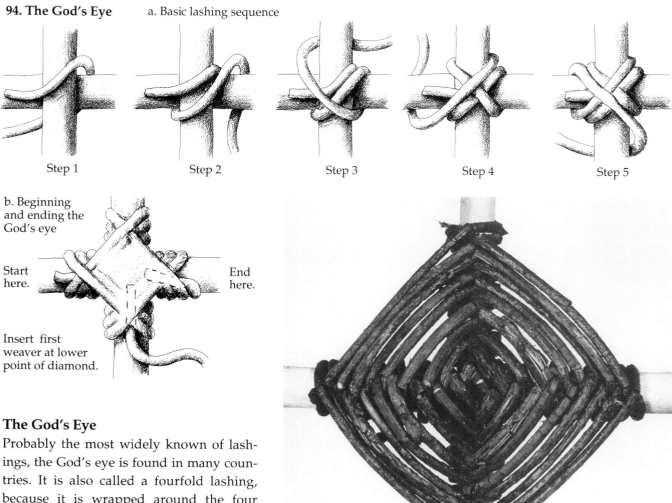

Step 1   Step 2   Step 3   Step 4   Step 5

b. Beginning
and ending the
God's eye

Start
here.

End
here.

Insert first
weaver at lower
point of diamond.

The God's Eye

Probably the most widely known of lashings, the God's eye is found in many countries. It is also called a fourfold lashing, because it is wrapped around the four members of a cross. The result is an attractive diamond shape with convenient spaces to hold the pointed ends of the ribs in place when first starting the weaving.

To make it, follow Steps 1 through 5 in Figure 94, then repeat Steps 2 through 5 until the God's eye is the desired size. If using round material, tuck the end of the weaver into the weave at the rim, opening up a space for it with the awl. It should end on the side opposite that from which it started. Keep the rows tight and close together.

If using a flat weaver, the beginning does not need to extend to the left. Just leave it under the first diagonal wrap and continue to wrap so that each row slightly overlaps the previous row. Do not cut the weaver off, but clamp it to the rim while the ribs are fitted; then continue weaving the basket with the same weaver.

*God's eye lashing
of unstripped
akebia.*

95. X-Lashing

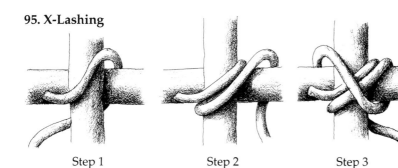

Step 1   Step 2   Step 3   Step 4   Step 5

X-lashing, above, and V-lashing at right.

The X-Lashing

This lashing is also called a threefold lashing because after the X, it is wrapped around only three members of the cross. Appalachian baskets more commonly employ X-lashings than God's eyes.

To make it, follow Figure 95. If using flat material, keep one wrap flat against the next as it goes over each cross member. With round material, keep the wraps very close together.

Because the lashing crosses itself between the handle hoop and the rim, it forms two pockets on each side. These, you will see, can hold the initial ribs in place.

Variations

One variation on the God's eye is the V-lashing (Figure 96). The V-lashing wraps around three members of the cross instead of four. The result is a V or half-diamond. It forms only one pocket on each side of the handle hoop because the crossings take place on top of the members, not between them. This lashing is seen less frequently than the previous two. Like all of the other lashings shown here, it can be made with flat or round material.

96. V-Lashing

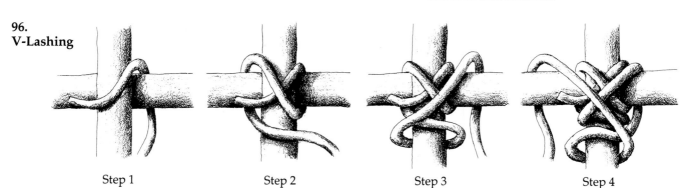

Step 1   Step 2   Step 3   Step 4

Two variations of the X-lashing are the double-X, used with a double handle (Figure 97a), and the triple-X, used for adding midribs to a one-hoop basket (Figure 97b). The X may be made once or twice around each section of the handle, depending on the type and thickness of your material.

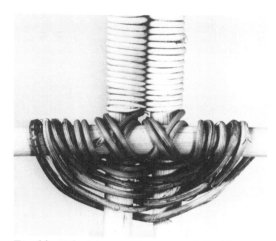

Double-X lashing, with wrapped double handle.

INSERTING RIBS

Some basketmakers begin inserting ribs immediately upon securing the hoops, alternating lashing with rib inserts. You can also complete the lashing and add ribs later.

In determining how many ribs your basket should have, here is a rough guide. For a simple melon-shaped basket 10 inches in diameter, use 12 ribs. Flat ribs may be tapered to be quite wide in the center of the basket, making a very solid basket with fewer ribs. (Take a look at John Long's basket pictured in the Gallery on page 182.) In this case there is just enough space between ribs for the weaver. Again, this is best done with a simple melon shape. If using narrow ribs or round ribs, or if your basket has a pouch shape, you will need more. I love the ones with many ribs; I have seen some with as many as 30 or 40.

97. Variations on X-Lashings

a. Double-X

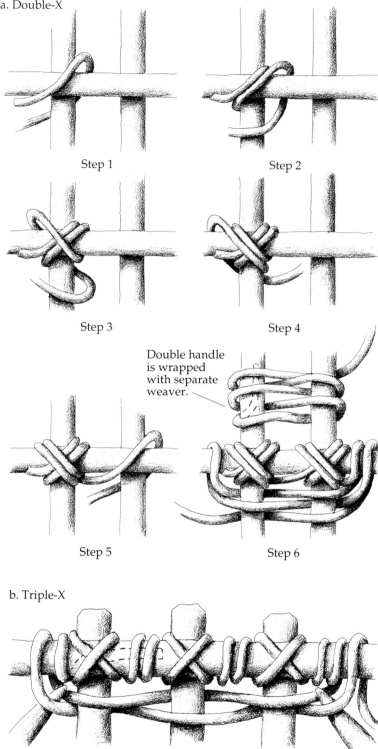

Step 1   Step 2

Step 3   Step 4

Double handle is wrapped with separate weaver.

Step 5   Step 6

b. Triple-X

Inserting Ribs into God's Eyes

The rib length will determine the shape of your basket. Decide where you want the widest point to be and cut your first rib to length by inserting one tapered end up into the inside corner of the God's eye near the rim and holding the other end at the opposite God's eye. When you are satisfied with the shape or curve, remove the rib, cut and taper the other end, and make an exact mate to this rib for the other side of the basket. Insert these behind the God's eye to form the middle rib in each half of the basket (Figure 98). Add matched pairs of ribs, gradually decreasing their lengths to form a smoothly rounded shape. Now weave several rows with the flat weaver remaining from the lashing to hold the ribs in place.

If using round material, insert a tapered weaver into the lower point of the diamond by making a space for it with your awl (see Figure 94b, page 143). If you start weaving to the right on one side of the basket, you must also start weaving to the right on the other side. This will ensure a proper weave sequence when the two weavers meet in the middle of the basket at the last row. Continue weaving over and under the ribs and from rib to rib.

Check the shape as the basket progresses and adjust the length of each added pair of ribs as necessary, shortening them or replacing them as necessary. Slip a short, tapered dowel into the rib's place to keep the weave open while you're working on the rib. Remove the dowel and carefully insert the reworked rib back into place.

Inserting Ribs into X-Lashings

If you're using flat material, you will see that the intersections between the two small pockets consist of tightly packed strips laid flat on top of one another. You can pierce the intersection with an awl and insert the middle rib there. Then add one (or two) ribs to the pocket on each side (Figure 99). This works quite well, particularly if you want to see how that middle rib will affect the shape of the basket. I have seen photos of old baskets having two or three ribs pierced into the lashing, which appeared to be ½ inch wide or more. Other early baskets appear to have ribs inserted a few at a time, starting right after the X or after only one or two rows of lashing.

If you are using round material for the lashing, you can put two ribs in each pocket. Try to maintain an even spacing.

Continue to add ribs in matched pairs by tapering their ends and inserting into the weave. Get them in as soon as possible. Alternate the weaving from one side of the basket to the other in order to maintain a constant tension and balanced shape.

98. Inserting Ribs into God's Eye Lashing

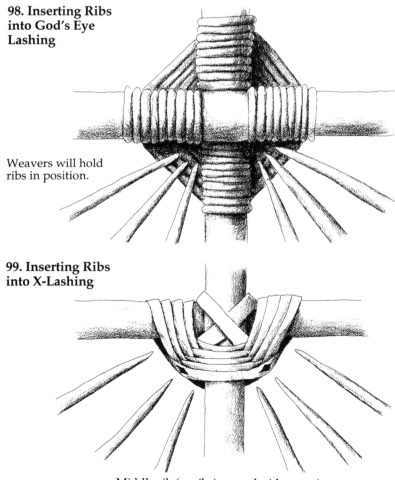

Weavers will hold ribs in position.

99. Inserting Ribs into X-Lashing

Middle rib (or ribs) on each side can pierce intersecting weavers.

Inserting Ribs into V-Lashing

Insert about three tapered ribs into each pocket as you would for the God's eye. You will notice that the V-lashing has a front and a back to its pockets, unlike the full God's eye, which has only a front.

PACKING

After all ribs are in place, it may be necessary to do some *packing,* that is, weaving over only some of the ribs and not going all the way to the rim (Figure 100 and photo, right). Baskets with ribs of larger circumference than that of the rim require packing to fill in and even out the weaving. When packing, do not return on the same rib as the previous row. Vary the returns, weaving to the rim often enough to avoid large gaps. Try to have all the packing done as you reach the center of the basket, so that you can weave this area from rim to rim on every row.

ONE-HOOP BASKET

The simplest and most common type of one-hoop basket is hemispherical, the hoop forming the rim of the basket and the ribs lashed to it. This is traditionally known as a potato basket (Figure 101a). Because it has no handle hoop, leave openings on each side of the basket at the rim as "built-in" handles. Simply stop the weave at the last rib instead of going all the way to the rim.

One, two, or three ribs (called *midribs*) are positioned on the inside of the rim at the halfway points on either side of the basket. Leave about ¼ to ½ inch protruding above the rim (Figure 90a, page 141). The midribs may also be shaped to a flat taper and folded over the rim (Figure 101b). Secure them by notching and tying with waxed linen. (Figure 101c). The triple-X lashing (see Figure 97b) is used on this basket, either with ribs protruding above the rim or with folded-over ribs. The lashing is worked right

100. Packing

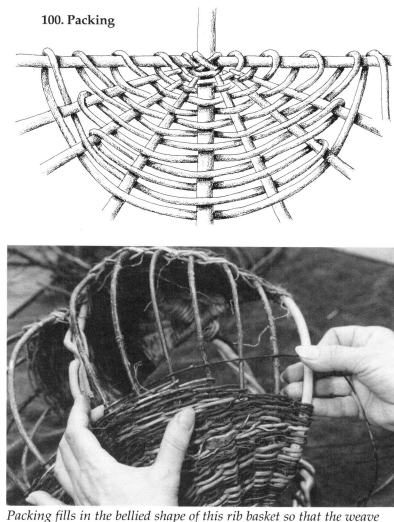

Packing fills in the bellied shape of this rib basket so that the weave will meet at the center. The weavers do not come all the way to the rim, but return at alternate ribs.

101. Adding Midribs to One-Hoop Basket

a. Potato basket

b. Fold tapered rib over hoop

c. Notch and wrap with waxed linen

102. One-Hoop Basket with Hoop as Handle

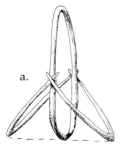

a.

b.

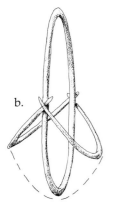

103. Simple Wrap Lashing

over the fold. With round or very fine weavers, more than one X may be made on each rib and the rim may be wrapped between X's to maintain spacing between ribs. Add more ribs and shape the basket as previously described.

Another one-hoop basket can be made with the hoop serving as the handle instead of the rim (Figure 102). The rim or opening is made by attaching two stout ribs to the handle hoop at a downward slant and using a simple wrap-type lashing (Figure 103 and photo below). The God's eye may be used also, but it results in an arrow shape, not a diamond.

The first two ribs may be long enough to reach the bottom of the basket, creating a wide opening and a flat bottom, as in a flower-gathering basket (Figure 102a); or shorter ribs will create a smaller a smaller opening and a somewhat pouchy shape to the basket (Figure 102b).

Ribs are held to hoop with a simple wrap-type lashing.

TWO-HOOP BASKET

In a two-hoop basket, one hoop forms the rim, the other the handle. Most students are introduced to rib basket construction by making a two-hoop basket. It's fun, attractive, useful, and full of possibilities for innovation and creativity.

For your first basket, I suggest that you make the shape hemispherical. Then you can experiment with various shapes as shown in Figure 104, making the ribs longer where you want the basket to belly out and shorter where you want it to come in, or positioning more of the handle hoop below the rim or above it. Using a large hoop for the rim and a small one for the handle will make the basket shallow. You can also vary the shape by bending a hoop at angles to flatten one side as for a wall basket (Figure 104d). Try square hoops, bending the ribs at the corners (Figure 104e). Keep in mind that these variations will necessitate more packing than a plain hemispherical one, particularly in extreme pouchy or fanny shapes.

You may also add ribs above the rim as in Figure 104f; or you may achieve similar results by starting with three hoops (Figure 104g). You may keep on adding ribs for a complete sphere (Figure 104h). (Is this a basket? Why not? A basket is a thing to put another thing in. Well, put the thing in before the last few rows are woven. Who said anything about taking the thing out?)

The handle may be wrapped by tucking one end of a round vine into the top point of the God's eye (Figure 105a) and wrapping to the other side. When the handle is completely wrapped, the remaining end should be bent and carefully tucked into the top of the other God's eye. If it becomes necessary to splice while wrapping, splice on the underside of the handle (Figure 105b) as follows: Wrap the end of the new strand with the old strand for several wraps. Lay the old end against the handle and continue wrap-

104. Two-Hoop Basket Variations

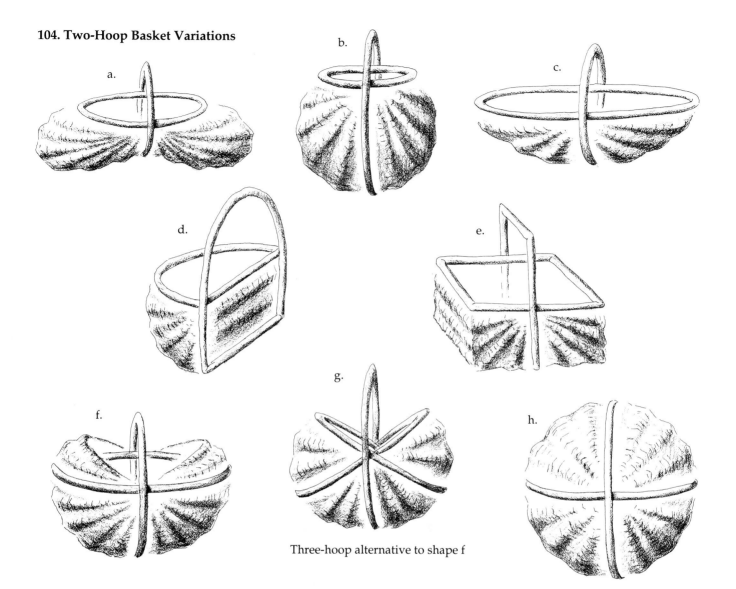

a.

b.

c.

d.

e.

f.

g.

Three-hoop alternative to shape f

h.

ping with the new strand over the end of the old. Bend both ends at a sharp angle so you can keep the wraps close.

Another treatment for the handle is to add a thinner rod to each side and then lace it as in Figure 105c. Use an awl to push down each row of lacing to keep it as tight as possible. This makes an attractive and comfortable handle and looks particularly good if the basket has a thin rod added just above the rim also, as seen in many Appalachian baskets. This, of course, will have to be decided at the very beginning of construction. The added rods should be tapered and put in after the God's eye is completed, or you may actually use three hoops

105. Wrapping the Handle

a. Starting the wrap

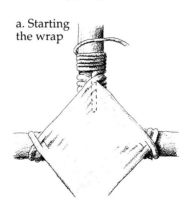

b. Splicing the wrap

c. Handle-wrap variation

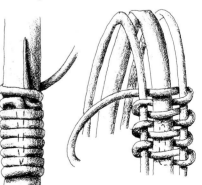

for the handle right from the start, making the God's eye right over them. Treat the three pieces as one in the body of the basket. The added rim rod is usually tapered and put in after the lashing is made.

If using flat material to wrap the handle, thin the end and lay it along the handle near the God's eye and wrap tightly over it. When you reach the other side, leave the last several wraps loose, insert the tail end, tighten the wraps and cut off the end. It is best to use a long splint so that no splicing is necessary.

A twisted hoop also makes a sturdy and attractive handle (as shown in the photo below). Soak a long rod and bend it into a circle. With the remaining length weave in and out of the original circle at least three times around.

Various roots, including hemlock and pine, are being used for this basket-in-progress, as well as some hardwood rods for the handle, ribs, and rim hoop.

THREE- (OR MORE) HOOP BASKET

Various shapes may also be made in the construction of a three-or-more-hoop rib basket. The shape or form probably seen the most is sometimes called a hen basket. It was traditionally used to transport brooding hens from one farm to another or to market.

Three (or more) hoops of various sizes are made and held together at the top where the weaving starts (Figure 106). Start at the center of the weaver and weave from the center top down in one direction. Go back to the center top and weave in the other direction with the other half of the weaver. Alternate the weaving from side to side.

Add ribs as soon as possible. Pack where necessary and continue to weave on alternate sides.

A flattened opening may be made by notching and bending the rods that border that opening (Figure 107; see also the photo on page 153). Notch the inside of the rod, bending toward the notch, for strength.

Changing the position of the hoops—the large ones for the openings and the small ones in the middle—will result in a more open, angle-ended cylinder (Figure 108a), which can be used for gathering flowers. A tapered shape will result if you arrange the hoops from large to small (Figure 108b), and this is the beginning of a cornucopia or a fish trap. If you arrange equal sized hoops parallel to one another, you get a simple cylinder (Figure 108c), which could be employed as a lamp shade. Some temporary weaving—or notched sticks—may be needed at the beginning to maintain the hoop spacing. Turn this shape into a doughnut section by spacing the equal-sized hoops closer at the top than at the bottom (Figure 108d). If the spacing is too wide, add ribs where necessary to keep the basket firm.

It is not always necessary for a basket to carry something or have a special use. Many of these forms can be purely artistic or design experiments. The curving cylinder can be curved even more to represent forms inspired by nature—a snail or sea shell. Shapes can be invented and combined for no other reason than to satisfy and delight your own creative talents and energies.

107. Rib Basket with Flattened Opening

a. Notch and bend first rods.

b. Add round hoops and ribs.

106. Beginning the Multi-Hoop Basket

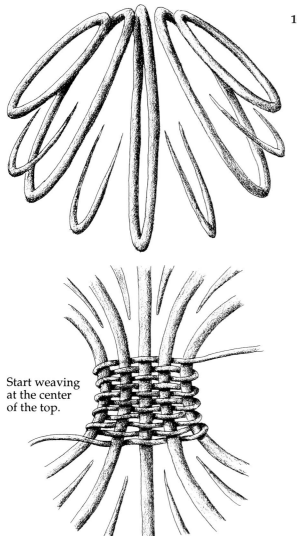

Start weaving at the center of the top.

108. Variations on Multi-Hoop Baskets

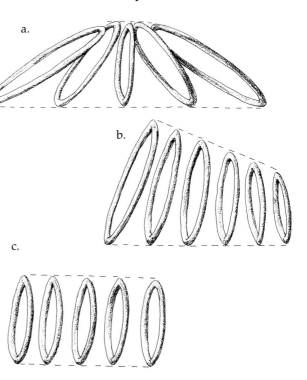

a.

b.

c.

d.

MELON BASKET

Basket Projects

Materials

- Hoops: 2 rods, each about ⅜ inch by 36 inches
- Ribs: 14 rods, a little thinner than the hoops, about 17 inches long
- Lashing and weaving: bark strips, split and cut to ¼ inch wide

THE SIMPLE MELON SHAPE of this basket will give delight to the new basketmaker. I used cedar bark, which is supple and pleasant to work with. You could, if you wish, dye some of the bark for a few contrasting stripes, and you can also wrap the handle.

Construction

Bend the two hoop rods (I used wisteria) and secure the scarf joint with waxed linen. The hoops can be 10 to 12 inches in diameter. Make one to fit inside the other. Join the two hoops together with God's eyes. Use a long splint of bark for each God's eye and do not cut it off. Continue the weaving with the same splint. Put in the same number of ribs on each side. (For this basket I started with five on each side and added two more where they were needed as the weaving progressed.) Work on both sides of the basket toward the middle, where the weaving from both sides meets. With this shape, no packing is needed.

Rib basket of wisteria and cedar bark.

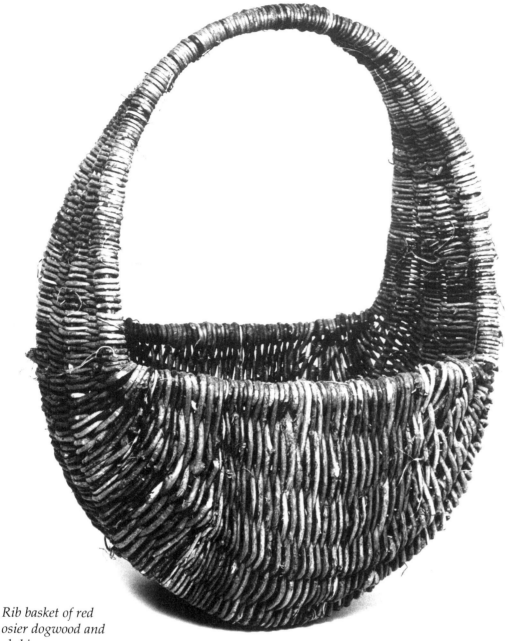

Rib basket of red osier dogwood and akebia.

RIB BASKET WITH FLATTENED HOOPS

Materials
- Stout rods for hoops and ribs
- Unstripped vine for weavers

AKEBIA ALWAYS DOES your bidding. Of all the basketmaking vines that grow in my area, it is my favorite. This basket, with red osier dogwood ribs and akebia weavers, is a variation of the hen basket, the opening being much larger than on the traditional basket used to transport a brooding hen. It measures 15 inches high, 10½ inches wide, and 7 inches deep.

Construction
Make two hoops flattened at the bottom as in Figure 107. Make two more hoops, oval in shape and begin weaving the four hoops at the top, as described in construction of a multi-hoop basket (Figure 106). Add ribs as soon as possible. Start packing after the handle area has been woven.

Chapter 9

Ornamentation

It is as if the pine-trees called me
From ceiled room and silent books,
To see the dance of woodland shadows,
And hear the song of April brooks!
　　　　　　　—JOHN GREENLEAF WHITTIER

Some baskets seem to cry out for a final touch and do not reach their peak of beauty without some form of ornamentation. This may be obvious at the very beginning of construction, and embellishments can be worked in as the basket progresses, or you may decide to decorate only after getting some perspective on an otherwise completed basket.

Textural decoration can be achieved within the basket's fabric by varying your weaves or the size of your materials. Negative spaces (open areas in the weave) can produce interesting sculptural and graphic effects. Ornamentation, the addition of decorative elements, can take the form of curls, tassels, beads, braids, strings, fringe, folds, ribbons, protrusions, and dangly-downs. It can also consist of paint or dye.

The basketmaker has a vast array of material for ornamentation in the plant, mineral, and animal worlds. Plant fibers, which compose the basket itself, are full of decorative possibilities, but various other plant parts,

A splintwork and plaited basket of palmetto with applied curls.

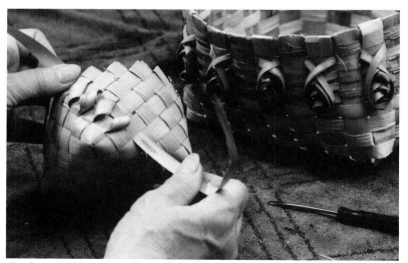

Curls are added after the basket is finished, and they can be freely related to the weave. Simply loop them through. Compare the splint basket in the background with the plaited one being decorated here.

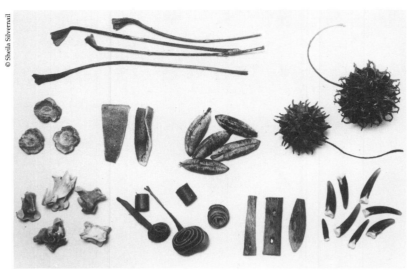

Some suggestions for applied ornaments. Top row: sycamore leaf stems. Second row, left to right: carrot, dried lemon rind, date pits, sweet gum balls. Third row: chicken neck bones, rolled hemlock bark, flat pieces of hemlock bark, and turtle claws.

109. Rolled Bark or Leather Buttons

These flat wisteria seeds will make an unusual basket decoration, attached to the weave through a drilled hole. Many other kinds of seeds and pods, when pierced or notched, can also be tied in place.

such as seeds, nuts, hollow stems, petioles, cones, dried fruit and vegetables, tassels, and moss, can also be used. Shells of both aquatic and land animals make exciting ornamentation, as do other animal products, such as teeth, bones, horns, claws, wings of insects, wool, skin, hides, sinews, feathers, and quills.

Decoration is limited only by one's imagination. Here are my favorite ideas:

Many seeds, nuts, beans, and pods can easily be attached to a basket if you first drill them or pierce them with a needle (you may have to soak dried seeds before piercing). You can often reveal intricate cross-sectional patterns by slicing or sawing larger pits or nuts. If you prefer the simpler shapes of hardwood rods, dowels, or even branches, prepare them by cross-cutting and drilling them for stringing or sewing. Consider carving, painting, or burning them for added decoration. Elderberry stems offer a special opportunity: you can push or burn out the pith with a length of heated wire coat hanger and use the hollowed stem sections as long beads.

Leather holds interesting possibilities. You can cut various shapes from flat pieces, drilling or punching them for attachment, or cut long strips from wet material, roll them, and secure the ends with string or tape until dry. If you begin with a long triangular piece, you can roll it most of the way up, starting at the wide end, punch through the center of the roll, and insert the long point through the hole (Figure 119). This long point can then be used for tying or weaving into the basket any way you like.

Many fruits and vegetables, such as peeled and sliced apples, pears, carrots or potatoes, will dry into interestingly wrinkled shapes. You might want to coat these with varnish or shellac. Pierce them for attachment. Try peeling the rinds of thin-skinned lemons and rolling them into cone shapes. They dry very hard.

The animal world is also rich in decorative materials. To make beads from clam shells, break the shell into small pieces, and drill a hole in the center of each one. Sand the edges by threading them onto a thin stick and rolling and rubbing them on a flat rock. Small periwinkles or snail shells can be used whole. Neck bones of chicken and other birds make interesting additions. Boil until the meat falls away and the sections separate. Wash and dry. You might want to give them a coat of varnish or shellac. There is already a hole in the center handy for stringing. Larger hollow bones can be sliced into rings, then polished. Claws or talons have long been used for ornamentation, as well as feathers, which can add gorgeous colors to a basket.

Dangly-downs of cordage or plaits can be attached to the rim of a basket (or elsewhere). You can knot or bead them on the ends, create a tassel by splitting the strand ends, or conceal the ends in a folded piece of leather or bark (photo, above right). Here's a method that works well with hemlock bark: Cut a long, tapering shape, as shown in Figure 110. Punch a hole in the center, insert the ends of the plait into the hole, and knot it or tie it to a little stick no longer than the width of the bark. Now fold and secure the bark (a clothespin works well) until dry.

Knobs from the ends of black walnut or sycamore leaf stems (photo, right), as well as others, can be secured into the weave as follows: Place a leaf stem, "bell" down, on the outside of the basket to the right of a spoke. You may place them randomly or in a pattern. Weave three rows over them as though they were part of the spoke. Bend and tuck the rest of the stem into the weave one spoke to the right (Figure 111).

Dangly-downs may end in a tassel or terminate hidden in a piece of bark.

110. Terminating a Dangly-Down

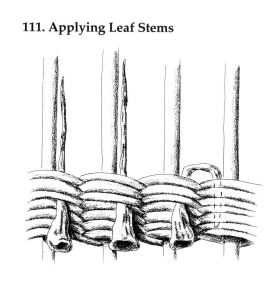

111. Applying Leaf Stems

Wickerwork basket of stripped akebia decorated with sycamore leaf stems.

Colors and Dyes

YOU CAN VARY THE COLOR of basketry material by dyeing, burying, harvesting in a different season, or altering the methods of curing and preparing the material. Native Americans buried basketry material in mud to obtain dark colors for patterns. Different mineral content in soils probably resulted in different colors. Soaking or burying with iron (an iron kettle, a railroad spike) will also darken many natural materials.

Plants used for weaving are so beautifully and subtly colored anyway that I do very little dyeing of materials I harvest myself. For red, you may choose sumac or red osier dogwood picked in the fall. Small red morning glory vine is also a lovely wine red. Inner barks can be cinnamon, rust, orange, brown, yellow, or red. Black walnut leaf stems, bark, and fern roots are a rich, dark brown. Iris leaves cured in the shade keep much of their green color, while those cured after frost and in bright light turn rust and tan. Different species of grasses and palms vary from gray-green to gold, white, tan, or yellow.

There are times, however, when you will want to dye basketry materials to achieve a particular effect. One of the most successful dyes comes from black walnut hulls. Gather the nuts in the fall (when you gather the leaf stems). Remove the hulls with a hammer, crush them, cover with water, and boil. Strain and immerse your material until it turns the desired shade. That's the recommended procedure. One time, I was not able to use my store of black walnuts when I gathered them. They sat in the dyepot and turned black and moldy. Later, I added water and boiled them, nuts, hulls, and all. The mix then sat on the porch all winter—froze and thawed. I boiled it again and strained it before throwing in some stripped akebia, cedar bark, corn husks, and iris leaves. I let them soak for about three days. They all turned various attractive shades of tan, medium brown, and dark brown.

Two other dye sources I have tried are iris and a garden variety of trumpet lily. The dye from fresh iris blooms is reportedly a rich and lasting purple, but the most I was able to get from rubbing the blossoms along a piece of stripped akebia was a beautiful silvery lavender. I might have obtained a deeper color if I had used more flowers. Additional experimenting, I know, is necessary. You try it! Let me know your results.

Walnut hulls for dyeing can be crushed with a mortar and pestle (or as at top, using a wooden bowl and rock), or by packing the hulls into a nylon (panty-hose) bag and hammering them into powder, above.

A wallpaper tray is an ideal container for dyeing basket materials. Cedar bark and palm leaves will turn a rich brown after a few hours in this bath made by boiling the crushed walnut hulls.

The color from the trumpet lily came about quite by accident. A friend gave me some flowers for the kitchen table. They looked a lot like daylilies, but much larger (they grow 7 to 8 feet tall) and dark yellow, with short pointed leaves. When the flowers wilted, I pinched them off the stalk and noticed that my fingers were stained yellow, and so was the tablecloth where a few anthers had fallen. I collected the anthers from all the flowers and let them dry. Later, I boiled and mashed them with a little water and put in some white corn husks. They quickly turned a gorgeous shade of deep yellow. This is a very potent dye; I had only six or seven flowers from which to gather the anthers.

A wide range of colors come from plants. Keep in mind the following basic information when you dye:

Most dyers use enamel pots. A copper or iron pot may change the color; nevertheless, it may be just the color you are looking for. Discarded enamel vegetable bins from old refrigerators are very useful.

The mineral content of water may affect the color. Choose rain water, soft water, or distilled water over deep-well or municipal water.

Vegetable dyes, though beautiful, are not readily absorbed into the woody fibers used in basketry. Dyeing leaves, shoots, and bark is different from dyeing wool fleece and yarn, because basketry materials are made of cellulose, and wool is made of protein.

Recipes for dyeing wool usually call for *mordants*—metal compounds that combine with the dye and the fiber to enhance the intensity and fastness of the color. For cellulose materials, the best mordant is alum (aluminum potassium sulfate), a white powder sold at grocery stores, pharmacies, mail-order supply houses, and sometimes garden centers. Use ½ cup of alum per pound of material; dissolve the alum in warm water and soak the materials overnight or longer. It isn't necessary to simmer the materials in the mordant. Mordanting is not required for all dyes—experiment first to see what happens without it.

Another approach is to rub the dyestuff onto the the basketry material, the way I rubbed the iris blossoms on the akebia vine. Usually it's easier to simmer the dyestuff in water, then strain off the fluid, called a *dyebath*. An hour's simmering is enough to make a dyebath from flowers or soft leaves. Hard twigs, bark, wood, or roots should be soaked for several hours or overnight, boiled at least an hour, and left to soak for several hours more. Mash ripe berries and fruits enough to make the juices flow, wait a few hours, then simmer briefly. To obtain rich colors, use plenty of dyestuff. Most dye plants work best if used fresh, but you can try drying or freezing them for later use.

Place the basketry material in the strained dyebath, simmer for an hour, and soak for additional hours. The time required varies, depending on the strength of the dye and the desired results. The color will vary with season of harvest and material to be dyed. The following chart, compiled from many sources, summarizes dye plants to try. For other dyeing supplies, here are two mail-order houses: The River Farm, Route 1, Box 401, Timberville, VA 22853; and Earth Guild, 33 Haywood St., Asheville, NC 28801, (800) 327-8448.

Wickerwork basket of stripped akebia dyed with black walnut hulls.

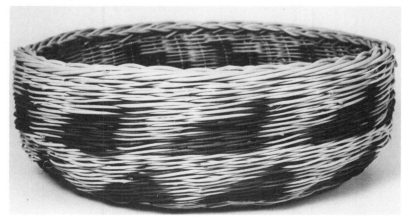

A Selection of Dye Plants

Dye Plant	Part	Color	Range, Habitat, and Notes
Agrimony *Agrimonia eupatoria*	Leaves Stalks	Yellow	Eur., w. Asia, N. Afr. Borders of woods, gardens, waste places of n. U.S.
Alder *Alnus* spp.	Inner bark	Rust	W. Id. and Wash., s. in mts. to s. Calif. Pound bark. Bring to boil. Steep material to be dyed.
Amaranth *Amaranthus* spp.	Flowers	Pink	Eur., N. Amer. Widespread weeds.
Barberry *Berberis vulgaris*	Stems Roots	Yellow	Eur. Common ornamental shrub, often planted in hedges.
Bayberry *Myrica pensylvanica*	Leaves	Gray-green	Ne. N. Amer.
Birch *Betula* spp.	Bark	Pink Tan	Alaska e. to Labr., s. into n. U.S. Local in mountains of N.C. With dogwood, oak, and cedar bark ashes, used to dye quills.
Blackberry *Rubus* spp.	Young shoots Berries	Gray Purple	Widespread in N. Amer. Dye in iron pot or add rusty nails as mordant.
Bloodroot *Sanguinaria canadensis*	Root	Red	Rich woodlands of e. N. Amer. Be careful: sap is poisonous; irritates mucous membranes.
Blueberry *Vaccinium* spp.	Berries	Purple	Widespread in N. Amer.
Broombeard *Andropogon virginicus*	Stems Leaves	Yellow	Open ground and open woods e. and cen. N. Amer. Also called broom sedge.
Butternut *Juglans cinerea*	Nut hulls	Brown Tan	Mixed hardwood forests of e. N. Amer. Also known as white walnut.
Cherry *Prunus* spp.	Bark	Tan Pink	Widespread.
Coreopsis *Coreopsis* spp.	Flowers	Brick red Orange	Cen. and w. N.Amer. Widely cult.
Cottonwood *Populus* spp.	Buds Leaves	Yellows Tans	Alta. s. to n. Mexico. Used to dye quills.
Dahlias *Dahlia* hybrids	Flowers	Yellows Oranges	Mexico. Common garden flower.
Dock *Rumex* spp.	Roots, chopped	Dark yellow	Eur. Roadsides, waste places.
Dogwood, Flowering *Cornus florida*	Bark Shoots	Gray Tan	E. U.S. Widely planted as ornamental.
Elderberry *Sambucus nigra*	Berries	Purple	Eur. Common in gardens.
Fern, Brake *Pteridium aquilinum*	Young shoots	Yellow-green Gray-green	Common, widespread. Also called braken.

Dye Plant	Part	Color	Range, Habitat, and Notes
Goldenrod *Solidago* spp.	Flowers	Yellow Tan	Widespread in N. Amer.
Grape *Vitis* spp.	Fruit	Purple	Numerous species throughout U.S.
Hemlock, Eastern *Tsuga canadensis*	Bark	Rust	Ne. N. Amer. from s. Canada to n. Ala. and w. to Minn.
Horsetail *Equisetum sylvaticum*	Branching stalks	Gray-yellow Green-yellow	Wooded swamps of N. Amer.
Iris *Iris* spp.	Flowers	Lavender Purple	Widespread. Many cult. for ornament. Flowers can be rubbed into the splint, or a dyebath made.
Larkspur *Consolida ambigua*	Petals	Blue	Rub on splints. Be careful: poisonous.
Lily *Lilium* spp.	Anthers	Yellow	Asia. Widely cult. Trumpet and other garden lilies may be used.
Lily-of-the-Valley *Convallaria majalis*	Leaves	Gray	Eur. Nat. in e. N. Amer. and widely cult. as ornamental.
Lily, Water *Nymphaea odorata*	Seed shells	Black	E. U.S.
Madder *Rubia tinctorum*	Roots	Red	Eur., Asia Minor. Cult. in U.S. for natural dyes. Best results with hard water or calcium hydroxide.
Maple, Red *Acer rubrum*	Inner bark and leaves Rotted wood	Black Purple	S. Canada and ne. U.S. Use to dye quills.
Mountain Mahogany *Cercocarpus* spp.	Roots	Rusty	W. U.S. Pound outer root bark and boil for 3 hours. Mix with juniper ash and powdered alder bark to make a red dye. (Navajo)
Marigold *Tagetes* spp.	Flowers	Yellow Gold	Mexico. Common in gardens.
Mullein *Verbascum* spp.	Leaves	Yellow	Eur., Asia. Widespread, waste places.
Nettle *Urtica dioica*	All, except roots	Greenish yellow	Eur. and Asia. Widely nat.
Oak *Quercus* spp.	Bark	Gray	Me. to Fla. and Tex. Add rusty iron to dyebath.
Onions *Allium cepa*	Outer bulb skins	Yellow Brass	Eur. Asia. Gardens.
Oregon Grape *Mahonia aquifolium*	Twigs Bark	Yellow	Nw. N. Amer. Cult. as ornamental. Also known as grape holly.
Osage Orange *Maclura pomifera*	Wood chips	Yellow	Lowlands of s. cen. U.S.; planted throughout the U.S. Also known as hedge apple or bois d'arc.

DYE PLANT	PART	COLOR	RANGE, HABITAT, AND NOTES
Peach *Prunus persica*	Leaves	Pale gold	China. Cult. in temperate climates.
Pokeweed *Phytolacca americana*	Berries	Pinks Purples	Rich, low ground, roadsides from Me. to Fla., w. to Mexico.
Rabbitbrush *Chrysothamnus nauseosus*	Flowers	Yellow	From w. Canada to Calif., Tex., and n. Mexico. Dry open places with sagebrush or open woodland.
Rhododendron *Rhododendron* spp.	Leaves	Grey	Se. U.S., Asia, Common ornamental.
St.-John's-Wort *Hypericum perforatum*	Plant tops	Yellow	Eur. Nat. N. Amer.
Sassafras *Sassafras albidum*	Bark	Orange-brown	E. deciduous forests from Me. to Fla. and Tex.
Smartweed *Persicaria hydropiper*	Plant tops	Yellow Gold	Widespread in damp soil. Garden weed.
Smokebush *Cotinus coggygria*	Shoots Bark	Yellow	Eurasia. Common in gardens.
Sneezeweed *Helenium* spp.	Plant tops	Yellow	Western U.S. Cult. in gardens.
Sumac *Rhus* spp.	Berries Leaves	Tan	Widespread in e. and midwestern U.S.; local elsewhere. High in tanins.
Sunflower *Helianthus annuus*	Seed hulls	Gray	Throughout U.S., s. Canada, and n. Mexico.
Tansy *Tanacetum vulgare*	Leaves	Yellow-green	Eur., Asia. Widely nat. in N. Amer. Also cult. as herb.
Walnut, Black *Juglans nigra*	Nut hulls and bark	Brown	E. U.S. Planted elsewhere.
Willow *Salix* spp.	Bark	Brown	Widespread.
Zinnia *Zinnia* spp.	Flowers	Orange Yellow	Mexico. Common in gardens.

Other Sources of Dyes

•Try coffee, tea, fruit, and other foodstuffs.

•Lichens, galls, algae, and mosses may be collected and used with varying results.

•An extremely wide spectrum of color can be obtained from wild mushrooms used fresh, dried or frozen.

•If you've got the gumption to chew salmon eggs, they are supposed to yield vermillion!

•A scale insect, *Dactylopius coccus*, gives cochineal, a red dye.

•Probably the most interesting dye source is the shellfish murex, which yields the royal and coveted purple. In the ancient city of Tyre, an industry was built around this one color. Battles were fought to keep control of the murex beds. Secret formulas were jealously guarded by families to be handed down to the next generation. Early Phoenicians developed tremendous lung capacity making a living diving for the creatures. This was the color of nobles—and subsequently responsible for the phrase, "born to the purple."

Miniatures

As soon as you make your first miniature, you will want to make another and then another. Relax, get comfortable and work under good lighting. Refer to the list of tools for those that may be helpful in constructing miniatures, particularly forceps, tweezers, and large, blunt needles.

Getting the material down to scale is so important in making the basket look right. Continue to experiment with fibers until you can split leaves and roots into thread-like strands, and make splints of wood and bark almost paper thin. Vines that are very thin, such as strawberry, red morning glory, and akebia, can be used whole as well as sedges, sweet grass, and other narrow leaves. Try splitting a leaf by sticking a needle into it and running it down its length.

You may want to work down to very tiny baskets. A good way to get the knack of working small is to start with a basket 2 or 3 inches high and make the succeeding ones

smaller and smaller. You will learn something from each one. Don't stay too long at it. Making a half-inch basket can be an extremely tense occupation.

Use the techniques you have learned in the preceding chapters. Most of them can be adapted. Shown on these pages are a few sample miniatures that I hope will inspire you to get started on this delightful form of basketmaking.

Splintwork basket of cane spokes and bulrush weavers The handle and cane-wrapped rim are of oak; the base is a ¾-inch diameter wood button.

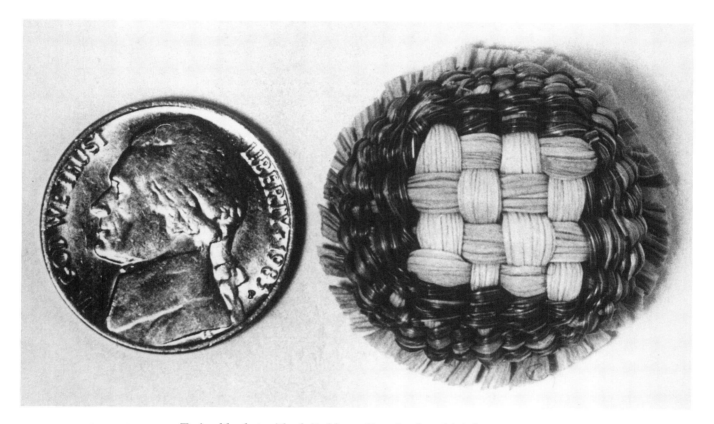

Twined basket with plaited base. Corn husk and iris leaves. Height ½ inch, width ¾ inch.

Gallery

*T*here is a web, it seems to me, that links basketmakers across America. It is as intricate, ethereal, and strong as any in nature. Reaching in all directions, it connects us by common regard for the beauty, usefulness, and skill of our craft. It reaches back in time, too, as we continue to learn from those who lived long ago.

Today we are enjoying a unique blossoming of basketry design and fabrication. It would be gratifying if some of this art were to contribute to the work of future generations.

I want to share with you the kind of work that's being done throughout the country, work that begins in fields and woodlands, and brings us in touch with the outdoors for our pleasure and use. In this gallery you'll be able to see many of the techniques described in this book, often applied to unusual materials and to forms that sometimes push the limits of what we have conventionally regarded as basketry. But the traditional is also represented here. Together they celebrate and honor nature's bounty.

Chapter 10

The Basketmaker's Web

*The spider taketh hold with her hands, and
is in kings' palaces.*

—PROVERBS 30:28

Annia Ulander
Högland, Sweden

MAIL BASKET
12 in. by 4½ in. by 11 in.
White birch bark and root

*This wall-hung letter holder is plaited,
turning down at the rim and weaving back
across the base, which displays the smooth,
brown inner face of the bark on both the
inside and outside of the basket.*

Facing page:
Char TerBeest
Baraboo, Wis.

STOLEN HEART
14 in. by 14 in. by 24 in.
Willow and unknown wood

*The free-form rib basket on the facing page
incorporates a slice of tree trunk whose
heartwood has rotted away leaving an outline
itself the shape of a heart, hence the title. The
form functions sculpturally as both a
container and a frame.*

Claude Medford, Jr.
Natchitoches, La.

UNTITLED
7½ in. by 3¾ in.
Dyed river cane

*Claude Medford used black walnut and
bloodroot to dye this traditional twill-
woven basket.*

Elizabeth A. Compton

Elizabeth A. Compton
Cambridge, Mass.

SUNSET WOODS
10 in. by 10 in.
Cattails, cedar bark, birch bark, spruce roots, white pine needles, cedar branches, cones, old man's beard lichen, jay feather with spruce branch handle

This little coiled basket captures a whole woodland, recreating its atmosphere in a visual potpourri of found materials. It is reminiscent of Japanese bonsai or haiku, wherein a large effect is made from miniature means.

Harold Shapiro

In these two baskets (above and on the facing page), Myrna Brunson shows something of the range possible from natural materials using the same technique, coiling. **Harvest,** *above, displays the abundance of a golden grassy field in fall. This soft, shaggy mantle portrays quite a different mood than the energetic coral-tipped pine needle surface on the facing page. With its dark, conical center and spiraling accents, the basket looks like a twister, concentrating and projecting its powerful form.*

Kenneth Porvancher

Myrna Brunson
Niantic, Conn.

UNTITLED, 1981
8 in. by 16 in.
Torrey pine
needles, dyed dark
brown with coral
tips

Facing page:
HARVEST, 1987
22 in. by 11 in.
Coiled wild oats

Carol Grant Hart
Salisbury, Conn.

BABY RATTLE
Stripped
honeysuckle

Baby's first basket.

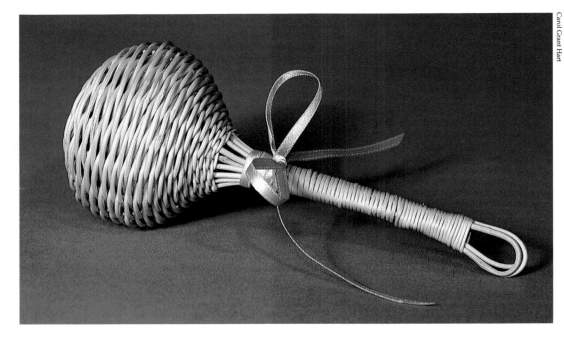

Carol Grant Hart

Photos: © Sheila Silvernail

Vivian Aron
Oley, Penn.

WILLOW
14½ in. by 15 in.

Vivian Aron grows her own willow in an area whose cultivation by basketmakers dates to the 19th century. Says Aron, "Nothing in my whole life has made me happier than making baskets."

Carol Grant Hart

Carol Grant Hart
Salisbury, Conn.

CORNUCOPIA
28 in. by 18 in. by 20 in.
Wild grape

How naturally this robust basket, as burly and strenuous as the vines it came from, rests in the sun. This is a serious working basket, capable of toting heavy loads and withstanding rough use.

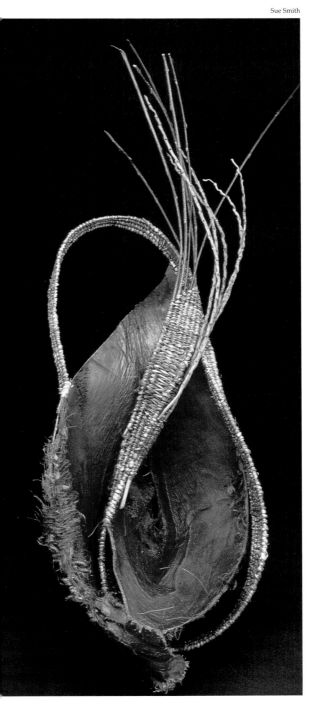

Sue Smith

Sue Smith
Fort Worth, Tex.

UNTITLED
22 in. by 8 in.
Palm cuff, palm seed sticks, willow, watsonia leaves

This basket opens like a seed pod or flower bud to reveal its interior.

Photos: Jean Greenwald

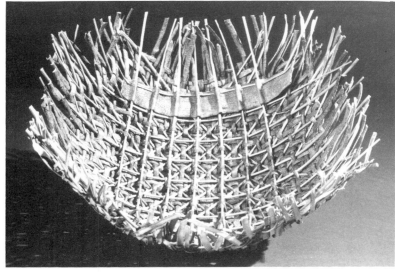

Dorothy Gill Barnes
Worthington, Ohio

WINDFALL RIDGE
20 in. by 20 in. by 6 in.
Pine bark and willow

The raw edge of this dished form offers a way for the eye to enter its densely layered structure. The pine bark is straight-plaited in a twill weave with willow rods captured on the surface. The result is a rich, beautifully complex texture.

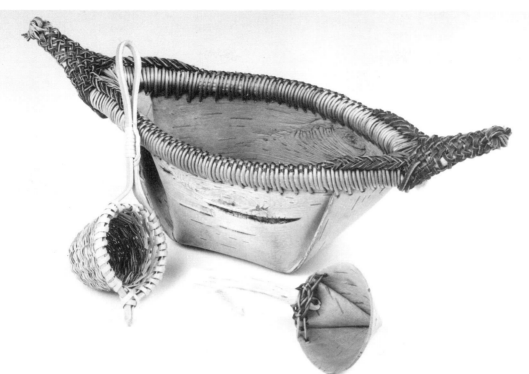

Alexander Photography

Liana Haubrich
Lempster, N.H.

MEDICINE TEA BOWL WITH STRAINER
AND LADLE, 1988
3 in. by 4 in. by 1 in.
Various barks and roots

*This tea bowl's elaborate detailing and exquisite
materials, which include barks from birch, elm,
and pin cherry, as well as spruce root and red
osier dogwood, give it a ceremonial stature.
How formal, for instance, to have two such
substantial handles on so small a bowl.
The strainer is of black ash and sunflower fibers,
while the ladle is made of birch bark and spruce
root with a maple handle.*

Char TerBeest
Baraboo, Wis.

FUNGUS ON A BIRCH POUCH
12 in. by 15 in. by 4 in.
Birch bark and leather

*The billowing fungus on this birch bark pouch
evokes the forest where it was found, and where
it can be used to gather more woodland riches—
berries, perhaps.*

Char TerBeest

Tom McColley

Connie and Tom McColley
Chloe, W. Va.

Above: Fields of Motion
24 in. by 32 in.
White oak, cherry

Facing page: Basket 89-52
White oak
14 in. by 26 in. by 26 in.

The McColleys call themselves "weavers of wood." They're production basketmakers who work in all natural materials, integrating wood splints with wood parts in consummate objects of craft. The rim and base of the vibrant piece above is lathe-turned cherry, drilled to receive the white oak spokes. Weavers are dyed with cold-water fiber-reactive dyes. The geometrically intriguing rib basket on the facing page is as much sculpture as basket. Need it hold more than your attention?

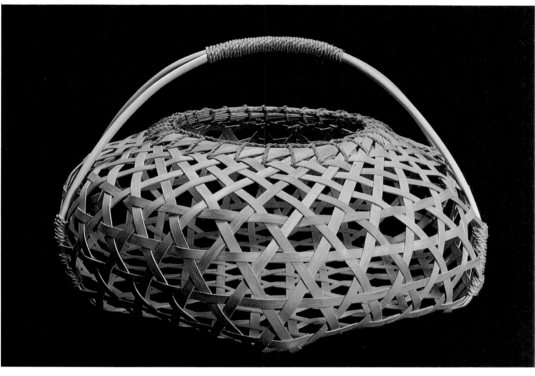

Tina VanDeWater
East Walpole, Mass.

LANTERN
13 in. by 13 in. by
7¾ in.
Black ash, white
ash, basswood bark

*The open weave of
this hexagonal-
plaited basket is full
of light, even without
a candle inside. The
handle, wrapped and
attached with
basswood bark
cordage, arches
over the form from
corner to corner like
a piece of sky.*

© Sheila Silvernail

Susi Nuss
Bolton, Conn.

TRIBUTE TO CORNELIA FRENCH
10 in. by 4 in.
Black ash and hickory

Patterned after a late 19th-century Shaker basket, which featured the same twill-woven quadrifoil design, this basket is the largest of a set of three. Its poise comes from perfect symmetry, the result of weaving the black ash splint over a mold. Handles and rim are of hand-riven hickory.

Fanie Carrier

Ed Carrier
Indianola, Wash.

UNTITLED
22 in. by 11 in.
Cedar bark

A nice example of crossed-warp fitching with a three-rod wale, this basket is easy for beginners to relate to because its structure is so evident. Actually, it can be a challenge to keep such a weave consistent with so much space between elements. The technique makes for a strong, light carrying bag.

Herbert Wages
Winslow, Ark.

ROUND SWING-HANDLE
BASKET, 1987
14 in. by 16 in.
White oak

OX MUZZLE, 1987
8 in. by 8 in.
White Oak

*This finely crafted splint basket leaves
undisguised a couple of the features of
its making. In the center of the front, for
instance, you can see the split spokes
(they're narrower) that create an odd
number necessary for a continuous
weaver. At the upper right, the beginning
and end of the rim lashing is tucked away,
but not elaborately hidden. These details
do not compromise, but rather evidence
the basket's integrity.*

*The hexagonal-plaited muzzle, designed
to prevent grazing, has a similar strength
that comes from using the appropriate
materials and techniques.*
Any ox would be proud to don it.

Photos: Philip Ezell

Photos: Brad Iverson

Kathleen P. Crombie
Garden City, Mich.

JUBILEE
14½ in. by 10 in. by 16 in.
Spruce bark, hardwood branch, datu rattan

Organic form is presented in a lively texture of twined spruce bark in this sculptural basket.

Tina VandeWater
Baraboo, Wis.

UNTITLED
8 in. by 11 in. by 6 in.
Elm bark and basswood bark cordage

Bold diagonals, in the twined crossed warp as well as the rim lashing, make this otherwise boxy basket surprisingly light and dynamic.

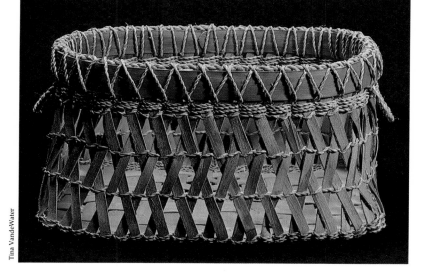

Tina VandeWater

Judith Olney
Rowley, Mass.

RIPPLE
13½ in. by 6 in.
Red maple

Judith Olney takes a plain, tight weave and gives it depth and intrigue by undulating it around the form.

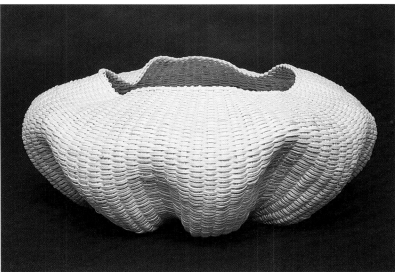

Betz Salmont
Manhattan
Beach, CA

POTATO BASKET
25 in. by 15 in.
by 10 in.
King palm seed
stems, grape vine
and driftwood
handle

Here's a freeform interpretation of a traditional one-hoop rib basket.

Phyllis Barrows
Bayside, Calif.

UNTITLED
Cottonwood pods

Phyllis Barrows describes the yearly cycle of her backyard cottonwood tree as a series of unpleasant phases. After periods of first sticky then crunchy-under-foot excretions, long green pods drop all over the place. Those that remain on the tree burst into messy drifts of cotton snow. Barrows tried making a basket of the stringy pods, placed it on her mantel when finished, and the next morning discovered it in a cloud of cotton. The pods had popped open and continued to spew seed for some time. She gathered the seed and filled the basket, a lovely greenish white fuzzy thing, pictured at right in transformation.

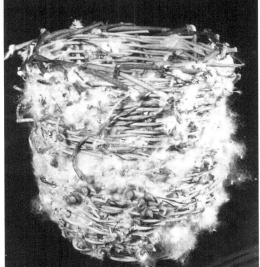

John Long
Slatington, Pa.

UNTITLED
3¼ in. by 4¼ in.
by 3½ in.
White oak

The structure of this small basket is conventional, but its handsome proportions and beautifully prepared white oak splints give it great presence. The rim, handle, and tapered ribs (requiring a total of six molds to shape) are unusually wide for a basket of this size, creating a feeling of solidity and permanence.

© Sheila Silvernail

© Sheila Silvernail

Misti Washington
Solana Beach, Calif.

GRANDMOTHER
BASKET
14 in. by 14 in. by 24 in.
Willow and unknown
wood

Misti Washington has extended the concept of the double-hooped rib basket by adding a half hoop spanning from side to side, then working four complete sets of ribs, rather than two. The result is four distinct pockets, a compartmentalized carrier inspired by childhood egg-fetching chores in a coop that housed four different breeds.

Judy Mulford
Los Angeles, Calif.

POTATO BASKET, 1983
13 in. by 10½ in.
Trumpet vine, dracaena, palm stalk,
philodendron sheath

Here's a potato basket that looks more like a slice of a melon. Omitting ribs near the rim results in generous openings that can be used as handles. This basket is clearly functional, yet makes a strong design statement.

Basket Plants

*T*he following is an alphabetical list of scientific names for plants used in basketry. For more information look up the common names in the Harvest Calendar, beginning on page 32, and Dye Plant chart, beginning on page 161.

SCIENTIFIC NAME	COMMON NAME
Acer circinatum	Vine Maple
A. macrophyllum,	Oregon Maple
A. rubrum	Red Maple, Swamp Maple, Scarlet Maple
Acorus calamus	Sweet Flag
Adiantum pedatum	Maidenhair Fern
Agapanthus africanus	Lily-of-the-Nile, Blue African Lily
Agave americana,	Agave, Maguey, Century Plant,
A. cantala, A. deserti,	Sisal, American Aloe
A. lecheguilla,	(*See also Manfreda*)
A. parryi, A. shawii,	
A. sisalana	
Agrimonia eupatoria	Agrimony
Agrostis gigantea	Redtop
Ailanthus altissima	Ailanthus, Tree-of-Heaven
Akebia quinata	Five-Leaf Akebia
Allium spp.	Onion
Alnus oregona	Red Alder
A. rhombifolia	White Alder
Aloe spp.	Aloe (*See also Agave, Manfreda, Yucca*)
Amaranthus palmeri	Amaranth
Amelanchier alnifolia	Serviceberry, Juneberry, Shadbush
Ammophila arenaria,	Beachgrass
A. breviligulata	

Andropogon virginicus	Bluestem, Broom Sedge (*See also Schizachyrium*)
Anthoxanthum odoratum	Sweet Vernal Grass
Apocynum androsaemifolium, A. cannabinum	Dogbane, Indian Hemp
Aristea spp.	Aristea
Artemisia ludoviciana	Wormwood, White Sage, Western Mugwort
Arundinaria gigantea, A. g. ssp. *tecta*	Cane, River Cane
Asclepias cordifolia, A. syriaca	Milkweed
Aspidistra elatior 'Variegata'	Cast-Iron Plant
Avena fatua, A. sativa	Oats
Bambusa spp.	Bamboo
Beaucarnea recurvata	Ponytail
Berberis vulgaris	Barberry
Betula lenta, B. papyrifera	Black Birch, Sweet Birch White Birch, Paper Birch, Canoe Birch
Bromus sitchensis	Bromegrass
Broussonetia papyrifera	Paper Mulberry
Butia capitata	Jelly Palm
Calamagrostis canadensis, C. c. var. *scabra*	Blue-Joint, Reed Bentgrass
Calamus siphonospathus	Rattan, Reed, Cane
Calocedrus decurrens	Post Cedar, Incense Cedar
Calycanthus floridus, C. occidentalis	Allspice, Strawberry Shrub, Sweet Shrub
Cannabis sativa	Marijuana, Hemp
Carex spp.	Sedge

Carya cordiformis	Bitternut Hickory
C. ovata	Shagbark Hickory
Catalpa bignonioides,	Catalpa, Cigar Tree
C. speciosa	
Ceanothus integerrimus	Buckthorn, California Lilac, Soapbloom, Deerbrush
Celastrus orbiculatus	Oriental Bittersweet
C. scandens	American Bittersweet
Cercis canadensis	American Redbud
C. occidentalis	Western Redbud
Cercocarpus betuloides,	Mountain Mahogany
C. ledifolius	
eropteris triangularis	Golden-Back Fern
Chlorophytum comosum	Spider Plant
Chrysanthemum spp.	Chrysanthemum
Chrysothamnus laricinus	Rabbitbrush
C. moquianus,	
C. nauseosus,	
C. tinctorius	
Cinna latifolia	Wood Reedgrass
Cladium mariscoides	Cladium, Twig Rush
Clematis virginiana	Clematis, Virgin's Bower
Cocos nucifera	Coconut Palm
Convallaria majalis	Lily-of-the-Valley
Coptis trifolia	Goldthread
Cordyline australis	Dracaena, Cabbage Tree
C. terminalis	Ti
Coreopsis spp.	Coreopsis
Cornus amomum	Silky Dogwood
C. florida	Flowering Dogwood
C. sericea	Red Osier Dogwood
Cortaderia selloana	Pampas Grass
Corylus cornuta	Hazelnut
var. *californica*	
Cowania mexicana	Cliffrose, Quinine Bush
Crocosmia aurea x *pottsii*	Crocosmia, Montbretia
Cycas spp.	Cycad
Cymbidium spp.	Cymbidium Orchid
Cynara scolymus	Artichoke
Cyperus alternifolius	Papyrus,
C. papyrus	Umbrella Plant
Dasylirion simplex	Sotol, Desert Spoon
D. wheeleri	
Deschampsia caespitosa	Tufted Hair Grass
Desmodium	Prostrate Tick Trefoil
rotundifolium	
Dirca palustris	Leatherwood, Moosewood
Dracaena draco	Dracaena, Dragon Tree

Elymus arenarius	Beach Wild Rye, AmericanDune Grass
Epicampes rigens	Epicampes, Deergrass
Epilobium angustifolium	Fireweed
Equisetum palustre	Horsetail,
E. sylvaticum	Scouring Rush
Eucalyptus globulus	Eucalyptus, Blue Gum
Evernia vulpina	Wolf Moss
Fatsia japonica	Japanese Aralia
Foeniculum vulgare	Fennel
Fragaria spp.	Strawberry
Fraxinus americana	White Ash
F. nigra	Black Ash
Fuchsia magellanica	Fuchsia
Gelsemium spp.	Jasmine
Gladiolus spp.	Gladiolus
Glyceria elata,	Manna grass
G. striata	
Gymnogramma	Golden-Back Fern
triangularis	
Helenium hoopesii	Sneezeweed
Helianthus annuus	Sunflower
Hemerocallis fulva	Daylily
Hierochloe odorata	Sweet Grass, Holygrass, Seneca Grass, Vanilla Grass
Hilaria jamesii	Galleta
Hypericum perforatum	St.-John's-Wort
Ipomoea coccinea	Small Red Morning Glory
I. purpurea	Common Morning Glory
Iris spp.	Iris, Flag
Jasminum spp.	Jasmine
Juglans cinerea	Butternut, White Walnut
J. nigra	Black Walnut
Juncus acutus	Rush
J. effusus	Soft Rush, Wire Grass
J. textalis	Basket Rush
Juniperus virginiana	Eastern Red Cedar
Laportea canadensis	Wood Nettle
Lavandula angustifolia	Lavender
Linum lewisii, L. perenne,	Flax
L. usitatissimum	
Liriope muscari	Lilyturf
Lonicera japonica	Honeysuckle

Lycopodium complanatum	Running Pine, Ground Pine
Maclura pomifera	Osage Orange, Hedge Apple, Bois d'Arc
Mahonia aquifolium	Oregon Grape, Grape Holly
Malus spp.	Apple
Mandevilla spp.	Mandevilla, Chilean Jasmine
Manfreda virginica (See also Agave)	Manfreda
Melaleuca quinquenervia	Melaleuca, Bottlebrush, Swamp Tea Tree
Mentha spp.	Mint
Morus alba	White Mulberry
M. rubra	Red Mulberry
Muhlenbergia rigens	Deergrass
Musa x *paradisiaca*	Banana
Myrica pensylvanica	Bayberry
Narcissus spp.	Daffodil
Nolina parryi	Nolina, Parry's Nolina, Bear Grass
Nymphaea odorata	Water Lily
Oryza sativa	Rice
Oryzopsis hymenoides	Ricegrass, Indian Millet, Silk Grass
Pandanus odoratissimus, P. tectorius, P. utilis	Pandanus, Lauhala, Screw Pine
Panicum miliaceum	Millet, Broomcorn Millet
Parthenocissus quinquefolia	Virginia Creeper, Woodbine
P. tricuspidata	Boston Ivy
Persicaria hydropiper	Smartweed
Phaseolus lunatus	Lima Bean
Philadelphus inodorus, P. lewisii	Mock Orange, Syringa
Philodendron giganteum	Giant Philodendron
Phleum spp.	Timothy
Phoenix canariensis, P. dactylifera	Date Palm
Phormium tenax 'Variegatum'	New Zealand Flax, New Zealand Hemp
Phragmites australis	Phragmites, Giant Reed
Phytolacca americana	Pokeweed
Picea glauca	White Spruce
P. mariana	Black Spruce, Swamp Spruce
P. rubens	Red spruce, Eastern Spruce, Yellow Spruce
P. sitchensis	Sitka Spruce

Pinus banksiana	Jack Pine
P. elliottii	Slash Pine
P. lambertiana	Sugar Pine
P. palustris	Longleaf Pine, Georgia Pine, Longstraw Pine, Southern Yellow Pine
P. ponderosa	Ponderosa Pine, Western Yellow Pine
P. sabiniana	Digger Pine
P. strobus	White Pine
Pityrogramma triangularis	Golden-Back Fern
Plantago spp.	Plantain
Platanus occidentalis	American Sycamore, Buttonball Tree, Buttonwood, American Plane Tree
Populus angustifolia, P. fremontii	Cottonwood, Aspen, Poplar
P. balsamifera, P. x gileadensis	Balsam Poplar, Balm-of-Gilead
P. trichocarpa	Western Balsam Poplar, Black Cottonwood
Proboscidea fragrans, P. louisianica, P. parviflora	Martynia, Devil's Claw, Elephant's Trunk, Unicorn Plant
P. pubescens	Screw Bean Mesquite
Prunus spp.	Cherry, Peach, Plum
Pseudotsuga menziesii	Douglas Fir
Psoralea argophylla, P. macrostachya	Scurf Pea, Leatherroot
Pteridium aquilinum	Brake Fern, Bracken
Pueraria lobata	Kudzu
Quercus alba	White Oak
Q. michauxii	Basket Oak
Raphia pedunculata	Raffia
Rhododendron maximum	Rhododendron
Rhus glabra	Smooth Sumac
R. trilobata	Threeleaf Sumac, Catclaw
R. typhina	Staghorn Sumac, Velvet Sumac
Robinia pseudoacacia	Black Locust, False Acacia
Rosa spp.	Rose
Rubia tinctorum	Madder
Rubus spp.	Raspberry, Blackberry, Dewberry
Rumex obtusifolius	Dock
Sabal palmetto	Cabbage Palm, Palmetto, Carolina Palmetto
Salix babylonica	Weeping Willow
S. discolor	Pussy Willow

S. exigua	Sandbar Willow, Narrowleaf Willow
S. humilis	Upland Willow
S. nigra	Black Willow
S. purpurea	Basket Willow, Purple Willow
S. sitchensis	Sitka Willow
S. triandra, S. viminalis	Basket Willow
Sambucus nigra	Elderberry
Sanguinaria canadensis	Bloodroot
Sansevieria longifolia	Bowstring Hemp
S. trifasciata	Snake Plant, Mother-in-Law's Tongue
S. zeylanica	Bowstring Hemp
Sassafras albidum	Sassafras
Schizachyrium scoparium	Broom Beard Grass, Bunchgrass, Bluestem
Scirpus americanus	Chairmaker's Bulrush
S. lacustris, S. pacificus, S. paludosus	Bulrush, Tule
S. robustus	Salt Marsh Bulrush
Secale cereale	Rye
Sequoia sempervirens	Redwood
Sesbania exaltata	River Hemp, Wild Hemp
Smilax spp.	Greenbrier, Catbrier, Smilax
Solidago spp.	Goldenrod
Sorghum bicolor	Broomcorn
Spartina spp.	Cordgrass, Salt Marsh Grass, Slough Grass
Stipa tenacissima	Esparto Grass, Spear Grass
Strelitzia reginae	Bird-of-Paradise
Symphoricarpos orbiculatus	Coralberry, Buckbush, Indian Currant
Syringa vulgaris	Common Lilac
Tagetes spp.	Marigold
Tanacetum vulgare	Tansy
Taraxacum officinale	Dandelion
Taxus spp.	Yew
Thuja occidentalis	Northern White Cedar
T. plicata	Western Red Cedar, Canoe Cedar
Tilia americana	Basswood, American Linden
Tillandsia usneoides	Spanish Moss
Torreya californica	California Nutmeg
Triodia flava	Tall Redtop
Triticum spp.	Wheat
Tsuga canadensis	Eastern Hemlock
T. mertensiana	Black Hemlock
Typha angustifolia, T. latifolia	Cattail

Ulmus alata	Winged Elm, Cork Elm
U. americana	American Elm
U. rubra	Slippery Elm, Red Elm
Urtica breweri, U. canadensis, U. dioica, U. gracilis ssp. *holosericea, U. lyallii, U. nivea*	Nettle
Vaccinium membranaceum	Blueberry
Verbascum spp.	Mullein
Vinca major `Variegata'	Vinca Vine, Band Plant
V. minor	Myrtle, Periwinkle
Vitis spp.	Grape
Washingtonia filifera	Fan Palm
Watsonia humilis maculata	Watsonia, Southern Bugle Lily
Wisteria floribunda, W. sinensis	Wisteria
Woodwardia spinulosa	Giant Chain Fern
Xerophyllum tenax	Bear Grass, Squaw Grass
Yucca aloifolia	Aloe Yucca
Y. baccata	Banana Yucca
Y. brevifolia	Yucca, Joshua Tree
Y. filamentosa	Yucca, Silkgrass
Y. glauca	Yucca, Soapweed
Zea mays	Corn
Zizania aquatica	Wild Rice, Indian Rice, Water Oats

Glossary

Base (also **Mat**). The bottom part of the basket. *Base* generally refers to a round, radiating bottom of either round or flat material. *Mat* generally refers to a square or rectangular base of flat material.

Base spoke. Spoke used for only the base of a basket.

Base stick. The warp material that composes the base of a square or rectangular basket.

Bi-spokes (or **Bye-spokes**). Spokes added alongside existing spokes to add strength or stability. Called **bi-stakes** in square or rectangular baskets.

Border (also **Lip**). The top of a basket usually finished off in a woven, braided, or wrapped technique. A *foot border* is a border woven on the bottom of a basket to give it something to stand on.

Breakdown. The separation of base spokes by the weavers.

Center (also **Button** or **Start**). The crossing of spokes that starts the base.

Coil. An element or bundle of elements forming spiraling rows of a stitched or sewn basket.

Core (also **Foundation**). That which constitutes the center of a coil in a coiled or stitched basket. A core may be single-strand or multi-strand, completely covered or exposed between stitches.

Green. Freshly cut and unseasoned plant material, having a relatively high moisture content.

Heartwood. The center section of a tree trunk, which no longer conducts sap. Usually darker in color than sapwood. It does not make the best splints, but it is useful for handles.

Hoop. A rod bent into a ring to serve as the basic structure of a rib basket.

Initial spoke. The spoke the weaving is started on. Changes of color or weave occur at the initial spoke; therefore, it should be marked so that you can easily tell when you have completed each round.

Lashing. The material used to sew or attach reinforcing pieces to the rim of a splint basket. Also used to describe methods of binding two crossed pieces or hoops together to form part of the frame in a hoop or rib basket.

Mat. *See* Base.

Midrib. The central ribs of a one-hoop rib basket that are lashed directly to the hoop.

Odd spoke (also **Half spoke**). A spoke added to create an odd number necessary in some weaves.

Packing. The technique of filling in an unequal space by weaving over only partial sections of one or more rows.

Plaiting. A weaving technique in which all elements perform the same function in the weave. There is no distinction between warp and weft.

Rib. A supporting elements, curved but not forming a complete ring, that functions as the warp in a rib (or hooped) basket.

Rim (also called **Lip**). The top of a basket (usually splint) that is lashed to the folded-over stakes.

Round. One complete row (or circuit) of the basket from initial spoke (or other designated point) back to the initial spoke.

Sapwood. The outer, usually lighter-colored portion of a tree trunk between the heartwood and the bark.

Scarf joint. A joint where two ends of splints or rods are spliced together to form a constant thickness or diameter.

Side spokes. Spokes added to base spokes to form the sides of a basket.

Sides. The body of the basket formed vertically after the base has been woven.

Splicing. The technique of joining the end of an old strand to the beginning of a new strand. This should be done so there is no break in the weave or pattern.

Splint. A thin, flat weaving material usually from a woody plant or a tree.

Splintwork. Basketry made from flat material.

Spoke (also **Stake** or **Warp**). The thicker element used in wickerwork, splint, or twined basket around which weavers are woven. I tend to use the term"spoke" when working with a round basket (as in the spokes of a wheel) and "stake" for rectangular or square baskets.

Stake. *See* Spoke.

Stick. *See* Base stick.

Stitch. A complete movement of a threaded needle (or other tool) that holds or binds together the coils of a coiled or sewn basket.

Stitching (also **Wrapping**). The element used to stitch or sew together the coils in a coiled basket.

Stroke. One complete movement (in and out) of one weaver.

Twining. A weave in which two weavers wrap around each spoke as they also twist around each other.

Upsett (also **Turning** or **Upstaking**). The transition of the base spokes from a horizontal to a vertical position; or the point where the base is turned up to start the sides of the basket. This may take several rows.

Weave. A series of strokes used to interlace the elements that create the pattern or fabric of a basket. A recap of weaves may be found on the charts that end the chapters on wickerwork, twining, and splintwork.

Weaver (also **Weft**). The elements that weave in and out of the spokes (or stakes) to create the body or fabric of the basket.

Wickerwork. Basketry that uses material round in section.

Tools and Equipment

A BASE-STICK CLAMP

Materials
• 2 pieces 1x2 stock, 12 inches long
• 3 carriage bolts, 2½ inches long, with washers and wing nuts
• 1 piece ¼ -inch stock, a little wider than the diameter of your base sticks and 8 inches long, for holding plate

Directions
Drill three holes in the two pieces of 1x2 stock as shown. Insert the bolts, and attach the washers and nuts. Drill two holes in the 8-inch-long piece large enough to pass the outside base sticks. The distance from the outside edges of the holes should be the same as the width of the base you want to weave.

In use, clamp your base stick at the appropriate intervals for weaving and slip the holding plate over the outside base sticks. The holding plate thus keeps the sticks from being drawn together by the weaving. Raise the plate as the weaving proceeds. Allow the inside base sticks to rest against the edge of the holding plate. You can drill other holes spaced for bases of different sizes.

*V*ery few tools are necessary in basket weaving. In many cases, a cutting tool of some sort is all you really need. But I like tools and use any that make the job easier or more pleasant. Fascinating to me, too, are tools of antiquity, and those that are altered or hand-made by innovative basketmakers to best serve a particular need. This list represents my own tool kit, with suggestions and recommendations for you.

Awl. A pointed stick, bone, knitting needle, or hardware-store awl will prove handy for various piercing and lacing jobs. Having a variety of sizes helps. Awls are also used to push the weavers down tight and to open up spaces where needed.

Clamps. Various types and sizes of clamps may be found in hardware, electrical, and automotive stores. Look for spring- and cam-action clamps as well as screw clamps. You can easily make a wooden clamp with holding plate to hold the base sticks for square or rectangular wickerwork baskets (instructions at left).

Clothespins. Spring-type clothespins are useful in splintwork and plaited baskets and elsewhere to hold elements together temporarily.

Crochet hooks. Crochet hooks are useful in pulling weavers down through the weave in twined baskets. Small hooks are indispensable in working with miniatures.

Tools, from left to right. Top row: awl, cutters, needle-nose pliers, scissors, screwdrivers. Bottom row: knives, leather skiver, tape measure, clothespins, crochet hooks, razor saw, needle file, flat file, steel needles, forceps, tweezers, dental bits.

Cutters. You'll use everything from very small wire cutters for fine vines to large pruning shears or loppers for grape vines and other tough fibers.

Dental bits. These are useful in working with miniatures. Simply twirl the bit between thumb and forefinger after starting a hole with needle or awl.

Drill. Electric or hand drills are used for making holes in material that is too hard for an awl to puncture.

Drawknife. A two-handled knife available in various sizes; one medium-sized blade will serve most needs. Use a drawknife in conjunction with a vise or shaving horse to remove bark from a log or to dress splints. (*See* photos, pages 22 and 27.)

Dyepots. Enamel pots will not affect the color of your dyes. Try discarded refrigerator vegetable bins. Don't use pots used for food preparation.

Forceps. Surgical forceps are wonderful for tucking ends of weavers down into tight spots and for use with miniatures.

Froe. A splitting tool with a straight handle set at right angles to the blade, used for riving a log into splints.

Gauge. A short section of drinking straw, tubing, or horn is helpful in maintaining a constant thickness of the core of a coiled basket (as shown in photo on page 132).

Gluts. These are wooden wedges used to split logs in preparing splint. Saw them from hardwood.

Holding Plate. *See* Clamps.

Knives. You'll need knives of several different sizes: small for tapering or whittling, large for scraping splints and harvesting.

Leather skiver. This useful tool, basically a razor-blade holder that bends a single-edged blade into a curve, can thin splints or barks to eliminate bulk in splices.

Maul. A section of hardwood shaped on one end to fit the hand and used for striking the froe or to pound a log before lifting splints.

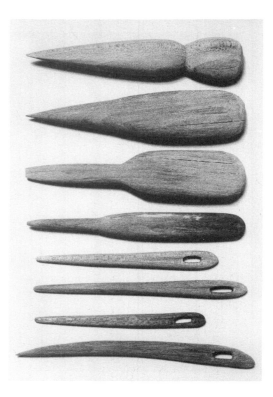

Molds. Molds or forms are used to ensure a symmetrical shape in many types of baskets. They were traditionally used in Shaker and Nantucket lightship baskets as well as in splint and sweet grass baskets made by some Indian tribes.

Needles. Collect all sizes of steel darning or tapestry needles for coiling and stitching. The making of handsome wooden needles is described below and of yucca needles on the facing page.

HAND-CARVED WOODEN NEEDLE

A ¼-inch-thick piece of seasoned dogwood, 3 inches long by 5/16 inch wide, will yield a good-sized needle for most work.

Step 1. Mark three pilot points in one end with an awl and drill small holes there to start the eye. (The finished eye should be about 3/8 inch long.)

Step 2. Using a sharp, pointed knife, carefully carve away the eye, removing the wood gradually. Shape the eye to a long oval, as shown. After carving, smooth the eye with a round needle file.

Step 3. Cut away excess wood along the length of the blank, shaping the top to a blunt, rounded point. Do not shape the point of the needle yet; keep it square for ease in handling until the top of the needle is nearly complete.

Step 4. Taper the point of the needle now, and smooth the entire length with a nail file and emery board. It should be satin smooth.

Step 5. Make the groove for the thread: hold a needle file flat as shown exactly in the center of the eye, and carefully file a shallow depression.

Step 6. Tip the point of the file into the eye to smooth all edges. Make sure there is nothing sharp inside the eye or along the groove. Finished needle should be about ⅛ inch by 3/16 inch by 2 to 3 inches long. It can be straight or slightly curved to help you in stitching tight or difficult areas.

Making a Wooden Needle

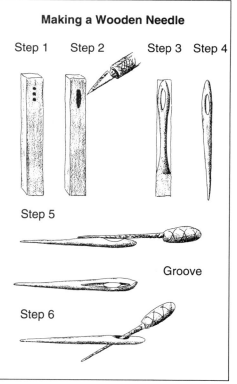

Step 1   Step 2   Step 3   Step 4

Step 5

Groove

Step 6

Needle file. A small round file used in shaping the eye of wooden needles.

Needle-nose pliers. Pinch or crimp a rod or vine before bending it, and it will more easily bend without cracking or breaking.

Razor saw. A very small, thin-bladed saw used to make fine cuts.

Rubber fingers. Purchase these in stationery or office supply houses; they're great for pushing a needle through a tight spot.

Screwdriver. Small sizes are useful for lacing splintwork baskets and tucking the ends of splints (before adding the rim) and weavers down into the weave.

Shaving horse. A foot-activated clamping bench that holds a splint while you smooth it with the drawknife.

Soaking tub. Most dried materials need to be soaked before using. Use any size or shape tub that fits the material. For material that cannot be coiled, such as catalpa beans, iris leaves and grasses, I use a wallpapering tray in the bathtub. Outdoors, a ditch lined with plastic, a canoe, boat, or a pond or stream will serve.

Thimbles. Use these to help push your needle while stitching.

Tweezers. These are especially helpful in making miniatures.

Work board. A scrap piece of wood, measured off in a one-inch grid is sometimes used for starting splint baskets.

YUCCA NEEDLE

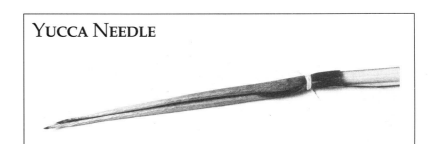

I discovered how to use a leaf of *Yucca filamentosa* as a needle while I was coiling with iris leaves that kept breaking over the eye of a metal needle going through tight spots. It works quite well with the soft leaves of iris, daylily, and other plants. You can also use it with bark or roots. Here's how to make one:

Step 1. Cut 2½ to 3 inches off the tips of yucca leaves. (You usually end up throwing this part away anyway.) They should be damp but still rigid. They will be cone-shaped with the edges rolled up.

Step 2. Carefully open up the rolled edges and lay an iris leaf on the opened cone.

Step 3. Reroll the edges around the leaf and tie with quilting thread. If using bark or root, make a little notch in the bark before tying where the thread will go around it.

Of course, you must cut the thread off and tie more material onto each new leaf—but it works in a pinch. If the needle is long to start with, you can simply cut off the end along with the thread. Repeat this until the needle becomes too short to use.

This needle really has some advantages. Not only does it save wear and tear on the iris leaf where it would usually be folded through the eye of a regular needle, but you don't have to contend with double thickness, helpful if your stitching material is heavy or if you're stitching through a tight spot. I have pulled on my yucca needle, grasping it with needle-nose pliers, and it did not break. Keep several in your tool kit along with a spool of quilting thread.

Making a Yucca Needle

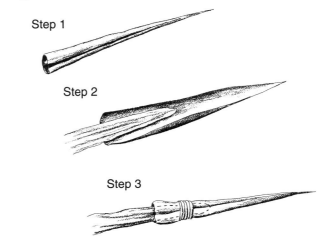

Bibliography

BASKETRY

American Indian Basketry Magazine (Oct. 15, 1980), Vol. 1, no. 3.

Anonymous. *Cane, Rush and Straw.* New York: Excalibur Books, 1977.

Belash, Constantine. *Braiding and Knotting.* Chas. T. Branford, 1947.

Cain, H. Thomas. *Pima Indian Basketry.* Phoenix: Heard Museum of Anthropology and Primitive Art, 1962.

Cary, Mara. *Basic Baskets.* Boston: Houghton Mifflin, 1975.

Cary, Mara. *Useful Baskets.* Boston: Houghton Mifflin, 1977.

Christopher, F.J. *Basketry.* New York: Dover, 1952.

Daugherty, Robin Taylor. *Splint Woven Basketry.* Loveland, Colo.: Interweave, 1986

DeLeon, Sherry. *The Basketry Book.* New York: Holt, Rinehart & Winston, 1978.

Eaton, Allen H. *Handcrafts of the Southern Highlands.* New York: Dover, 1973.

Faust, Patricia L. "Collecting Old Baskets." *Early American Life* (Dec. 1977), Vol. 3, no. 6.

Gilman, Rachel Seifel, and Nancy Bess. *Step-by-Step Basketry.* Racine, Wis.: Western Publishing, 1977.

Glashausser, Suellen, and Carol Westfall. *Plaiting: Step-by-Step.* New York: Watson-Guptill, 1976.

Hart, Carol and Dan. *Natural Basketry.* New York: Watson-Guptill, 1976.

Harvey, Virginia I. *The Techniques of Basketry.* New York: Van Nostrand Reinhold, 1978.

Hoppe, Flo. *Wicker Basketry.* Loveland, Colo.: Interweave, 1989.

James, George Wharton. *Indian Basketry.* New York: Dover, 1972. (This edition is a facsimile of the fourth edition of *Indian Basketry,* published by Henry Malkan in 1909.)

Land, Marie. *The Art of Pine Needle Basketry.* Lilburn, Ga.: Corner Cupboard Crafts, 1978.

LaPlantz, Shereen. *Plaited Basketry: The Woven Form.* Bayside, Calif.: Press de LaPlantz, 1982.

LaPlantz, Shereen. *The Mad Weave Book.* Bayside, Calif.: Press de LaPlantz, 1984.

Lasansky, Jeannette. *Willow, Oak and Rye.* University Park, Pa.: Pennsylvania State University Press, 1979.

Mason, Otis Tufton. *Aboriginal American Indian Basketry.* (Reprint of the 1904 edition published by Government Printing Office, Washington, D.C., 1976.)

Meilach, Dona Z. *A Modern Approach to Basketry.* New York: Crown, 1974.

Meilach, Dona Z., and Dee Menagh. *Basketry Today.* New York: Crown, 1979.

Miles, Charles, and Pierre Bovis. *American Indian and Eskimo Basketry.* Santa Fe: Pierre Bovis, 1969.

Navajo School of Indian Basketry. *Indian Basket Weaving.* New York: Dover, 1971. (Originally published by Whedon and Spreng, Los Angeles, 1903.)

Newman, Sandra Corrie. *Indian Basket Weaving.* Flagstaff, Ariz.: Northland Press, 1974.

Rauch, Mary. "Pine Needle/Raffia Basketry." *Creative Crafts Magazine* (Feb. 1981), Vol. 7, no. 7.

Richardson, Helen, ed. *Fiber Basketry, Homegrown & Handmade.* Kenthurst, N.S.W.: Kangaroo Press, 1989.

Richardson, Sandra Lee. "Baskets." *Decorating and Craft Ideas* (June 1976). Vol. 6, no. 8.

Rossbach, Ed. *Baskets as Textile Art.* New York: Van Nostrand Reinhold, 1973.

Schneider, Richard C. *Crafts of the North American Indians.* New York: Van Nostrand Reinhold, 1972.

Siler, Lynn. *The Basket Book.* New York: Sterling, 1988.

Stephens, Cleo M. *Willow Spokes and Wickerwork.* Harrisburg, Pa.: Stackpole Books, 1975.

Stephenson, Sue H. *Basketry of the Appalachian Mountains.* New York: Van Nostrand Reinhold, 1977.

Teleki, Gloria Roth. *The Baskets of Rural America.* New York: E.P. Dutton, 1975.

Teleki, Gloria Roth. *Collecting Traditional American Basketry.* New York: E.P. Dutton, 1979.

Tod, Osma Gallinger. *Earth Basketry.* Bonanza, 1972. (Originally published by Orange Judd in 1933.)

White, Mary. *How to Make Baskets.* New York: Doubleday, Page, 1902.

Wright, Dorothy. *The Complete Book of Baskets and Basketry.* New York: Charles Scribner's Sons, 1977.

BOTANICALS

Anonymous. *Guide to Trees.* New York: Simon and Schuster, 1977.

Brown, Charlotte Erichsen. *Use of Plants.* Ontario: Breezy Creeks Press.

Cobb, Boughton. *A Field Guide to the Ferns.* Boston: Houghton Mifflin, 1956.

Collingwood, G.H., and Warren D. Brush. *Knowing Your Trees.* Washington, D.C.: The American Forestry Assoc., 1964. (First printing, 1937.)

Fernald, Merritt L. *Gray's Manual of Botany,* 8th ed. New York: D. Van Nostrand, 1950.

Harlow, William M. *Trees of the Eastern and Central United States and Canada.* New York: Dover, 1957. (Originally published by McGraw-Hill, New York, 1942.)

Hitchcock, A.S. *Manual of the Grasses of the United States, Vol. 1 and 2,* revised by Agnes Chase. New York: Dover, 1971. (First edition published in 1935.)

Jaeger, Ellsworth. *Wildwood Wisdom.* New York: Macmillan, 1945.

Knobel, Edward. *Field Guide to the Grasses, Sedges and Rushes of the United States.* New York: Dover Publications, 1977.

Little, Elbert L. *The Audubon Society Field Guide to North American Trees (Eastern Region)* and *(Western Region).* New York: Alfred A. Knopf, 1980.

Niering, William A. *The Audubon Society Field Guide to North American Wildflowers (Eastern Region)* and *(Western Region).* New York: Alfred A. Knopf, 1980.

Niethammer, Carolyn. *American Indian Food and Lore.* New York: Collier Books of Macmillan, 1974.

Peterson, Roger Tory, and Margaret McKenny. *A Field Guide to Wildflowers.* Boston: Houghton Mifflin, 1968.

Petrides, George A. *A Field Guide to Trees and Shrubs.* Boston: Houghton Mifflin, 1958.

Shosteck, Robert. *Flowers and Plants.* New York: Quadrangle/N.Y. Times Book, 1974.

Spellenberg, Richard. *The Audubon Society Field Guide to North American Wildflowers (Western Region).* New York: Alfred A. Knopf, 1979.

Staff of the L.H. Bailey Hortorium. *Hortus Third.* New York: Cornell University and Macmillan, 1976.

Symonds, George W.D. *The Shrub Identification Book.* New York: William Morrow, 1963.

DYEING

Adrosko, Rita J. *Natural Dyes and Home Dyeing.* New York: Dover, 1971.

Beebee, Dorothy M., and Miriam Rice. *Mushrooms for Color.* Eureka, Calif.: Mad River Press, 1980.

Brooklyn Botanic Garden. *Dye Plants and Dyeing—A Handbook.* Brooklyn: Brooklyn Botanical Garden, 1964.

Buchanan, Rita. *A Weaver's Garden.* Loveland, Colo.: Interweave, 1987.

Denver Art Museum, *Indian Vegetable Dyes I,* Denver Art Museum Leaflet 63, 1934.

Denver Art Museum. *Indian Vegetable Dyes II,* Denver Art Museum Leaflet 71, 1936.

Kramer, Jack. *Natural Dyes, Plants and Processes.* New York: Charles Scribner's Sons, 1972.

Index